The Gift of Education

The Gift of Education

*How a Tuition Guarantee Program
Changed the Lives of Inner-City Youth*

Norman A. Newberg

WITH A FOREWORD BY
Michelle Fine

State University of New York Press

All royalties due to the author as a result of this book will be directed to the Say Yes To Education Foundation, in support of future scholarships.

Funding for this research was provided by the Lilly Endowment and the Say Yes to Education Foundation.

Published by
State University of New York Press, Albany

For information, address State University of New York Press, 194 Washington Avenue, Suite 305, Albany, NY 12210-2384

Production by Kelli Williams
Marketing by Fran Keneston

Library of Congress Cataloging-in-Publication Data

Newberg, Norman A.
    The gift of education : how a tuition guarantee program changed the lives of inner-city youth / Norman A. Newberg ; foreword by Michelle Fine.
        p. cm.
    Includes bibiographical references and index.
    ISBN 0-7914-6619-1 (hardcover : alk. paper)
    1. Urban youth—Education (Secondary)—Pennsylvania—Philadelphia—Case studies.   2. Urban youth—Scholarships, fellowships, etc.—Pennsylvania—Philadelphia—Case studies.   3. Youth with social disabilities—Education (Secondary)—Pennsylvania—Philadelphia—Case studies.   4. Youth with social disabilities—Scholarships, fellowships, etc.—Pennsylvania—Philadelphia—Case studies.   5. Student assistance programs—Pennsylvania—Philadelphia—Case studies. I. Title.

LC4093.P5N48 2005
373.12'23'0974811—dc22   2005000651

10 9 8 7 6 5 4 3 2 1

This book is dedicated to George Weiss,
founder and sponsor of Say Yes to Education,
to the Belmont 112 and their families, and to the Say Yes staff.
Each of these participants believe that poor people deserve a better future.

Contents

Foreword

I watched this book grow. Norman Newberg and I have been in conversation for over a decade about Say Yes to Education. I have been honored to watch as Newberg's distinct blend of passion and rigor, compassion and impatience, scholarly deliberation and activist sense of urgency have labored to produce *The Gift of Education*. I have witnessed relationships grow and graduations celebrated, surprises and disappointments, revisions and political speed bumps, treacherous assertions, and delightful break throughs. To have traveled with Norman on this journey is a privilege, for he is a scholar, a writer, a progressive, and a mensch. And so we have much to thank him for. But before I begin my foreword, I will scribble a note to Norman (feel free to look over his shoulder).

Dear Norman:

I've read through the book and I write this thank you note, for me and the rest of the nation, who need to hear what you have delicately told us. As you document the cumulative and devastating costs of poverty and racism in America, so too you chronicle the magic made possible with a simple gift of redistributing wealth. As an aside, I thank you for not conducting this research in my neighborhood. It would, of course, embarrass and shame us if you displayed the stories of crime, teen sexuality and pregnancy, school failure and parental cover up, drug use and abuse that litter middle-class America. We'd have to sue you. But that's the privilege of privilege—no one really gets to write about these troubles here, because our records are sealed, confidential, whited out, cleaned up by lawyers and psychiatrists. We've had this discussion before—the gaze you so brilliantly place on the lives of poverty should of course be cast, as well, on lives of privilege. But with this book, you force us to recognize that lives of wealth and comfort are, indeed, shameful parasites to poverty. As you bear witness to the collective cost and responsibility, I write, then, to thank you for your wisdom and for introducing us to the Belmont 112.

Michelle

Foreword: An Invitation to use Bifocals

You are about to read the vibrant story of the Belmont 112; a cohort of young people whose futures have been blessed and lives made visible by a "gift" promised to them upon graduation from high school. And yet before you begin, I ask that you read the text bifocally, through the dual lens of individual lives and critical policy analysis. For as much as we learn about the Belmont 112, *The Gift of Education* offers readers a searing biography of neoliberal America. During the time period documented, 1987–1999, the nation was fortifying our prison-industrial complex, dismantling the welfare system, and retreating from the public financing of public education. Through this labyrinth of policy shifts to the Right, the Belmont 112 grew up. Learning to ride bicycles and public transit, they entered puberty, fell in and out of love, enjoyed slumber parties at George and Diane Weiss' house, lost parents, got classified as learning disabled, dropped out of high school and graduated, had babies, traveled, went to prison, and even more went to college. Like most teens in America.

But during their formative years, the nation was aggressively pursuing a get tough on crime strategy that propelled a mass incarceration of youth and young adults in communities of color. In their neighborhoods, during the final quarter of the twentieth century, while violent crime in the nation decreased, incarceration rates quadrupled. In 1974 153,500 African-Americans were in prison or jail; this figure leapt to 635,000 in 1994, and 884,500 in 2002 (The Sentencing Project, 2004). Today, in the state of Pennsylvania, Blacks account for 10 percent of the general population, and 49.7 percent of the incarcerated population. During the decade of Newberg's watch, the correctional system had its eyes on the mothers, fathers, and siblings of the Belmont 112, while George and Diane Weiss pinned their hopes on the youth.

During these same years, the Belmont youth perhaps caught a chill as the early winds of "welfare reform" whistled through the cracks in their living room windows. In 1993, the number of children living in low-income families reached a national high of thirty-one million, with 31 percent of white children and 69 percent of Black children living in "low income households" (measured as 100–200 percent of the Federal Poverty Level). Just as the Belmont 112 were entering their senior year in high school, anticipating the college education they were promised six years before, they were haunted, consciously and not, by those they would leave behind—family and friends not lucky enough to be touched by the "gift."

And from 1980–1990, federal budget funds for elementary and secondary schools dropped by 12 percent; for postsecondary the drop was even more significant at 22 percent. Pennsylvania's cities suffered then, as now, from a ruthless commitment to educational finance inequity that devastated schooling and possibility in urban and rural communities. During the years Newberg journals, the long arm of prison entered the Belmont community, as jobs, welfare, and educational funding walked out. And the Belmont 112 watched. While readers may *believe* they are reading about the lives of youth touched by a gift, I would ask you to read for a doubled biography of youth and a nation [placed] at risk, with justice and democracy under siege.

Newberg's monograph bears poignant witness to the systematic abandonment of poor communities of color and the magnificent strength distributed across 112 young people who had access to the well-cushioned life raft subsidized by George and Diane Weiss. From the pages of Newberg's powerfully crafted book, we learn about resilience, strength, struggle and pain in their souls, bellies, minds, and imaginations. Like watching a fast speed photograph of a flower blossoming, only in reverse, we witness lives disabled by a *state* of neglect and fiscal abandonment, flourishing unevenly and despite, with the sweet nectar of what Newberg critically theorizes as the "gift."

But Newberg offers no sentimental applause for the gift. Intrigued by the promise and stunned by the complexities of living in systemic poverty, he asks us to confront a set of tough questions about the State, privilege, privatization, social and personal responsibility in the dawn of the twenty-first century. Recognizing that Say Yes to Education is indeed an act of enormous generosity in times of economic and racialized injustice, Norman Newberg asks us to think hard about what a gift means for youth in families and communities threatened by the treacherous tides of high unemployment, federal abandonment of poor urban communities, the crack/cocaine epidemic, and relentless racism. In communities perhaps vibrant in spirit but withering in fiscal resources, how do we respectfully acknowledge that SYTE may have been charity of great magnitude, and a trivial nod toward justice? Troubling questions like these are raised by Newberg's text, which is at once ethnography and Talmud: close, careful observation joined with colorful and contested interpretations of responsibility, justice, and guilt in unjust times.

A word about the educational model embedded in SYTE: In September 2004, George Weiss and colleagues announced to a packed audience in the APOLLO theatre that the kindergartners in the audience, drawn from five Harlem elementary schools, would be granted college tuition if they completed high school. Tossing footballs into the audience, with ecstatic parents, educators and youth, the scene was another "miracle" on 125th Street. But this model of SYTE was dramatically modified from the 1987 original. This model recognized the need to support not only youth but schools, families, and communities. The siblings of the new cohort will also enjoy academic supports; their schools will be supplemented and the parents of these youth will be helped should they opt to pursue further education. With a thicker and more engaged model of family, community, and youth support, SYTE has evidenced an institutional capacity to reflect, reform, and extend what's needed in these very hard times as youth are being lost to the blades of finance inequity, poverty, racism, high stakes testing, lack of hope, and dreams deferred. We can only watch and hope that this new cohort will be a hopeful and stinging reminder to state policymakers that all children need, deserve and crave educational challenge, justice, and opportunity.

For now, we learn from the Belmont 112 and from Norman Newberg that young people who have endured too much still dream, hope, yearn. Most long for an educator who will listen, extend a hand, take a walk, excuse mistakes, and open doors. Newberg shows us through stories and cost benefit analyses that it takes so little to make a difference, to help young people beat the odds in a system designed to devastate. And yet we also meet the haunting ghosts; the effects of multigenerational federal, state, and local betrayal etched in their eyes. We hear mothers thanking the program for giving their children "the privilege to dream." And we hear parents doubting the sincerity, and refusing, the gift.

In this book, Norman Newberg speaks in the voice of Gramsci's public intellectual. He asks us to think through the promise, the State, privatization and "gifts." he dares us to imagine *what could be* in a nation eating so many of our young. The Belmont 112 also ask us, from their college classrooms, corporate jobs, hair braiding salons in their living rooms, the streets and from prison, to respond with urgency to the structural crime scene we call "poverty" in America.

References

Chaikan, J. *Crunching the numbers: Crime and incarceration at the end of the millennium.* Bureau of Justice Statistics: Washington DC, January 2000.

Fine, M., M. E. Torre, K. Boudin, I. Bowen, J. Clark, D. Hylton, M. Martinez, Missy, R. Roberts, P. Smart, and D. Upegui. *Changing minds: The impact of college in prison.* The Graduate Center: City University of New York, 2001. www.changingminds.ws

Lu, H., and H. Koball. "Living at the edge: The changing demographics of low income families." New York: National center for children in poverty, August 2003.

Mauer, M., and R. King "Schools and prisons: 50 years after Brown." Washington, DC: The Sentencing Project, 2004.

"Racial disparities in incarceration rates." *Prison Policy Institute Newsletter.* Washington, DC: Prison Policy Institute, 2000.

Preface

On June 19, 1987, one hundred and twelve sixth-grade students in Philadelphia's Belmont Elementary School received a remarkable offer from George and Diane Weiss of Hartford, Connecticut. Upon graduation from high school, the students' college or vocational training tuition would be paid in full by the Say Yes to Education Foundation (SYTE), which the Weisses sponsored. Sixty-five percent of the Belmont students came from families living at or below the poverty line, and all were African-American. Of the group, 47 percent were identified as "learning disabled," an unusually high percentage. Students and their parents at first found this opportunity difficult to comprehend. One parent described the impact the offer had on parents and students:

> For a single mother of four, working every day to support my little ones and having known first hand the struggle to try to educate yourself despite the knowledge that this education will put you in debt for years to come, there could have been no greater gift given to my son or to me. Many of the parents of the children who received this special gift have not grasped the importance of it, for they, too, lack the education that affords them the privilege to dream. The Say Yes to Education Foundation has rekindled in many of our families the hopes and dreams we once believed were out of reach.

Many of the 112 would eventually obtain a college degree. Others would define success differently, using the resources provided to them to chart their own course. Still others would not complete high school despite the efforts of SYTE staff, mentors, and family networks. This book tells these stories and explores the reasons some were able to use the gift and some were not.

Data Collection

Because students continuously changed and developed, the staff could not make assumptions about their needs. Therefore, the program coordinators kept an ongoing journal of student narratives, so that staff and sponsors could review running records of students' development. Several different data sources were assessed in order to produce a well-rounded portrait of each student and of the program's impact on the entire group. An outside researcher collected records of students' academic performance on standardized tests and teacher-given marks from sixth through twelfth grades. Of the twenty-five interviews from which I have culled material for this book, seven were conducted by Randall Sims and eighteen by the author. Prior to each interview, groups of parents and students reviewed the protocol of questions to check for clarity and appropriateness of wording, and generated additional questions that reflected their interests. Key questions were repeated in two or three of the subsequent years to assess changes in student growth over time. The first interviews were held in 1993 as students were preparing to graduate high school. Eighty-eight students out of 110 participated (two of the original Belmont 112 were deceased); twenty-two dropouts did not. The 1993 interviews explored students' interest in school, their assessment of the quality of education they received, the obstacles encountered and strengths employed as they progressed through grade school, and their hopes for the future.

The second round of interviews was conducted in 1996, when SYTE high school graduates were three years out of secondary school, attending two- or four-year colleges or vocational training centers, or working. Dropouts worked at low-level jobs and/or were involved in the drug trade. The 1996 interviews explored five major topics: students' ability to benefit from a postsecondary school education, students' capacity to make decisions, the effects of racism, the motives of students who became teenage parents, and the ability of students to imagine positive roles for themselves that might guide them into young adulthood. By 1996, four of the Belmont 112 had died; sixty-four out of 108 students participated in these interviews.

The third set of interviews, in 1999, sampled forty students in or out of two- and four-year colleges, and thirteen high school dropouts. Analysis of these interviews was organized within these categories: issues of independence and dependence, choosing careers, overcoming environmental influences such as drugs, alcoholism, violence, and poverty, exploring student interest in giving back to the younger generation, and examining student beliefs about their future. Each time interviews were conducted, a sample was drawn to reflect these basic categories: high school as a terminal degree, two- and four-year college attendees or graduates, pursuing vocational training certification, and dropouts. In addition, parents' views on these subjects were surveyed in small focus group discussions. Finally, we interviewed persons who provided perspectives from complementary vantage points, including the program sponsor, George Weiss, program coordinators, and high school and elementary school teachers and administrators.

Each round of interviews was analyzed to reflect the impact of program interventions and the nature of individual student and group development. Thus, these interviews provided a form of action research for program staff and sponsors that probed the state of the program and marked those areas needing attention. Whenever possible, outcomes were compared with those of similar populations that did not have the benefit of the SYTE intervention. An external researcher studied the Belmont 112 from 1987 to 1992, and 1993 with regard to standardized test achievement, attendance, and high school graduation rates, and compared them with those of students from the same school one year behind and one year ahead of the SYTE group (Schlesinger 1993). By 2000, the group used to compare Belmont outcomes in high school could not be found in sufficient numbers to use at the postsecondary level. Instead, two surrogate comparisons were made. One used census tract data and the other used the outcomes of Tell Them We Are Rising, a similar tuition guarantee program in Philadelphia. The high school portraits of Michelle and Roger first appeared in Urban Education in 1996 (Newberg and Sims 1996).

Telling the Story

The book is based on the three stages in Marcel Mauss' theory of gift-exchanges: giving, receiving, and paying back. I use these broad theoretical markers to provide structure for the narrative of how the gift was given, the ways in which it was received and the effort put forth to give back. Gift-giving, according to Mauss, exposes ". . . the freedom and obligation inherent in the gift," and how "generosity and self-interest are linked in giving . . ." (Mauss 1954, 68). The Say Yes to Education story describes the individuals involved in the various stages of gift-giving and receiving and the obligation to give back. There are three relevant actors in this story. First, I explore the motivation of the sponsors, with a focus on their generosity and self-interest. Next, I closely examine the students, looking in particular at their quest for freedom to set their own life course, their obligation to use the gift productively and the necessity of returning in some form the gift they had received. Along the way the reader learns about the staff, who managed the middle ground between sponsors and students so as to facilitate realization of the gift.

Part one (chapter 1) tells about the giving of an unusual gift, an all expenses paid postsecondary education, to a group of students who did not ask for it. After the initial excitement about the scholarship quieted, students and parents slowly came to understand that the gift was really not free. There was no magical pot of gold one could collect at some office. Rather, Say Yes was an invitation to an uphill struggle to make going to school an everyday rule. The sponsors and staff expected their students to work hard to master school subjects and to seek help when they were having trouble understanding assignments. These were foreign expectations that many students and their parents did not always meet as a part of their daily routine. The sponsors communicated that the gift was real, but came at a cost to the beneficiaries. Who were these sponsors who made such a generous offer quite blindly to a group of students who, prior to the public announcement, were complete strangers? Who were the sponsors' role models? What kinds of relationships did students and sponsors develop? How did the sponsors understand their role as advocates for the students? What class issues emerged between sponsors' and students' values?

Part two (chapters 2, 3, and 4) explores how students acted out their responses to the gift at home, at school, and on the street. Parents, students, teachers, SYTE staff and sponsors were the actors in these arenas through middle and senior high school—removing barriers, opening doors, and hacking out a pathway that made learning possible and important. Each of these actors shaped the meaning of the gift to motivate inner-city students to achieve. However, staff and sponsors understood that for those who were "achieving failure" in school subjects, oppositional behavior seemed like a functional response, rather than a negative one, to an opportunity that appeared unattainable (Varenne et. al. 1998). Elijah Anderson, an African-American ethnographer of urban communities, notes that individuals in poor inner-city neighborhoods live some combination of "decent" and "street" lives (1999). These categories are global and include most of the behavior in inner-city neighborhoods. It is necessary to add that any community encompasses a range of responses to its environment. With that caveat in mind, Anderson's categories provide a useful first cut in analyzing SYTE student behavior. The students who pursued academic studies so that they might be able to use the scholarship seemed to align themselves with inner-city people who live in "decent" households. The "decent" people conform to the norms and values espoused by middle-class Americans (punctuality, a serious attitude, and commitment to academic studies, respect for authority, belief that hard work is eventually rewarded) even though, from an economic standpoint, the "decent" people may be part of the working-class strata of society. Students whose lives are focused on being "street" join drug gangs, frequently drop out of school, solve problems violently, and believe that authorities are to be "gotten over" (duped, ignored, or defied). For those who live in both worlds, some form of code switching is necessary to manage the contrasting expectations (Anderson 1999).

The Belmont 112 played out their roles as decent, street, or code switchers in their schools, homes, and streets. The facts of their lives were determined by forces they did not control, such as neighborhood, segregated living, racism, the underworld drug economy, and a scarcity of role models who demonstrated that education paid off. SYTE attempted to counteract these powerful negative stressors by instilling in its charges a culture of academic press in which students would become ambitious to learn and accountable for their behavior.

The gift fomented tensions and pressures in students to become academic achievers. In turn, their teachers were challenged to teach more effectively, knowing that these students had a guarantee of a fully paid postsecondary school scholarship. And since 39 percent of the population was schooled in special education classrooms, these children posed particular challenges to SYTE staff as they searched for opportunities to improve the odds that as many students as possible could use the scholarship. The gift had a broad impact across the community. The response of students, teachers, and parents to the challenges and pressures exerted by the program form the content of part two.

Giving back comprises part three (chapters 5 and 6). Gifts do not come free. The giver of the gift underscores that his or her relationship to the students and their families is an unequal one. The sponsors provided resources that necessarily caused feelings of indebtedness. What power resides in the gift that causes some recipients to pay it back? (Mauss 1954). In what ways were they able to pay back their debt? In what ways was it impossible to find a way to give back? Chapter 5 focuses on how those students first mentioned in chapter 4 experienced postsecondary schooling. Several questions shape this analysis: First, for those attending a postsecondary school, how did they experience advanced education? Embedded in this question are concerns about the preparation students brought to college, the ability to study and use support services, and their socialization to an academic environment. Second, how does racism affect their lives? Third, how did the postsecondary experience help them clarify their career goals? And fourth, how do students understand the concept of giving back? With that in mind, how do these students think about their futures? In particular, how do they define success for themselves?

In chapter 6, the book concludes with a perspective on lessons learned: a set of policy recommendations and implementation strategies for school systems and communities derived from this study. The value of programs like SYTE lies in their capacity to re-think who is capable of learning and what it might take to see that more become so. This chapter reflects back on America and what it does (and does not) offer these youth, their families and their communities. It raises questions about what these data mean for our understandings of youth development, schooling, special education, and the corrosive effects of poverty in a society where social safety nets are shredding. While the reader will see the value of the generous philanthropy of the sponsors of Say Yes, it will also become apparent that philanthropy alone cannot take the place of governments' responsibility to provide quality education for all children.

Acknowledgments

This will be an incomplete list of people I wish to thank, but I will mention those who had the most direct influence on making the writing of the book possible: Joel Goldstein, Peter Buttenweiser, Joan Lipsitz, Henry Koppel, Tsvi Yisraeli, Maria Casillas, Peter Kuriloff, Renee Fox, Margaret Beale Spencer, Lee Ann Gorfinkle, Chana Joffe-Walt, Wayne Higley, Barbara Stevens, Sheldon Hackney, Marvin Lazerson, and Mona Basta. Randall Sims, senior Say Yes project coordinator, was invaluable in helping to develop question protocols for the interviews. He also skillfully conducted several of the interviews. Diane Greenberg, teacher of writing and good friend, helped me to find an authentic voice to tell the students' life histories. I am grateful to Lisa Chesnel, acquisitions editor at State University of New York (SUNY) Press, who expressed interest in my book proposal and marshaled it through the review process and Board approval for publication. Kelli Williams, production editor for SUNY Press, capably guided me through the various stages of editing to final production. Ellen Frankel read early drafts and offered suggestions about how to think about the structure of the book. Mary Helen Spiri helped me shape a first cut at analyzing the 1993 and 1994 student interviews. Natalie Jaffe used her sharpened pencil to offer editorial advice on several chapters. Deirdre Martinez wrote the section on cost analysis found at the beginning of chapter 6. She was particularly helpful in finding appropriate national statistics and read the book numerous times, editing various drafts. Michelle Fine, as she notes in the foreword, has been a witness to the development of this book. Her penetrating observations moved me to reconsider how I presented the lives of the Belmont 112. I value her friendship and her honest criticism.

My children, Josh, Liam, Jeremey, and Noga were encouraging advocates. Noga read many of the interviews as they were being transcribed.

She was twelve-years-old at the time and asked those innocent questions that made me reconsider some of my assumptions. Adina, my life partner, never doubted that I would finish this book. I could count on her incisive comments to move my writing forward. As always, she knew when to offer advice and when to listen.

PART 1

Giving the Gift

CHAPTER 1

Giving the Gift

Catching the ball

The Genesis of Say Yes to Education

The University of Pennsylvania in the mid-1980s was at the beginning of a cycle of involvement with its surrounding community in an effort to establish a more open and responsive relationship. Central to the community's and university's concerns was the quality of the neighborhood schools. I formed the Collaborative for West Philadelphia Schools in 1986 as a vehicle for initiating dialogue and seeking solutions. It was chaired by Sheldon Hackney, then Penn's president, and the presidents of Drexel University and the Philadelphia College of Science and Pharmacy. Two bank executives, representing commercial interests, an associate superintendent for the city's schools, the superintendent for West Philadelphia, local teachers and principals, and several community activists comprised the committee's membership. The Collaborative was charged with researching the schools' needs and enlisting the institutions in finding appropriate solutions. As executive director of the Collaborative, I surveyed thirty area schools and learned that teachers, administrators, and parents were most concerned about the need for scholarship funds, the high dropout rates, and the lack of after-school tutoring services. Parents were particularly distressed by the fact that too few of their children were academically able to compete successfully for college admission. The agenda the Collaborative pursued based on that survey included: producing a resource guide for schools and

3

parents; identifying the kinds of services available through various agencies in the community; a massive recruitment and training of over six hundred students from the three colleges to act as tutors in thirty area schools; the College Access program in West Philadelphia, which raised $1.2 million for students who were likely to be accepted by a college, but had insufficient funds to attend; Bridging the Gap, a research and implementation project designed to stem the dropout rate and improve planning and communication across school boundaries; and a program for a group of students entering seventh grade, who were selected for intensive educational support through high school and into a postsecondary education. In the spring of 1987, George and Diane Weiss agreed to sponsor such a program, which was named Say Yes to Education.

Bridging the Gap

In response to the dropout concern, I initiated an action research study that involved eight elementary schools and three middle schools, all feeding into one high school. The project, Bridging the Gap, analyzed student test data, grades, attendance patterns, and styles of teaching at each level (Newberg 1991). The organizing hypothesis asserted that students who accumulate histories of failure between grades one and eight are most likely to drop out by the end of ninth grade. Early warning signs are most apparent in the transition between elementary and middle schools, when academic expectations change. Often by fourth or fifth grade, students who eventually drop out are one to two years behind grade level in reading and math. These deficits compound as the students move through grades without ever catching up. Some of these problems were addressed by investing teachers and administrators in the success of a cohort, rather than a single grade of students, over multiple years and across school levels. Particular attention was given to the redesign of ninth grade into small "houses" or learning communities so that teachers could monitor student progress carefully and intervene quickly when students were failing. As a result of this work, the entire school district of Philadelphia was restructured into feeder pattern clusters in an attempt to reduce the scale of management and supervision. This work was replicated in the North Hollywood and Sun Valley schools in the Los Angeles Unified School District.

Tuition Guarantee Programs

Bridging the Gap functioned at a systemic level, affecting school organization, monitoring of student performance longitudinally, and providing teacher professional development (Newberg 1991). At a more micro level, Say Yes to Education attempted to demonstrate what could be accomplished when 112 low-resource inner-city students were supported by a sustained supplementary program over multiple years, providing some of the educational and social assistance available in more affluent school districts.

Tuition guarantee programs were first developed in the 1960s, as part of Lyndon Johnson's War on Poverty and funded by the Economic Opportunity Act of 1964 and the Carnegie Foundation. (Levine and Nidiffer 1996). Efforts to focus energy and expenditures on minority children, like the struggle to end segregation, reflected the belief that minority school failure could be remedied. A. Levine and J. Nidiffer identify three kinds of programs, each designed to address the academic and social needs of children born in poverty: transition, early intervention, and comprehensive programs (1996). At the federal level, the creation of Upward Bound in 1965 was intended to serve as a transition program between high school and college. There are currently 566 Upward Bound projects serving about forty-two thousand students. At least two-thirds of each project's participants must be selected from low-income households (under 150 percent of the poverty level) and neither of whose parents has graduated from college. Upward Bound projects offer extensive academic instruction as well as counseling, mentoring, and other support services. Students meet throughout the school year and generally participate in an intensive residential summer program that lasts from five to eight weeks. Most students—about 90 percent—enter Upward Bound while in the ninth or tenth grade, and about 35 percent remain with the program through high school graduation. Upward Bound projects are generally operated by two- or four-year colleges. The annual average cost per participant is about $4,200. An initial evaluation of the program that followed a group to high school completion found that Upward Bound makes a substantial difference in the lives of certain groups of students, especially students entering the program with lower educational expectations, students with serious academic problems, and boys. Results also show that duration of participation is linked to positive program outcomes (Myers and Schirm 1999).

In addition to transition programs such as Upward Bound, the 1960s saw the creation of a number of early intervention programs, including A Better Chance (ABC). To date, ABC has placed more than eleven thousand middle and junior high school students in college preparatory schools, both public and private, nationwide. According to ABC's own statistics, more than 99 percent of A Better Chance graduating seniors immediately enroll in college. It should be noted that although ABC originally targeted low-income youth, their program has always focused on youth who have already demonstrated academic potential. More recently, changes in funding have resulted in a change in their target group, to largely middle-class youth. Their outcomes, therefore, while impressive, cannot be compared to programs such as Say Yes to Education, which targets low-income minority urban youth, regardless of academic ability.

Comprehensive programs, including tuition guarantee programs, move beyond academic counseling or short-term involvement; comprehensive programs provide not only mentors and academic, social, and cultural enrichment, but also make a long-term commitment to each individual in the program. Tuition guarantee programs are comprehensive programs that go one step further, by providing guaranteed college funding.

While characteristics of tuition guarantee programs differ, the typical program "adopts" a group of elementary school students, provides mentoring and academic supports, and guarantees some amount of money for college. The first and most widely known tuition guarantee program was started in 1981 by Eugene Lang in New York City. With nearly 180 projects in sixty-four cities across twenty-seven states, "I Have a Dream" (IHAD) has now served over thirteen thousand students during its more than two decades of operation. Most "Dreamers" who go to college are the first members of their families to do so. However, results vary among IHAD programs. Related to this finding, Levine and Nediffer expose a significant weakness in the IHAD programs. Because "there is no research base to indicate which elements of the program work and which do not, there is no way of understanding what makes IHAD effective" (Levine and Nidiffer 1996, 178). Beyond understanding the key elements of their success, IHAD has neither published data on postsecondary school outcomes, nor have they provided a comparison group to evaluate the program's effectiveness.

While Say Yes is in many ways similar to IHAD, association with universities differentiated Say Yes from its progenitor. IHAD prided itself on being a freestanding organization without an institutional home. Eugene Lang believed that each sponsor should have complete freedom to develop his or her program. It was his way of preventing bureaucratic tangles that might get in the way of serving IHAD children's needs. George Weiss and I held an opposite view, believing that there was much to gain by associating SYTE with universities, including research opportunities, a prodigious pool of student volunteers, and academic colleagues who could assist in meeting program needs or those of individual students. Association with a university would also provide the capacity to conduct systematic evaluation of a tuition guarantee program, up to and including postsecondary attainment rates of participants. Previous literature, including a report by the General Accounting Office, has recognized the need for evaluation that identified a comparison group at the outset (U.S. GAO 1990). The comparison group for SYTE is described in the data collection section.

A year after the start of SYTE, a second last-dollar scholarship program, Tell Them We Are Rising, was established in North Philadelphia by Temple University, with participants comparable to SYTE's in terms of the special education population, neighborhood influences, teenage pregnancies, and kinds of inner-city schools attended. This project allowed us to compare SYTE's postsecondary school outcomes to a similar scholarship program.

Say Yes to Education

The final agenda item from the work of the Collaborative was the creation of a program to support a cohort of students starting at the end of sixth grade and extending through postsecondary education. The program was operated by an executive director (the author of this book) who hired two project coordinators. As students worked their way toward high school graduation, SYTE coordinators provided such services as tutoring, counseling, regular home visits, advocacy, mentoring, college visits, internships, and summer school enrichment programs.

But for the recipients of the promise, the SYTE students, the pledge seemed distant and unreal. Few students could imagine in 1987 that they might be able to take advantage of the gift in 1993, the year they were scheduled to graduate from high school. The staff discovered in their first meetings with students that they were reluctant or unable to describe the kind of person they wished to become. They had little or no orientation to the future.

Initially, the two African-American project coordinators, Randall Sims and Lily Holloway, visited each student's home to discuss the gift with their families, and to interview the students about their strengths, weaknesses, talents, and interests. The coordinators picked up a wealth of information about available family supports, and assessed the gaps in a family's ability to provide for their children. Fifty-three percent of the mothers and forty-seven percent of the fathers of these children had not completed high school. The program was asking a large proportion of parents to help their children achieve educational goals the adults had not attained themselves.

Each introductory student interview concluded with the following question: What would you like to be when you finish school? Fewer than twenty-five percent of students responded; they couldn't imagine a possible future. They did not see their parents as models of school success, and did not connect school with the ability to construct a viable future. Further, the school system they attended communicated, through its tracking and grade retention policies, that success in school was not for all children and, more precisely, not for them. Minority students from low-income families are particularly at risk for subject failure, retention in grade and, finally, dropping out. They feel devalued and, as a result, become alienated from school.

The SYTE program set out to create an alternative vision of the future for SYTE students, their families, and the schools they attended. The ensuing years of support provided by staff and sponsors required students to work hard, be persistently motivated to succeed, and believe that education could make a positive difference in their life chances. SYTE staff members were responsible for communicating the vision and translating its meaning into the incremental steps that students had to take to achieve their goals.

The staff carefully monitored students' academic performance. Regularly scheduled meetings with classroom teachers, counselors, and administrators assessed student progress and explored alternative methods of instruction when that seemed indicated. If SYTE was going to change the odds for student success, the staff believed that a comprehensive approach was essential—one that combined an array of social supports, academic monitoring, advocacy for school reform, and deep parental involvement. In a sense, the program was much more than a gift that changed the opportunity structure for students from low-income families. The program was making a critical point: without transforming relationships and widening the sense of possibility, students would not be able to take advantage of better opportunities.

The Penn Connection

I have served as executive director since the program's inception in 1987. I recommend policy and implementation strategies, and provide general oversight to the five existing programs. Philadelphia has three chapters, each connected to the University of Pennsylvania. Both Hartford, Connecticut, and Cambridge, Massachusetts have established chapters in cooperation with Hartford University and Lesley University, respectively. For the Belmont group, Penn provided medical and dental services at no cost. Consultation on mental health issues was provided by the Penn Council for Relationships on a sliding scale. Close connections developed between the Penn football program and Say Yes, under the aegis of George Weiss. The football program supplied free tickets to games; but more importantly, Penn's winning team coach, Ed Zubrow, took a particular interest in the students. He ran football clinics for them and gave inspirational workshops on the dangers of drug use and dealing. Later, he became an active member of SYTE's board of directors. George Weiss, president of the board, had received his bachelor's degree from Penn's Wharton School of Business and Finance; students at Wharton who admired an alumnus's financial success and public largesse supported SYTE. Wharton's MBA program organized a Say Yes to Education club and sustained it for over a decade, recruiting hundreds of tutors and mentors. The Graduate School of Education offered office space and counsel from faculty. Former Dean Marvin Lazerson, also a board director, was instrumental in promoting the program within the university and nationally. He sponsored a national conference on university/community partnerships that brought practitioners and academics together to share ideas on how to deepen these connections. SYTE was featured in the conference program. The Penn connection offered a complex network of physical and human resources that would have been almost impossible for an independent entity to duplicate.

Meeting the Sponsors

In the spring of 1987, as executive director of the Collaborative for West Philadelphia Schools, I was searching for potential sponsors for the Say Yes to Education program. Sheldon Hackney, chair of the Collaborative, thought George and Diane Weiss of Hartford, Connecticut might be interested. George Weiss and Sheldon Hackney had met at an earlier time, and George had expressed his interest in setting up something like the I Have a Dream program. Based on that conversation, Dr. Hackney arranged for me to meet the Weisses in George's Hartford office. George was an associate trustee of the University of Pennsylvania and had founded a highly successful money management and brokerage firm. Diane was an activist who fought for integration in the schools her children attended in West Hartford, Connecticut. In addition to activism as a parent, she was also a knowledgeable educator with two master's degrees: one in student counseling and a second in school psychology with an emphasis on special education.

When I entered George's office, he stood up slowly from behind his desk and, with the aid of a cane, walked painfully to greet me. He explained that he was suffering from a severe back injury that was probably related to his training as a skull racer during his undergraduate years at Penn. George invited me to sit down and asked if I minded him reclining on the floor; being prone released pressure on his back and made it easier for him to talk. Orienting myself to his spacious office, I admired the giant photos of Penn football players in action displayed on the wall behind his desk. George had been a recruiter for Penn football, especially successful in bringing talented athletes to the team.

George's wife, Diane, came in, sat down on the floor with George and joined the discussion. I described several projects the Collaborative sponsored, including Bridging the Gap and Say Yes to Education. Very quickly George asked: "In that Say Yes program, would we be able to have direct contact with the kids? I don't want to just give money. We want to know the kids. We want to get involved in their lives." Diane concurred but added, "If we get into their lives, they'll want to be in our lives. It's a two-way street. Are we prepared for that?" Diane, with a background in counseling was sensitive to the nuances in relationships. George seemed to have made up his mind. "Yeah," he said, "that's OK. But in the beginning I may not be as involved as you might be. I won't be able to hop a plane and spend a day with them. Maybe later I could, if my back improves. So a lot would ride on your availability and interest in this." Diane was cautiously interested and said she'd like to think about it. George followed up with some questions about costs and urged me to get back to him in a week.

Who were these strangers who eventually agreed to take on the support of 112 inner-city students? How did their backgrounds prepare them for this unusual commitment?

Both of their parents were Jewish immigrants who fled Europe at the start of World War II. Diane's mother was raised in Czechoslovakia. Her father, one of six children, was born in Russia and worked his way through college, eventually obtaining a law degree from Yale University. George's father was born in Carlsbad, Austria. He aspired to be a doctor, but quotas during the mid-1930s in Vienna, as in the United States, restricted Jews' attendance at medical school. Instead, he studied music and chemistry. As a young man he had a career as a conductor and composer.

As a child, George saw his father as the eternal student, taking numerous advanced courses at universities. Although a high achiever academically, he lacked the ability to express warmth for his son. George, by contrast, was a jock who felt challenged and rewarded by athletics, but was not interested in music or the sciences, his father's passions. George thought of himself as "emotionally disadvantaged." He longed for affection from his father.

During his youth, George's father attempted a kind of intimacy with his son by posing difficult algebra problems for him to solve. This challenge earned George's respect for his father's brilliance, but left him with a longing for more ordinary ways of sharing with a son, like playing ball or going fishing. George's room, above the family garage, was often freezing cold in the winter, but nonetheless gave him sanctuary. As an adolescent, he reflected that "I would just go off and listen to hockey games and study and I was sort of . . . a lot of people block emotionally and I was sort of in my own world. The aim was to just survive." The lack of overt affection from his father left a void in George's life, one he continuously searched to fill. He felt a closer affinity with his mother.

Born and raised in Vienna, George's mother escaped Austria in the late 1930s. Having held a high administrative post in Vienna, she was able to transfer some of her administrative skills to hospital management when she immigrated to the United States. She commanded the higher salary; his father never cared about money. Lessons in financial matters were better taught by his mother, who understood money and knew how to manage it. George thought he probably took after her.

Both parents were clear about how to use their "disposable income," a term George learned at Penn's Wharton School of Business, where he studied finance as an undergraduate. As Austrian refugees, the Weisses had seen how the Jewish community had been destroyed by the policies of the Third Reich. Therefore, once they earned salaries in America, George said they took "a large percentage of their disposable income and gave it to Israel. They felt that if Israel doesn't make it, there'd be no hope for the Jews." George was struck by his parents' insecurity, but also their commitment to ensure a future for Jews. They modeled for him that giving had to have a purpose that was larger than ones' immediate self-interest.

A precursor to his approach to philanthropy occurred when George was an undergraduate at Penn. One year his fraternity sponsored a Christmas party for a gang of Irish and Italian boys from south Philadelphia. The "12 Apostles," as they called themselves, returned to the frat for other occasions, and George would often play basketball with them. After his graduation from the Wharton School of Business, George stayed in touch with the group. At one point, he invited the group to lunch. In the course of conversation, George realized that all twelve of these young men had graduated high school. George was stunned; he told them how proud he was of their accomplishment. He recalled they said: "George, we would not be able to look you in the eye if we dropped out." At that moment, George made a promise that if he ever had the financial ability to make a difference, he would do it through education. But he did not want to just give money for scholarships; he wanted to get to know the people he was helping in a more "hands on" manner. He was successful and believed that now it was his turn to give back.

Two heroes shaped the values George believed influenced the way he lived his life; the biblical David and former ambassador to England and newspaper magnate Walter Annenberg. David represented a childhood hero: ". . . the little guy that conquered the all-powerful giant, Goliath. Maybe that's part of my Jewish background. I used to get into a lot of fistfights as a kid and, being a Jew, when I was attacked I stood up for myself and my people, like David in the Bible did." In adulthood, George didn't abandon his self-image as the scrappy David who fights for the underdog. By the time George entered his mid-40s he had established a highly successful investment firm that traded electric utilities worldwide.

The moment that captured the man George aspired to become occurred at a meeting of Penn trustees. Walter Annenberg announced that he would give $120,000,000 to the university and George, a newly elected trustee, led the applause. Annenberg shook his head in disapproval. He approached the podium and said: "It is simply a matter of good citizenship." In that moment, Annenberg taught George how to think about wealth: its object is to do good in the world, not to accumulate things; it is about opening oneself up to others and demonstrating caring. In a reflective moment George comments: "I'll tell you what I'd like to see on my tombstone: 'here lies a man who made a difference.'" Establishing the Say Yes to Education college scholarship program in June 1987 gave George the opportunity to make a difference in the lives of 112 sixth-grade students who were about to graduate from an inner-city elementary school.

In its first five years, Diane participated actively in program development. She visited SYTE regularly and was a significant presence in all its aspects. Students grew to expect her unannounced visits to their schools, when she would counsel individual students about their academic work or personal concerns. Each summer she would move to Philadelphia for six weeks to teach writing and literature in SYTE's summer school. George was inactive the first year of the program, but when his back improved, he taught vocabulary development classes during summer school and hosted students in his West Hartford home. Because the Weisses were visiting Philadelphia on a regular basis, they bought a condominium in center city Philadelphia and entertained the students and their families in their home. These were times to meet in small groups over spaghetti dinners; they offered a chance for casual conversation. Not only did Diane and George meet with students and their families, but they also established close ties with the superintendent of schools and local politicians that gave them the opportunity to be effective advocates for the students' needs. In the spring of 1992, Diane addressed Philadelphia's City Council in support of the school district's plea for adequate funding for public education. She reflected on SYTE's work with the Belmont 112 over the previous five years, opening her address with this question:

What had we learned about the support of inner-city youth? The investment in human beings is unlike any other investment. There are no quick profits, no quick fixes, no easy solutions, but there are thousands of unknowns. The investment in human beings has to be taken seriously, early and long term—if it is to pay off.

She continued by urging the Council to maximize education dollars so that more children might benefit.

In his public statements, George often talked about how much the students had taught him—that they had made a better person of him. They taught him how to be a "mensch"—a Yiddish word meaning "a caring person" who could be touched by the pain poverty inflicted on innocent children. Giving the gift gave him access to his own feelings. It was much more than a tax break, as some critics suggested. The program connected him to the lives of individual students, their dreams, their limited horizons and opportunities. By providing the gift of a free higher education and supplemental social and academic supports to attain that goal, George felt he was redistributing some of his wealth so that more could share in the American Dream.

The combination of direct contact with students, their families, and political and educational leaders won recognition for the Weisses as people committed to making the program work. The purpose of Say Yes, from George's perspective, ". . . is to show people out there that these kids are in every way as bright as your kids, or my kids. The difference between these kids is that the SYTE kids have the odds stacked against them. Give these kids the same nourishment and support and they will make it." He summarized his reason for starting the program by reintroducing a basic theme in his life—"making a difference." "If other people are encouraged to stand up and make a difference," he asserted, "because we've shown the way, I think that's basically what I wanted." He wanted his message to reach people in business, school officials, government, and volunteers from all walks of life. In this instance, George made a difference by publicizing Say Yes so that others would follow his example.

George saw the program as a mix of the opportunity to go to college without the worry of loans, and sustained academic and emotional support by adults who cared. "You have to give kids hope," he urged. "If there's no hope, then they will drop out. The easiest thing to do is to drop out. Their parents have done it," alluding to the fact that half of the Say Yes students' parents had not completed high school.

"You have to give poor kids alternatives. Flipping hamburgers," punching his point home, "is not a great incentive to stay in school."

The Parents

Most parents appreciated the hope and the opportunity the Weisses extended. But George was concerned about those parents who did not attend the kick off meeting; some of those parents were less enthusiastic about the program. George remembered William Crandall's father who was paraplegic: "He didn't want to speak with me. He told me not to call him again. 'And don't come to my door,' Will's father said. 'And don't help my kid. I can take care of my kid.' " George was stunned "because I knew what my motives were and I didn't really understand why Will's dad didn't understand what the program was about. So that really threw me." He pondered: "I was sitting here saying, all I'm trying to do is help. So I tried to argue with him. But I still don't get it. I told him, 'Your kid is important to me.' Then he hung up on me." George was incredulous. He couldn't imagine that a parent might question his motives, which he believes were "pure." It was a hurtful rejection from a man in a weak physical and financial condition who did not want charity from a rich white man. Mr. Crandall's situation was unusually difficult, but he insisted on taking care of his own son in whatever way he felt was appropriate.

Poor people are placed in situations where they often need help. Unfortunately, that help is not always given in a way that respects the person receiving help. In fact, African-Americans can point to countless examples of abuse disguised as help. Consider the infamous Tuskegee Syphilis Study, in which 399 poor black sharecroppers in Macon County, Alabama were denied treatment for syphilis; they were deceived by physicians of the Unites States Public Health Service for forty years. The Tuskegee Syphilis Study was government-sponsored racism disguised as benevolent aid (Tuskegee Syphilis Study Legacy Committee 1996). In the private sector, there is an extensive history of African-American singers and songwriters who signed away lifetime rights to wildly successful songs and scores in return for a pittance. The number of African-American inventors in the early twentieth century will likely never be known, for their works were often appropriated by white men. Mr. Crandall's reaction may have been difficult to understand from the perspective of the sponsors, but for many African-Americans, skepticism would be a natural response to an offer that seemed too good to be true.

For sponsors and staff, Mr. Crandall's response was an early warning signal that we needed to be sensitive about how we gave support and to be aware of the message sent to those who were recipients.

Most parents, unlike Mr. Crandall, were pleased by the offer of the gift and embraced the Weisses for their generosity. Terrance's grandmother contrasted sharply with William's dad. "Terrance's grandmother always touched me," George remembered. "She has an artificial leg and we always joked about when we both get better we'll go dancing. So every time I've seen her, which is twice at Terrance's home, I kid with her saying, 'I'm ready when you are.' I always saw her as very supportive. She was in a tough situation, but she was there for Terrance and she was open with me."

Terrance's grandmother was not unusual in her capacity to be a giving person. Reviewing his experience with Say Yes families, George noticed: "I see very strong and loving mothers and grandmothers, but very little emotional support from the fathers. In a way, I see the SYTE families as even warmer than my own family." He reflected further on some of the differences between his own family and the students: "My father was distant, and my mother had to support the family, and I didn't get as much warmth and caring as some of these kids got."

If his parents could not give George the warmth and overt affection he craved, they did give him the unequivocal expectation that he would be an "educational success." His parents did not assume that George would necessarily go to an Ivy League college, "but there never was any thought that I wouldn't go to college. It was like not being a drug dealer. It just wasn't a factor. It was assumed I would go to college." George was aware that these students faced a different set of circumstances. George's father was a success in his academic pursuits and transmitted to his son a belief that education was important and necessary. George felt morally indignant with those whose sense of entitlement gives them the surety that they "have an earned privilege to a college education." "These kids," referring to the SYTE students:

> from the moment they get up in the morning, have the whole system against them. They lack meals, quality schools, being taught by disinterested teachers, fighting their way through drugs. Some of our kids take three buses to get home and then have to take care of siblings, losing your childhood because you're an unwed mother. What opportunity have these kids had except Say Yes? It's almost nonexistent. That's why drugs. They are looking for some-

thing to substitute for real opportunity. They want the power of dollars in their pocket. So they deal. Sometimes it's money to support a family. It's not right? It's not right that their family is starving either. When I talked to the Say Yes kids, I noticed that some of them are very anti-Asian. And I said to them: "Don't be jealous of what the Asians achieved. They worked hard and got what they deserved. Take their success as motivation to work harder to get what you deserve."

George viewed inner-city life as a paradox. On the one hand he understood that "the whole system is against them." He knew that poor Blacks lack opportunity to make a better life through the legitimate economy and therefore they are reduced to making money through drug deals or other marginal legal or illegal pursuits. But he was also impatient with SYTE students, hearing them complain about Asians crowding out Blacks from the limited opportunity that may exist in the poor neighborhoods they share. George implied that the capitalist dictum of "picking yourself up by your own boot straps" has worked for other minorities and felt impatient with those Blacks who will not exert sufficient effort to improve their lot. He believed, for a moment, that hard work is rewarded by the creation of opportunity.

Choosing the School

The first major step in creating the SYTE program was the selection of a school; it was important to do so without bias. Therefore, I asked Dr. Constance Clayton, superintendent of Philadelphia public schools (1982–1994), to select the school and a particular class in which the scholarships would be awarded. I asked her to consider two criteria in selecting a group of students: they should reside in West Philadelphia within a short drive from the University of Pennsylvania and should come from low-income African-American families. She recommended Belmont Elementary School. The day before the public announcement of the gift, I learned that forty-four of the 112 students slated to leave sixth grade for middle school had learning disabilities and required instruction exclusively in special education classrooms. How did Belmont Elementary School attract such a large special education population? That question remained unanswered for several years. After some probing, I learned from Dr. Ronald Brown, director of special education from 1990 through 1993 in West Philadelphia, that Belmont, because it was an underpopulated school, was designated as a regional special education center. Elementary schools throughout West Philadelphia sent their more difficult special education students to Belmont. However, the school had recently been selected for restructuring. A new principal, Sophie Haywood, was appointed the previous August 1986 with a mandate to whip Belmont into shape and quickly demonstrated that she was prepared for this task. During the year, she had reorganized reading instruction, welcomed parents and community members into the school, and focused everybody's attention on improving student achievement. When she learned of the Weiss' gift, she urged teachers to socially promote every student they possibly could into the commencement class. Mrs. Haywood "cleaned house" and insisted that Say Yes take the special education students who comprised 47 percent of the graduating class (Mezzacappa 1999b).

When I received the news about the large percentage of students enrolled in special education, I asked for a meeting with Penn's President Hackney, Marvin Lazerson, dean of the Graduate School of Education, and Barbara Stevens, executive assistant to the president. George Weiss was not able to come, but he and Diane contributed to the conversation via a conference call. I opened the meeting by stating that if we agreed to take on the special education students, we needed to accept the fact that many of these children had histories of chronic school failure. I raised the question of our ability to meet their needs within the context of a college-bound program. President Hackney, the father of an adult daughter who has an intellectual disability, weighed in quickly: "It's clear to me that we either include all of the students in the program or withdraw." George concurred: "It's like having two kids at Christmas or Chanukah and only giving one a present. I'm not going to have half of those students walk out of the auditorium disappointed. It's not what I'm about." Diane Weiss, who had experience evaluating special education students, argued that society saw these children as expendable. She asked us to fight against labeling and appreciate the potential each child has. Say Yes, the group concluded, was about hope, opportunity, and caring. Excluding the special education students seemed antithetical to the values the program espoused. SYTE should not deny any child the chance to make a better life through education.

After some debate, we agreed that all 112 students would be included. With this in mind, it was apparent that the Say Yes mission needed revision to include a wider range of student abilities. No longer could we think of it as a program for regular education students bound for college. Some special education students might gain admission to a four-year college, but for others, that aspiration seemed unrealistic; more likely, these students would attend community colleges or vocational schools. So the program made provision for possible attendance at these schools. Initially, Say Yes was designed to challenge inner-city regular education students to achieve high academic standards so that they could avail themselves of an all expenses paid four-year college scholarship. This was an ambitious goal because of the low academic standards and expectations common in inner-city schools. In a sense, Say Yes attempted to compensate for the failure of the public schools to educate children who had largely been abandoned by society. If that were true for regular education students, the problems were compounded for those in special education. Special education classrooms in the mid-1980s had become dumping grounds for children in urban school systems that did not know how to educate or lacked the will to try.

Announcing the Gift

George's chronic back problem prevented him from making the June 17, 1987 public announcement of the scholarship; he asked Diane to speak for both of them. She opened her remarks to the graduates with a stunning offer: "We are making you an offer none of you can refuse. I promise you. You have won the lottery. How can you collect? I'm here this morning to tell each and every one here that we will guarantee your college education. My family will pay for every bit of it." She clarified the terms of the deal with more specific details. "That means if each and every youngster on this stage graduates from high school with a diploma and is accepted to a college or technical training school, we'll pay all the costs." She closed by affirming that her family would do more than give money. Each member of the Weiss family, including George, Diane, and their daughters Debbie and Allison, would be involved personally as tutors and mentors. At the very end, she threw several footballs into the crowd of students on the stage. She said it was now the students' turn to catch the ball and run with it. The symbolism was unmistakable. The football represented the scholarship each student was promised. Now it was the students' responsibility, with the program's help, to grab hold of the opportunity and work hard to earn the prize on the other side of the goal post—high school graduation, a college education, or an appropriate postsecondary education. In the case of the Say Yes program, the givers of the gift (the Weisses) and those receiving it (the students) were connected in a way quite different from that of traditional gift-giving. The exchange did not end the day the scholarship was announced; the relationship between the donor and the recipient continued to develop and grow more complex over time. Although it would be some time before the students themselves would comprehend the power of the Weiss' gift, some of the parents had an immediate response. One parent explained her feelings:

> That was something that never in a lifetime. . . . We walked through the streets celebrating and my neighbor met us at the door and said, "I seen it on the news" and everyone was ecstatic. And it was something, we growed up down here, and it was something in a lifetime we never would have seen. We have never, we would never have seen this opportunity in a lifetime.

The Role of the Media

On the day the scholarship was announced at Belmont Elementary School, three major television channels, *The Philadelphia Inquirer* and *The Daily News,* the premier city newspapers, and the *Philadelphia Tribune,* a prominent African-American newspaper, covered the story. Periodically over the succeeding thirteen years, national newspapers and television featured updates on SYTE students who became known to the public as the Belmont 112. While other media followed the story through infrequent updates, *The Inquirer* published several front-page stories about the program annually, giving it prominent visibility in the greater Philadelphia community and beyond. Dale Mezzaccappa, *The Inquirer's* education reporter, wrote these major stories and made Say Yes a regular part of her news beat.

Early on, George saw the value of publicity. He wanted to "market" the SYTE product to the public. In order to do so, George needed a public forum for telling its story. An alliance formed between the media, the Say Yes sponsors, and the program staff. George used SYTE publicity as a local and national platform to talk about education in the inner city, the ravages of poverty, and the need for a communal commitment to alleviate these problems.

I felt that the program also had an obligation to protect its students from the press. As young adolescents who were mostly twelve years of age, I did not think it would be constructive for them to see their names in print. George and I met with the education editor of *The Inquirer* to discuss the matter. The newspaper argued it would be discreet in how it described the children, but felt that using names would promote public recognition of individual students. And since *The Inquirer* intended to follow the school career of these children "until the bitter end" (said ironically) of the program, the editor wanted to use real names. After some discussion, we reached a compromise. The paper agreed not to use student names for the next two years—through the end of eighth grade. When the students entered high school in ninth grade, the reporter, Dale Mezzacappa, would be required to ask each student's permission before his or her name could appear in print. The agreement was honored through junior high school and even into ninth grade, but by tenth grade it was abandoned. Students were not always told that what they said in an interview would appear with their name in the newspaper. My response was to tell the students they had the right to refuse an interview and to be aware that if they did agree to speak with a reporter, their names would appear in the newspaper.

Parents and students had an uneasy reaction to the constancy of the press in their lives. Some parents felt the press was only interested in the seamy side of ghetto life. As one parent said at a SYTE meeting, "If Dale came to my house, she might be surprised to see that my son has a bed of his own made up with clean sheets and blankets. That might disappoint her." Other parents said, "They're only interested in how many of our girls get pregnant." "They love to talk about drug dealers and how our boys end up in jail or get killed." Robin Wall Hill, a SYTE project coordinator, who was with the program for the first five years, interrupted the parents' complaints when she explained: "They need to sell newspapers. They need an angle that's going make people read the paper. And often the angle is about how things are bad in the ghetto."

The announcement of the gift at the Belmont graduation in June 1987 was a major public event. With newspaper and television media present that day, there was little opportunity for the students and their families to get to know the sponsors. But in the fall of that year, George and Diane met about seventy-five of the students and many of their parents at an inaugural party held in Gimbel Gym on Penn's campus. George, still nursing his bad back, walked around the large room holding on to a cane. He shook parents' hands and hugged students. He wanted a sense of intimacy with these families so that he might develop some appreciation of their lives, especially their hopes and fears for their children. This kind of disclosure necessarily takes time. But he and Diane and their daughters had committed themselves to a long-term relationship. The program acknowledged that students might not be able to finish the traditional four-year bachelor's degree in four years. The program understood that many of the students had familial responsibilities and might need more time. Therefore the program gave students seven years to complete a bachelor's degree. In practice, most completed the program in five years. In two exceptional cases, one student took six years and another took six and a half to complete their studies. This night in the fall of 1987 was the beginning of that journey.

The Communities

How realistic and how probable is it that inner-city Blacks can succeed in education without an intervention like SYTE? The following section reviews the literature and describes the Belmont feeder pattern—those communities or census tract neighborhoods that send children to Belmont Elementary School—whose statistics speak of the conditions that existed in the very communities where the Belmont 112 were raised.

Over the last twenty years, a large body of literature has demonstrated that certain structural problems pervade inner-city communities. W. J. Wilson (1997), D. S. Massey and N. A. Denton (1993), and E. Anderson (1990, 1999) present evidence that segregated inner-city Blacks are trapped in an environment characterized by low income, unemployment, and underemployment. Businesses and manufacturing entities that provide employment have abandoned these neighborhoods. Segregation perpetuates poor schools that inadequately prepare the next generation, produce an inordinately large percentage of unwed mothers who are destined for welfare dependency, and increase crime and drug sales. In particular, the decade of the 1980s saw an increase in income inequality and a polarization between the haves and the have-nots. The term widely used in the 1980s for the urban poor was the "underclass," which carried with it pejorative ideas of criminal, antisocial, and dysfunctional behavior. This "blame the victim" mentality often masked the reality of poverty in urban centers; the societal factors imposed on people living in poor neighborhoods inhibited their ability to move beyond their position. In an effort to more accurately define these externally imposed obstacles, Joel Devine in 1993 developed a definition of "underclass" that tried to focus the problem more appropriately:

> Persons living in urban, central city neighborhoods or communities with high and increasing rates of poverty, especially chronic poverty, high and increasing levels of social isolation, hopelessness, and anomie, and high levels of characteristically antisocial or dysfunctional behavior patterns. (p. 94)

Anderson, who has written ethnographic studies of two of the neighborhoods in the Belmont feeder pattern, observes that with the United States' shift from a manufacturing economy to a service and high-tech economy, workers with limited education and minimal work skills are displaced by those in more affluent communities who have the education and the competence that match the needs of the new economy. "In cities like Philadelphia," Anderson (1999) states:

> Certain neighborhoods have been devastated by the effects of deindustrialization. Many jobs have been automated, been transferred to developing countries, or moved to nearby cities like King of Prussia. For those who cannot afford a car, travel requires two hours on public transportation from the old city neighborhoods where concentrations of black people, Hispanics, and working-class Whites live. (p. 110)

The casual observer is fast to moralize about the inability of the poor to find work, and resents their substitutions for work such as welfare dependency, teen pregnancy, and drug trafficking. These and other rackets are there to pick up the economic slack. In addition, quasi-legal hustling, like holding down three and four jobs and other under-the-table cottage industries that go unreported, teach the younger generation how to survive in an economy in which they can not compete directly (Anderson 1999). In what ways did the neighborhoods in which SYTE students were born and raised conform to these patterns? How did the demographics of Belmont Elementary reflect on the lives and families of the Belmont 112?

The feeder pattern for the Belmont Elementary School comprises the following neighborhoods: Powelton Village, West Powelton, Mantua, Belmont, East Parkside, and Mill Creek, all located east of 52nd Street and north of Market Street, the main east–west thoroughfare through the city. They straddle Lancaster Avenue, the main commercial district for this area.

Poverty was widespread in this part of West Philadelphia, an underlying cause of the physical deterioration. In four out of seven of the census tracts within these neighborhoods, 1990 median incomes were less than 53 percent of the city median. The Belmont 112 were not alone in their struggle to escape poverty. By 1992, the national poverty rate had reached its highest levels since the 1964 War on Poverty, with 40 percent of the poor being children (J. Freedman 1993). Like many inner-city neighborhoods, the Belmont area was characterized by high unemployment, low-educational attainment, high rates of infant mortality, and very low birth weights. Many of the neighborhoods in the area were plagued by drug use, drug trafficking, and crime. Residents of these neighborhoods called their area "the bottom." Prior to the major shutdowns of local factories and other sources of employment, "the bottom" was a term of intimacy and pride. By the 1980s, the term had taken on a negative connotation descriptive of the down and out feeling of pervasive poverty.

The Belmont neighborhood itself, located just north of Lancaster Avenue at 41st and Brown Streets, displayed significant contrasts between blocks, some well-kept with houses in good repair, and others in which the housing was deteriorating and vacant lots were frequent. The bleak and desolate appearance of the area surrounding the school was matched by a devaluing of human life through poverty, drugs, and violence. Between 1987 and 1993, over half of SYTE students' parents had been involved in taking illegal addictive drugs for at least two years. While the number of SYTE students using drugs was relatively small, the percentage involved in selling drugs was high. A veteran teacher who taught at Belmont for over thirty years noted that when she asked her "third-graders to describe the things they see on their street, twenty-five years ago children talked about people sitting on front stoops, kids playing, and dog poop by the trees. Now kids talk about hiding behind front steps to escape gunfire, covering their ears when they hear police sirens, and finding drug caps strewn along the pavement." The high incidence of black-on-black murder is directly related to drug trafficking. One community member mourned the loss of an increasing number of young black men murdered in the early 1990s. She noted with despair that:

> A lot of children that graduated from Belmont, a lot of males that graduated from here, were killed in gangs and a lot of them got killed, you know around here in the neighborhood. With drugs and, you know, dealing in drugs and things like that. At one point I was going to funerals like crazy.

Of the Belmont 112, five were murdered in drug-related incidents. The scholarship offer did not spare them.

School personnel estimated that 60 percent of Belmont school children during the 1980s lived in households headed by single females and 70 percent were on welfare. SYTE parents were on the high end of this range, with 75 percent of families headed by single mothers and between 65 to 75 percent on welfare.

The average poverty rate for the entire feeder pattern was 35 percent or nearly four times the citywide poverty rate of 9 percent in 1980. By 1990, the feeder pattern for Belmont had changed little; the poverty rate was 33 percent while the citywide poverty level had doubled to 16 percent. Predictably, family incomes attest to the level of poverty in the Belmont feeder pattern. Incomes ranged from $6,124 to $16,957, less than half the median income for the city in 1980 and less than the national median income of $21,023. By 1990, the median income ranged from $7,710 to $19,195, approximately 50 percent less than the citywide family median income of $30,140 which was also less than the national median for all families of $35,353. Black median incomes nationally were similar to the median incomes in Belmont, at $12,674 in 1980 and $21,423 in 1990.

Apart from the percentage of welfare recipients in the Belmont feeder pattern, a large number of residents were unemployed. The number of those included as unemployed in the U.S. Census is a drastic undercount because only those people actively looking for work are included. The chronically unemployed are not counted. In 1980, the average unemployment rate was approximately 26 percent, or more than three times the citywide rate of 8 percent. In 1990, the average for Belmont was still three times higher than the citywide rate, at 20 percent vs. 6 percent.

Looking just at the national unemployment rate in 1988 for black males between the ages of eighteen and nineteen, nearly one in three males were out of work (31.7 percent). Also in 1988, the Congressional Research Service determined that key measures of standard of living, including real wages, had fallen since the 1970s. They found that the average worker entering the workforce in 1988 was likely to earn less than someone who had entered the workforce fifteen years earlier (Bingaman 1988). The effect of a chronic lack of adequate employment has far-reaching effects at the individual and the community levels. For the individual, long-term entrenched poverty is the direct effect. For the community, the limited tax base results in a substandard infrastructure that is unable to support quality schools, provide health and housing assistance, or encourage entrepreneurship.

Not surprisingly, Belmont feeder pattern residents had attained lower educational status than residents of other areas. They fell short of citywide and national rates by percentages roughly analogous to the difference in income levels, poverty levels, and the percentage of welfare recipients.

These demographic factors probably contributed to the low level of academic accomplishment many area adults experienced when they were in high school. In 1980, 48 percent of residents in the Belmont feeder pattern, on average, had attained less than a high school diploma. Similarly, only 50 percent of SYTE parents had completed a four-year high school education. These figures worsen when compared to the number of students who graduated from the high school most Belmont students attend. Only 25 percent of the entering ninth grade class had graduated from University City High School four years later in 1992, one year earlier than the SYTE students were scheduled to graduate.

Segregated high schools in inner-city communities are notorious for the poor quality of instruction. And low expectations from educators combined with poverty-stricken home lives produce outcomes for students that condemn them to marginal futures with few options. When Richard DeLone studied histories of inner-city children for the Kenniston Commission at Yale University during the 1970s, he determined that there was little reason for these children to hope for a better future than their parents,' hence the title of his book *Small Futures* (1979). Jonothan Kozol's *Savage Inequalities* documented the vast differences between spending in urban districts and suburban districts (1991). Stories of crumbling buildings, not enough chairs for students to sit on, and no textbooks to read contrast with suburban schools housed in glittering buildings filled with the latest technology, new textbooks every year and small class sizes.

One contributor to the inequality in per pupil spending is the declining role of state spending on local school systems in Pennsylvania.

The share of local school costs that comes from the state has been shrinking for three decades (Gewertz 2001). In the 1970–71 school year, the state provided an average of 54 percent of the cost of schools statewide. In 2000, the state covered an average of only 37 percent of the cost of public education. The level of state funding provided in Pennsylvania is low by national standards; only thirteen states contribute less than 40 percent. To compensate for the loss of state funding, local tax rates have risen. In the late 1990s, local property taxes rose by $1.7 billion to compensate for the loss of state funding. The increased reliance on property taxes exacerbated funding inequality, due to the fact that the tax base in the suburbs was considerably higher than the base available for taxation in the city. Of the dollars that do flow from the state, the formula used to distribute these dollars does not provide a foundation amount to the districts with concentrated poverty sufficient to ensure an adequate education. A foundation formula, which is used by at least forty states nationwide, would guarantee all districts a minimally adequate level of funding. In the 1999 school year, Pennsylvania's highest spending school district spent $222,000 more on a class of twenty-five students than the state's lowest spending district (Gewertz 2001).

Quite possibly as a result of these spending inequities, nearly half of Pennsylvania's students are failing to demonstrate proficiency in math and reading as determined by the Pennsylvania System of School Assessment (Donley and von Seideneck 2003). Nationally, urban students perform far worse, on average, than children who live outside central cities on virtually every measure of academic performance. As studies show that achievement is directly related to the quality of teaching, statistics also reveal the difference in the quality of teachers urban districts can afford compared to suburban districts. Lower per pupil expenditures in urban districts, combined with the additional challenges urban teachers face, restrict the quality of teachers urban districts can attract. Secondary students in high-poverty schools are twice as likely as those in low-poverty schools (26 percent vs. 13 percent) to have a teacher who is not certified in the subject taught (Olson 2003). Students in high-poverty, high-minority schools are also more likely to be taught by inexperienced teachers. Schools serving high-poverty, high-minority, and low-achieving students have a harder time not only finding qualified teachers, but also keeping them. In high-poverty middle schools in Philadelphia, for example, 46 percent of teachers in 1999–2000 had come to their schools within the previous two years (Neild et al. 2003).

This inequality in the schools ironically is occurring at the same time spending on prisons is skyrocketing. A recent report shows that during the 1980s and 1990s, average state spending on corrections grew at six times the rate of state spending on higher education, and by the close of the millennium, there were nearly a third more African-American men in prison and jail than in universities or colleges (Justice Policy Institute 2002).

For those who managed to complete high school, college costs were climbing out of reach. College costs went up by approximately 60 percent in the decade of the 1980s and by approximately 40 percent in the 1990s (College Board 2002).

In summary, the Belmont feeder pattern reflects some of the more daunting aspects of segregated life for Blacks in the inner city, with high unemployment and underemployment leading to poverty and the need for government assistance. Lack of employment opportunities often seduces young black males to improve their lot by selling drugs. Drug-selling gangs in the inner city take care of their homies by offering them a false sense of security through incomes they do not have the skills to earn in the dominant society. Frequently older men, twenty to thirty years of age, direct these gangs and deliberately hire school-age kids to sell drugs. Juveniles, if arrested by police, receive light sentences and are soon out on the street looking for the drug lord who would employ them. It is a fail-safe compact that protects the adult who makes most of the profits off the kids' backs. These gangs are also the source of violent rivalries that contribute to the tragically high number of deaths among black males.

Schools offer little relief or refuge from life on the streets. This is the backdrop against which the Belmont 112 played out their lives. Generally, within constrained conditions, people have some choice. They can choose to be "decent" or "street" in Anderson's language. But certain conditions and circumstances can predetermine direction. Racism, poverty, and lack of opportunity perpetuate and reproduce negative conditions. The paucity of opportunity makes escape from poverty through education precarious.

The Social Context

Despite the reality of inner-city life, the idea that Blacks and other minorities lack ambition, motivation, and persistence to work their way out of poverty has currency in this country; poverty is viewed as self-inflicted. Initially, George seemed to agree with Shelby Steele's (1990) critique in his book *The Content of Our Character: A New Vision of Race in America*; Steele chides fellow Blacks for whining about the bad cards fate dealt them and urges them to take charge of their lives. Steele is fully aware that discrimination against Blacks has been a destructive force for generations. Therefore, he urges that while Blacks and Whites must fight racism, Blacks must simultaneously find the energy and motivation to support themselves. This line of reasoning is consistent with black conservatives' argument against welfare entitlements, perhaps best articulated by the work of Thomas Sowell, a black economist at Stanford University (1981). Interventions such as welfare and affirmative action, Sowell believes, deaden initiative among Blacks to compete for a better standard of living. George concurred with this analysis; but as his earlier statements attest, he understood that the system has not created a level playing field.

Of course, this belief is not a new one for Americans. In the 1860s, Ralph Waldo Emerson published his essay, "Self-Reliance," in which he stresses the importance of taking responsibility for one's own situation and depending only on oneself for support. "But do your work, and I shall know you. Do your work, and you shall reinforce yourself" (Emerson 1865, 54). Not only does Emerson declare the importance of self-reliance, but criticizes social institutions whose mission it was to aid those in need: "Then again, do not tell me, as a good man did today, of my obligation to put all poor men in good situations. Are they my poor? I tell thee, thou foolish philanthropist, that I grudge the dollar, the dime, the cent I give to such men as do not belong to me and to whom I do not belong" (Emerson 1865, 52). Some Americans do "grudge the dollar" paid through taxes for social programs. Though Say Yes is not supported by the taxpayer's money, public criticism continued to be directed at a program that sought to break the cycle of poverty and teach 112 students to help others do the same.

In the United States, there is a general feeling that "holds disadvantaged groups, such as inner-city Blacks, largely responsible for their plight" (Wilson 1997, 159). In fact, a survey administered between 1969 and 1990 consistently identified "lack of effort by the poor themselves" as the most popular noninstitutional explanation of poverty (Wilson 1997, 160). The Say Yes students were assumed to be responsible for their own economic situation and therefore could not ignore the feeling that perhaps they should work themselves out of poverty, without assistance from social programs. More specifically, Say Yes students had to contend with public opinion in their own community as the local press tracked the progress of the program. From the day they received scholarship pledges in front of cameras and reporters, the students were made all too aware of the criticism not only of their program, but their lives. Headlines such as "More Felons than College Graduates" and "The $5 Million Lesson" raised concern as to whether or not the students "deserved" the time and money that had been invested in them (Mezzacappa 1999b). Some of the students even faced angry parents and teachers who believed the program was "wasting good money on those Say Yes kids" (Mezzacappa 1999c).

With increasing exposure to the lives the Belmont 112 led, George Weiss came to understand some of the obstacles that affected students' ability to use the scholarship productively. The demographics of the Belmont feeder pattern predicted that the Belmont 112 would have "small futures." Perhaps these data explain why fewer than 25 percent of SYTE students could offer any answer when our staff asked them to imagine a vocation they hoped to pursue. If students believe they will inherit "small futures," it is unlikely they will construct positive dreams they cannot realize. The Weisses and the SYTE staff helped students frame images of "possible selves" (Markus and Nurius 1986), representing ideas of what they might become, shaped by exposure to neighborhoods outside the "bottom." Students began to see different ways of living and slowly tried on new roles and foreign ideas.

Gift-giving engenders an asymmetrical relationship between the giver and the recipients of the benefactor's magnanimity. The scales are out of balance and, from the recipient's perspective, the debt may feel unpayable. Hence, a feeling of dependence can ensue. How the SYTE students received the gift and the meanings they attached to it form the framework of the next chapter. As the reader will see, the scales were not always out of balance, particularly when the students taught the sponsors and staff about their lives and the need to recalibrate the kind of support offered if the students were to become successful users of the gift.

PART 2

Receiving

CHAPTER 2

Raising the Level of Play

Junior High School

This chapter scans events and educational programming in the first few years of SYTE. I start with a description of Sulzberger Junior High School, where most of our students were slated to start seventh grade in the fall of 1987. At Sulzberger, staff and sponsors learned how to advocate for students' academic needs by paying close attention to the quality of their education. We were particularly aware that our special education students required careful monitoring to avoid getting stuck in the education pipeline without the possibility of reasonable progress.

Early in the life of the program, we traveled with our students to Fellowship Farm to learn at a deeper level how they understood the SYTE opportunity. That experience, the second topic in the chapter, crystallized the racial and class differences that existed between the staff, the sponsors, and the students. The third section depicts our first summer school program and foreshadows subsequent ones, underscoring the objectives of the educational program and its persistent effort to expose SYTE's students to a range of role models they might emulate. The chapter closes with a description of one of our students' funeral, the first exposure for the sponsors to the most awful consequence of persistent poverty and the drug economy.

Life at Sulzberger

Sulzberger had a bad reputation. School officials knew that crime was rampant, a by-product of daily drug dealing in and around the building. Not much teaching went on. Children ran wild. Learning was not on the agenda. Teachers yelled for order and shouted for discipline. But the results were temporary, and not persistent enough for academic learning. Gangs ran roughshod over authority—any authority: parents, teachers, the principal, and the police. It was a kid's world. For some, it meant fun for the moment. But in the long term, the fun was pernicious. It trapped children in ignorance; they imitated adult lives they couldn't manage.

The new principal, Dr. Patricia Harris, had come with a solid reputation as a no-nonsense, innovative leader. Her appointment promised change. But as I walked the halls with her and saw the decay of the building and the mayhem, I wondered how realistic a turnabout could be.

The community, too, was daunting. Three massive housing projects loomed a short distance from the school; 80 to 85 percent of the school's students lived in these towers, including many SYTE children. Built in the 1950s, the towers tell a story of planning for poor people gone amuck. In the late 1990s, cities began to raze these citadels of failure and despair and replaced them with low-rise houses or duplexes—two-story buildings with an apartment on each floor. These lower buildings often had a small lawn or garden attached, which made room for some recreation and maybe a flowerbed. But in September 1987, the towers stood, all thirty floors occupied. One teacher referred to the towers as the "cages," suggesting entrapment. The elevators often didn't run, leaving residents the arduous task of walking up fifteen flights of stairs, if they lived in the middle of the tower, in a poorly lit stairwell smelling of urine and littered with garbage.

Seventy-eight of the 112 SYTE students were slated to attend Sulzberger; another thirty-two attended junior high schools dotted around the city. Of the remaining students, one had moved to Maryland and another to South Carolina. Those parents who wanted "something better" for their children enrolled them in schools in the far northeast section of the city. In compliance with court orders to integrate the school system, five SYTE children boarded school buses at seven in the morning to make the hour trek from West Philadelphia to Rush Middle School, a predominantly white middle-class school in Northeast Philadelphia.

The poverty rate for the Sulzberger population was extremely high; the entire student body was entitled to free or reduced price subsidized lunch. Several children were homeless and lived in shelters. For example, Roger, a tall handsome seventh grade SYTE student, started Sulzberger in September 1987, but moved to four different schools that year. His mother was a crack addict who couldn't sustain her costly drug habit and maintain a place for her family to live. For part of that year he was homeless, bedding down wherever he could. Because of his many absences from school, Roger was retained in seventh grade. Eventually, a grandmother of another SYTE child took Roger into her house and kept him for the rest of his school career. When his home situation stabilized, he attended Drew Elementary School, which included seventh and eighth grades.

The majority of SYTE students spent two years at Sulzberger. Dr. Harris, in that short time frame, saw to it that the building was repaired, painted, and made to look a bit more hospitable for children and adults. She restored a sense of order and purpose, and made the school feel less impersonal by reorganizing it into small "houses," each with about two hundred children working with a team of teachers. She put teachers on notice that teaching was the business of the day, and introduced several new programs to strengthen teachers' capacity to teach. Student attendance improved, from 68 percent when she started in 1987, to 90 percent when she left four years later. But many of these changes took time to realize. And while SYTE children benefited somewhat, they were also influenced by the negative habits that were only slowly starting to change for the better. SYTE caught the beginning and the transitional periods, but not the full flowering of progress.

Entering a junior high or even a middle school may pose a formidable barrier for students. Often there is a poor fit between the preparation of the children entering and the expectations of the receiving teachers of the new level. Teachers may expect a higher standard of work than children can easily produce. And there is often little or no communication between teachers and principals at the receiving and sending schools. As a result, an entering junior high or middle schooler, especially in inner-city settings, may feel unprepared for the new level of work. Proof of this condition was revealed when 25 percent of the SYTE students were retained in seventh grade. Of those children who did not pass, few caught up as a result of being retained in grade. Rather, many were retained again in ninth grade and, soon after, dropped out of school.

Retaining failing students in grade seems an appropriate strategy to help those students master the grade's material. However, a recent review of the research on retention finds a clear connection between retention and eventual dropout (Jimerson et al. 2002). Retention in grade results in lower self-esteem, a lack of fit among classmates, and contributes significantly to a long-term process of school disengagement that often leads to dropping out.

Special Education at Sulzberger

Both Dr. Harris and Pat Sannaghan, chair of the special education department at Sulzberger, were surprised at the low level of academic skills among the forty-four SYTE students assigned to special education classes. They reported that many of the forty-four students functioned at a second grade level in seventh grade. Generally students make one year of progress annually. If students start out with a second grade skill level in seventh grade, there is little possibility of catching up by age eighteen, when most students graduate high school. For those students experiencing failure early in their school careers, the road to success seems very long and they give up. They may find other routes to earning a living and building a life, but academics will not be the vehicle.

With a large number of SYTE children in special education, it was incumbent on the program to know what was happening to them. Initially, SYTE staff and sponsors found it almost impossible to understand precisely how a child in special education was progressing. Several times I requested their cumulative pockets, where all transactions about a child are kept and presumably passed on to the next grade. I had difficulty gaining access to these records, and those few that I was able to see contained little useful information. When I questioned Sannaghan about the incompleteness and poor quality of the records, he concurred that "records were kept in a cursory manner and often not kept at all. It was not unusual to find only 50 percent of a class' records." When I asked Sannaghan to explain this, he feigned a sarcastic manner in illustrating the kind of statement teachers make if confronted with this problem:

> "Oh well, that's the way it is, the records are never right. And anyway that's what people do. Well, it's not my problem." But, if you know that someone is coming in to inspect those records, teachers are more likely to be prudent in taking care of them. It

got to a point that out of a whole group of special education kids, only five of their records would be missing, because we were told to go to the sending school and track them down. And so now there was a record. And so when people held a meeting about a kid, I would pull the record and get a perspective on a child. That's pretty important.

To strengthen our knowledge and increase our effectiveness with the Sulzberger staff, I asked Randall Sims to act as an in-school intermediary who would look after the SYTE students' needs almost daily. This was particularly effective with regards to the children in special education. These children by law were examined periodically to determine their progress and to identify the next round of academic and social goals students and teachers should work toward. The examinations, called C-sets (child study evaluation teams), generally involved meetings of the child's parent, a school psychologist, a special education teacher, and sometimes the child. The outcome of each meeting was a written Individual Educational Plan (IEP). Randall was especially helpful in explaining the process to the parents and advocating for the preferred kinds of school services for the child. And because Randall was knowledgeable about the school system, he was able to look out for the child's best interests. Sannaghan remarked on Randall's influence at the C-sets:

> I mean you get Randall Sims to sit in on a C-set, I can't bullshit him. And he was sitting there, and he brought the parent, I mean all of a sudden I have to make sure that whoever is coordinating this C-set process has to be on target, on the ball, has their records, knows the kid. . . . You know, so it raised the level of play, there's no doubt about that . . . you raised the level of play and expectations of standards simply because you were there and expected certain things. . . . And so you really did have a strategic intervention in many ways by raising the level of expectations of excellence not just for your kids, but for the whole school.

While Randall's presence at a C-set made a difference and helped a child's parent understand the proceeding, I hoped we could find ways to empower parents by using other parents who were in similar circumstances to coach and model how to interact with school personnel. Frequently, parent organizations are of little help to poor families and especially to those parents with special needs children. Philadelphia Parents' Union, founded by concerned parents and led by Happy

Fernandez, was designed to be an alternative to the traditional Home and School Association. The word "union" in its title was chosen to alert school professionals that this was a serious group that knew their rights and was not afraid of confronting the establishment. Parents' Union used knowledgeable parents to train their peers to be more effective in advocating for their children. Because the special education population of the city was exploding, especially in poor African-American neighborhoods, Parents' Union developed workshops for parents on the following topics: understanding a student's test scores, representing your child at a C-set, talking with a teacher about your child's failure, and speaking to the principal about a decision to expel your child. The topics were of immediate practical use to parents. The workshop presenters were parents like SYTE parents; hence they were able to establish rapport and trust. In addition to the workshops, Parents' Union encouraged their parent educators to accompany less confident parents to school meetings where they felt the need for support. SYTE established a close working relationship with Parents' Union and engaged their parents of special needs children to conduct workshops so that our parents could begin to see that they could have a voice in making decisions about their children's education.

Becoming Advocates

C-sets are conducted every couple of years and are only meant for special education children. But I believed that the program should monitor the regular education students as well, and suggested to the area superintendent that we hold quarterly meetings at the school just before children received report cards. The superintendent asked Dr. Harris to hold the first meeting at the school. Teachers, the area superintendent, Diane Weiss, the project coordinators, and I sat around a table in the school library to discuss students' strengths and weaknesses displayed the previous quarter. We also brainstormed possible interventions for students lagging behind in their class work. The initial meeting was strained and confrontational; SYTE was asking school personnel to be accountable for the quality of their work. The principal felt we were usurping her authority, "boxing her in." I felt we had to have access to students' data. We could not wait for a reform movement to take effect. SYTE students were not strong academically. I suggested that we institute early warning notices and meetings about student failure so that the program could intervene quickly in collaboration with the school. The strategy from the SYTE program point of view was to create strong ties with the staff and administration of the school, and simultaneously establish a range of support services for children and their parents.

In order to accomplish these goals, SYTE needed office space and a place to hold meetings and workshops. Prudential Insurance Company occupied a large complex of buildings located a few blocks east of Sulzberger. The company decided to relocate their offices to center city and was prepared to donate the building to the community with the understanding that the space would house a variety of programs that could assist community development. The building was renamed the Urban Education Foundation and SYTE became one of its first tenants. The program rented a large room, big enough to house a section for the coordinators' offices and a larger section for meetings. In addition, we had access to space for after-school tutoring, which was held four afternoons each week. SYTE students were required to attend at least one session weekly, but were welcome to come as often as they felt they could use help. Tutors were obtained from student bodies at neighboring universities and a few older tutors were recruited from local government offices. Students attended tutoring for various reasons. Some recognized they needed help with schoolwork and came on their own. To find more reluctant students, Randall Sims periodically polled their teachers at Sulzberger to identify students they felt would benefit from tutoring. Randall would wait for those students until school was over and escort them to the tutoring center. Still others came for the snacks and juice. And a few came because the lights and heat were on, unlike the situation in their public housing apartments. SYTE's tutoring center also provided a place where students could babysit their younger siblings.

By Christmas 1987, SYTE parents expressed interest in preparing a holiday dinner for all SYTE students and their families. Staff members Randall Sims and Lily Holloway organized a committee that planned the menu, shopped for food, cooked the meal and served it. Diane, George, and their daughters were guests of honor. Students capped the evening by presenting George and Diane with a gift. The dinner was a success. It gave the parents a chance to reciprocate for the gift that had been awarded their children. The entire process helped build an intimate family-like feeling among those who served on the dinner committee and extended to those who attended. The holiday dinner became an annual event and was soon followed by an Easter talent and fashion show organized by a particularly strong parent, Omaira Stally, in collaboration with staff. The experience of working with a competent and confident parent gave students a role model from their community they could admire. Students were motivated to work hard. They wanted to feel good about their performance and make their friends and families feel proud.

The annual Christmas dinner and Easter show were ways students and parents could give back to the sponsors by sharing favorite foods they prepared and by students displaying their talent for performing. An important part of these events was an exchange of gifts. The Weisses would distribute tee shirts and jackets with the program's moniker, dictionaries and calculators; the parents and students would also offer their gifts, such as a framed picture of the Belmont 112.

A Retreat at Fellowship Farm, Spring 1988

We had been working with the SYTE students since the fall of 1987. By the next spring, the sponsors and staff thought we understood some of the issues our students faced. However, we were not at all sure students grasped the program's purposes or knew how to align their individual goals with those Say Yes espoused. Arriving at this deeper perception of program goals and discovering how to make personal connections with those aims were tasks that required uninterrupted time for discussion and reflection. A retreat center located away from the distractions of the city seemed to be the appropriate setting for our discussions. I suggested that we organize a retreat, facilitated by outside consultants, at Fellowship Farm, located in a semirural area, where I had attended other retreats. Seventy-five students, their junior high school principal, six teachers, twelve parents, Diane Weiss, the two project coordinators, and I boarded buses on a chilly spring day in West Philadelphia for the hour-long ride to the retreat center.

The March skies were clear and the view from the bus was unimpeded by large buildings. Students noticed that the houses were mostly single with lots of land surrounding them, very different from the tightly packed row houses ubiquitous in their neighborhoods. Students were excited and expectant as we pulled into the parking lot. In the early afternoon, they scrambled off the buses and scattered to explore the foreign landscape. Once rooms were assigned, students found them, selected their beds, and stored their gear for the one and one half days that we would spend together.

Before the start of the first session, students were invited to the dining hall for a snack of popcorn, cookies, and soda. The coordinators tried to keep an orderly line as students raced up to the food counters, tripping less assertive peers on their way. At some point, a group of students had amassed enough popcorn to start a fight. A snowstorm covered the dining hall as popcorn was hurled back and forth and kids ducked for feigned shelter. All the adults helped break up the melee. When the group quieted, the coordinators gave orders on how the cleanup would proceed. Some students balked, screaming, "I didn't do anything. Why should I need to clean up?" Since the mess was widespread, it was impossible to say who was responsible. Instead, cleanup became a communal responsibility. Some of the students continued their protest. They were offended by collective punishment and wanted distinctions drawn between those who committed the wrong and those who did not participate. The mess was reluctantly cleaned up, with a few students refusing to get involved.

When the dining room was clean, the first workshop began in a spacious barn with exposed rafters. The students huddled on the carpeted floor, catching up with each other. Three quarters of the group attended Sulzberger Middle School, but the fourth quarter was enrolled in schools outside their neighborhoods. One student recalled that, "for a long time we did not see some of our friends that much. And when we got together it was fun."

After some icebreakers that helped reintroduce students to one another, the facilitators described the objective of the retreat: an opportunity to clarify personal and group goals as members of Say Yes. The following questions set the tone for the discussions: What does it mean to you to be in Say Yes? What responsibilities should students have in this program? How should staff and sponsors help? How do you reach a long-term goal such as gaining admission to college?

In response to the last question, the facilitators asked group members to show how they would get to college by creating physical representations of the strategies they might use to achieve this goal. Two volunteered to show how they would solve this problem. They set up other students as physical barriers in their way, and then burrowed their heads and shoulders to get to their objective. The students didn't try to imagine a range of strategies. They didn't know how to decode the steps it takes to get to college, such as doing well in school subjects, studying for tests or class work, and graduating from high school. They quickly fixed on just battering their way through. When I discussed this incident with Randall several years later, he reflected on the students' reasons for their strategy: "The blind determination to bowl over any object in sight by sheer force seems like a metaphor for the group. These are working-class kids who believe that if you exert the effort, you will get the reward without regard to skill or level of achievement."

The facilitators fed back to the group that they were using only one strategy to accomplish their objective and urged them to brainstorm additional ways to achieve the goal. The brainstorming activity was tough going. But, with coaching from the facilitators, some new strategies did eventually find their way up on the newsprint posted on the front wall. Suggested strategies included: "Find someone in your neighborhood who graduated from high school and then finished one or two years of college. Ask that person how he or she did it. What helped this person? Find a teacher that grew up in the 'bottom,' but graduated from college. How did that happen? Did they ever fail? What did they do then?"

Middle-class children learn how to decode the system. For them, there is a correspondence between the language and styles of interaction in their homes and in the schools they attend. However for minorities who live in poverty, ". . . Schools rarely provide working-class minority students the necessary training for effective decoding; such children are systematically denied true opportunities for long term success" (Stanton-Salazar 1997, 15). SYTE students were demonstrating that they did not receive the knowledge from their families on how to operate in a middle-class environment and that the schools they attended, in Richard DeLone's words, "discriminate by expectation" (1979, 107). Inner-city schools often assume poor minorities will not succeed and, therefore, do not support and challenge them so that they might be successful in school. SYTE was designed to interrupt that cycle of failure.

The afternoon session ended with an overview of the rest of the retreat and a reminder that dinner would be served in the dining hall at 6:00 P.M. Students had an hour to get ready for dinner or roam around the farm. A group of students clustered around the animal sheds, entreating the sheep to meet them at the fence so they could pet them. Being close to animals was a new and fun experience for many. I rang the dinner bell and students and adults filed into the dining hall. The menu included spaghetti. The adults were on alert, not wanting a repeat of the afternoon's popcorn fight with a messier medium like spaghetti. Dinner was full of animated talk about friends and new experiences on the farm. After dinner, the entire group gathered for the evening program. After various announcements were made, Randall asked for some time to "process" the popcorn fight.

Randall opened the discussion with two questions addressed to the entire group: "Raise your hands if you feel you acted appropriately during the popcorn fight this afternoon." Several hands were raised. Randall's second question: "How many people feel they were acting wild and inappropriately?" A few hands were sheepishly raised. Randall continued, "I see a few of you have enough character to recognize when you've done wrong. But what I can't figure out is why, why did you carry on the way you did and make a spectacle of yourselves?" No one answered his question. The group was still. Slowly a low buzz of conversation moved around the room. Randall pressed harder to get a response: "I don't get your behavior. You don't act this way at home. Why did you think you could get away with that kind of foolishness here? Your parents would not tolerate those kinds of carrying on. Will somebody give me an answer?"

Richard, the only student dressed in a white shirt and tie, stood up: "Mr. Sims, I think we did wrong. Personally, I didn't do anything. But I am my brother's keeper. I should have spoken out." A few students nodded in agreement. "Is there anyone else who agrees with Richard or has . . ." and before Randall finished his sentence, Christina was up on her feet looking visibly upset. "I don't feel bad about nothing. I didn't do anything wrong, and I'm not my brother's keeper," she shouted out to Richard. "And I'm not going sit here and take punishment for something I didn't do." Then turning sharply to face Randall, she said, "And I don't think you're being respectful to us the way you're talking and I don't like that." A loud debate ensued, with students lining up behind Christina's or Richard's positions. Randall interrupted the group's talk, and pressed his point further with Christina: "OK. Let's say you didn't get into that fight. But you saw what was going down. You saw people acting wild. You're a leader. Why didn't you get in there and help stop it? You're not shy and people listen to you. Why did you sit back and just watch?"

Christina's cheeks flushed: "Mr. Sims, why are you picking on me? Am I the only person in here? Why is all this coming at me? I didn't do nothing and I don't like being blamed for stuff I had no part in. And I don't think it's democratic the way you pick on people." Diane Weiss and I felt the discussion was turning into a confrontation between Randall and Christina. The rest of the group at this point seemed disengaged. Diane came to Christina's defense: "I think Christina and Richard were brave to stand up and speak their minds. We might disagree with someone, but we have to make room for their voices. Christina needs to be heard. She's a leader." Christina smiled broadly and sat down. Randall responded, "I agree with you, Ms. Weiss; Christina is a leader. That's why I want to know why she didn't help stop the fight? And I'm not just talking to Christina. Other people could have . . ." At this point, I motioned to Randall to wrap up the discussion. The hour was getting late and the group discussion, which did not appear to be making much headway, was eating into the evening program.

Before the program began, I met with the facilitators to reevaluate the plan for the evening session. The facilitators felt that it didn't seem appropriate to proceed with individual goal-setting without bringing the discussion about the fight to closure. The dining hall discussion had probably stirred up feelings that needed a safe and less confrontational forum for discussion. We decided to divide into small groups of ten with adults, staff, and consultants facilitating the meetings. The focus would be on the kinds of situations in which students would take individual responsibility for their actions as members of Say Yes. We were beginning to forge a community whose members needed to support each other over the next several years. Giving more people a chance to voice their opinions seemed to be a good way to help students appreciate some of the values that felt important to students as well as to the staff and the sponsors.

At the end of the evening session, students left the barn and noticed a sky bright with stars. They found their way to their dormitories and began to prepare for bed, or so we thought. But, instead of settling down, they had a long night of mayhem. Some boys visited the girl's dorms much to the consternation of the adult supervisors. Back in their cabins, boys started to throw sneakers and pillows. Most of the activity was harmless—young adolescents away from home enjoying unbridled freedom. For the adults it was not fun. Many of us spent a sleepless night trying to keep one step ahead of the students' creative commotion.

The next morning the students looked tired as they walked slowly into the dining room. Breakfast was uneventful. The morning workshops helped students think about how they cope with distractions and how to stay focused so they achieve their goals. Students left with plans for how they would stay on task in their academic subjects over the next month, including resolving to attend after-school tutoring regularly; asking the teacher for help in the classroom or before and after school if they don't understand something; and doing homework every night it is assigned. Asking for help turned out in the years ahead to be one of the most difficult behaviors for students to master. The staff would revisit this issue repeatedly.

After a quick lunch, students packed their things for the ride back to Philadelphia. They took their seats on the buses and asked staff if they could return to Fellowship Farm a second time. Most people slept on the way home. The principal of the junior high school, Dr. Harris, said about this trip, ". . . for many of them, that had been the first time they had been outside the city. For many of these kids, they never get any farther than Lancaster Avenue (a shopping strip of stores in their neighborhood). They don't know anything beyond that. They haven't even been to center city." Rasheed, a SYTE student, remembered the trip as a turning point for him. He describes the scene vividly:

> We got into trouble that night. And you all [staff] got frustrated with us, because we didn't clean up or something like that. That was a good time; we had a lot of fun. We were wild. It was wild, too wild at times even. And Mr. Sims, he had my number. I knew it. We were throwing shoes and we knew that we would get into trouble. But that trip was one of the most useful trips I ever had. Yeah, 'cause that was away from society. And we had time to really think. We were wild, but it did a lot for a lot of us. I know a lot of us wanted to go back for a second time. And then meeting the animals [sheep and cows], and seeing how people live out there—that was kind of fascinating.

Rasheed had fun. He and his classmates acted wild. He knew he had crossed a line at times and accepted that his behavior would have consequences. Mr. Sims would be on his case. But then Rasheed stepped back from the fun and looked at the deeper meaning of the trip. Fellowship Farm was a place apart from urban society. In the city you can't think, he insisted. The retreat offered a chance to see a different way of living. It invited an opportunity to be a "kid," but also a time and place to be reflective, to imagine other ways of being and becoming.

Not many people in Rasheed's neighborhood finish a four-year degree (only 6 percent according to the 1990 census). The trip proposed a reach and a stretch for something intangible: high school graduation and a college education.

Another student, Cherice, remembers the small group session after dinner. Like Rasheed, she thought the retreat allowed people to interact in more caring ways. She said: "Like when we took that trip to Fellowship Farm and was acting wild. And we got really a chance to sit down and talk to the staff and tell them why we were acting the way we were. And we really got everything off our chests."

The retreat allowed students to speak their minds and adults listened, an experience not too common for young adolescents. The retreat was a reflective time, too, for the SYTE staff and Diane Weiss. In the exchange between Christina and Randall, students saw Christina confront an authority figure. She objected to being treated as part of the crowd. In her eyes, when Randall did not see her behavior as distinct from the crowd, he acted undemocratically. She determined to assert her right to be different and to be treated as an individual.

Randall, for his part, wanted the group to accept responsibility for its inappropriate behavior. He saw the public confrontation as an opportunity to educate the group about appropriate behavior in public places by establishing a "collective set of expectations." He made the point that they were taught how to behave in their homes and, by acting "foolishly," the students brought disgrace on their parents, themselves and SYTE. At another level, Randall's public confrontation was also meant for the white sponsors and executive director. The subtext appeared to be "don't coddle these kids. They need discipline. Now is the time to establish proper authority relations. These students need to develop the courage to intervene with their peers if they do something wrong. How else can we establish a sense of responsibility to the group and its goals?" Randall's personal life reveals some parallels with the lives of the students. He acknowledged: "So my life and my history basically mirror that of the children I work with now in the program and children I've worked with throughout my adult career." Randall expanded on his history, noting:

> I was born to parents who did not have much. In their view, they came up on the hard side of things. They couldn't go to school when they wanted to. They came under Jim Crow and segregation. So a kid who could go to a free school, who could train to be

anything he or she wanted to be in this country, and who didn't take advantage of it, was not a kid that they wanted to raise in their home. It was just incomprehensible to them—people who had to struggle and fight to learn and read, who had to teach themselves to read well, just couldn't tolerate kids who could do that for free, and who didn't take advantage of it. It was unconscionable to them, something that was inexplicable. There never was a reason for it. Bad behavior anytime, but especially in school, would not be tolerated. Poor performance in school was inexcusable.

Randall's parents set high standards for his behavior at home and in school. He carried those expectations with him and wanted to pass on that "social capital" to his charges (Coleman 1988). Opportunity for advancement through education must not be frittered away by foolish street behavior by Blacks, Randall might argue. For middle-class families, the popcorn fight would be judged as trivial: kids being kids. However, Randall was searching for, in Coleman's language, a "set of effective sanctions that can guide and monitor behavior" (1988). For Randall, the popcorn fight symbolized a luxury Blacks could not afford. Bad behavior was not to be tolerated. It needed to be nipped in the bud so that it would not weaken the potential of poor children to escape from poverty. Perhaps also implicit in Randall's statements was a challenge to white liberals. Black parents often insist on swift verbal and physical punishment for children who misbehave. Middle and upper-class Whites are less likely to use physical punishment and more often will listen to a child's version of an incident before taking action. There is a presumption that a child has rights too. Randall certainly did not mete out physical punishment. But there was a sense among the Whites that he pushed too hard to make his point and, in doing so, may not have respected Christina's rights as an individual.

Fellowship Farm was a unique experience. Students reacquainted themselves with their peers. Through testing and resisting adult limits, students learned about freedom and responsibility within this emerging temporary community. Staff and Diane experienced some of the class differences between Black and White values and expectations. Everyone perceived, not always clearly, the distance these students needed to travel to make productive use of the gift. Randall remarked that, "The retreat gave us the first opportunity to see the students' mental preparedness to tackle the program's objectives." The lessons derived from the retreat sketched out some of the competencies that would make the gift attainable, and those skills, attitudes, and behaviors were in evidence in the first summer school conducted by the program.

Summer Schools: Shaping the Program's Objectives

It has been documented that poor children lose skills and knowledge over the long summer vacation (Bracey 2002). SYTE staff wanted to prevent this loss of competence by keeping school-related activities present in children's lives. SYTE's summer school combined a review of areas of academic weakness with a preview of work students would encounter the next fall. The first summer program had the following objectives:

- develop group cohesiveness so that Say Yes students identify positively with the program, its sponsors, and staff;

- instill in students a positive feeling of self-worth, a sense that each person can learn and contribute to his/her own growth, and the development of the group;

- demonstrate how learning can be fun and exciting, as well as requiring diligent, hard work;

- expand the range of experiences and knowledge so students will be curious about a variety of careers and professions;

- gain a deeper appreciation of what it means to be a responsible male or female;

- understand that all behaviors have consequences, and choose behaviors that affirm constructive values for themselves and others;

- value written and oral expression and search for ways of communicating ideas and feelings effectively.

These were ambitious goals, certainly not to be attained in one four-week summer program. The goals, rather, announced an agenda the program would follow over the next five summers. Some of the goals were personal and interpersonal; others promoted academic skill development and career exploration.

In the summer of 1988, for example, career exploration mostly happened during a one-week intensive program at the Philadelphia

Zoo. Students studied animal adaptation as part of a science unit. But the zoo's staff offered an opportunity to observe and speak with African-American employees who held jobs in maintenance, food services, accounting, animal keeping, and veterinary medicine. Thus, SYTE students observed in one setting a variety of employment opportunities that require different levels of education. The zoo was a particularly good setting for this kind of exploration, since it is situated in West Philadelphia, close to SYTE students' homes. And the zoo administration had made a good faith commitment to employ African-Americans in a range of jobs, and gave priority to qualified applicants from West Philadelphia. Students heard reports from employees who had worked their way up from maintenance to animal keeper and from bookkeeper to supplies procurement manager. The latter employee started his employment as a high school graduate, but over several years paid his way through college, earning a degree in business administration. The veterinarian was a leading African-American scientist who headed research at the zoo. He held a doctorate in Veterinary Medicine and was also a professor at the University of Pennsylvania's School of Veterinary Medicine. SYTE staff wanted students to see, at work, African-Americans employed in careers that required little education and those that required advanced college degrees. These employees shared personal stories of how their careers progressed, their satisfaction with their work and compensation, and particular problems they have encountered in the workplace and how they coped with them.

In the summer program of 1988, all students were engaged in writing workshops that also combined an academic component with career exploration. George Weiss' sister, Elizabeth Saunders, a consultant in the writing process for a suburban Cleveland public school system, and Marilyn Boston, a Philadelphia public school teacher, worked with SYTE students three times each week. Children maintained personal journals on a daily basis and produced edited pieces that were published in a summer report to parents. In general, the teachers were concerned with the poor quality of student writing. It was characterized by lack of engagement; sentences were fragmentary, and production of material too limited. But when topics touched on an important life experience or event, some students' writing became vivid. One thirteen-year-old boy, who lived with his invalid grandmother, wrote the following statement after a class discussion on how drug abuse affects family life:

I know what it is like to have a parent that is on drugs because my real mother is on drugs. I feel really sorry for her. I still love her because she is still my mother. I would send her to jail because she steels from me and my grandmother. I know this sounds dumb but I threatened to kill my mother and I meant it very much. I never saw my mom after that day. (Mezzacappa 1988b)

The previous example illustrates how youth who are classified as not succeeding in their school literacy practices can demonstrate remarkable power and fluency in literacy forms—journal writing—that have direct and emotional relevance to youths' lives.

The summer program of 1988 made it clear that SYTE students would need repeated coaching to improve their school literacy practices. Other attempts included an intensive, literature-based writing program offered between eighth or ninth grades; writing skills required to produce research papers taught during the summer between tenth and eleventh; and brainstorming ideas, drafting and editing essays for college applications the summer between eleventh and twelfth grades.

The writing activity in the summer of 1988 culminated in a meeting with two prominent African-American journalists, Chuck Stone of the *Philadelphia Daily News* and Acel Moore of the *Philadelphia Inquirer's* Editorial Board. Both men told stories about their education, how they searched for employment and their rise in their profession. These initial meetings with African-Americans employed in various vocations and professions were superficial, one-shot events. Later in the program, however, students in tenth and eleventh grades experienced more in-depth opportunities to explore career interests through long-term internships and mentoring. The program's objective for the first summer program was to show students that people like them sustained employment in productive careers. Because unemployment and underemployment were so high in the students' neighborhoods, and because African-Americans in poor communities often have low aspirations for employment, it seemed essential that SYTE students have ongoing exposure to role models who could explain how they succeeded.

Many of the programs, like writing, introduced in summer 1988 were recycled and deepened as students' schoolwork demanded more sophisticated effort. Some summer school courses were more episodic, lasting one or two summers. For example, in summer 1988, students studied concepts such as adaptation and the ecology of the habitats of animals at the zoo. The next time they studied science was in the summer between tenth and eleventh grades, when the curriculum included Chemistry. In this instance, teachers introduced the first topics in Chemistry so that students felt knowledgeable when they encountered these lessons in the fall. Chemistry often becomes a horror for students whose academic skills are weak. By introducing beginning topics in the summer before they officially took the subject, students actually performed quite well, according to their first report card in Chemistry. Similarly in math, students had an introduction to Algebra in the summer before ninth grade and an overview of Geometry the summer before tenth grade as a preview of class work they would have in the fall.

Part of the summer school's agenda was devoted to academic skill development and career exploration, but an equally important part of the work was to instill positive social attitudes that would make it more likely for students to take advantage of the gift. The staff, sponsors, and I were aware that young teenagers are subject to experiences that can jeopardize their health and their psychological well-being and, therefore, decrease their ability to use education productively. These stresses include drug dealing and using, teenage pregnancy, and resolving conflicts through violence (Spencer 1997). To begin addressing these dangers, Randall recommended an expert from the Crisis Intervention Center who discussed, in graphic, unvarnished language, the destructive effects of drug abuse, and raised awareness about how adults ensnare children and adolescents in gangs that form the personnel of drug businesses. Over time, a handful of our students used or became addicted to drugs, but at least half of the 112 was involved in drug dealing. The need to make large amounts of money fast was too compelling to resist.

Since teen pregnancy is a known problem among poor white as well as black teens, we hoped that an up-front discussion of sexuality and the responsibility necessary for parenthood would help our students to be thoughtful about premature sexual experiences. With that goal in mind, I hired a highly respected black sex education specialist to teach a course that covered the biology of reproduction and raised awareness about those behaviors that were likely to promote responsible male/female relationships. The staff revisited this topic numerous times over the subsequent years in one-on-one private counseling sessions.

The summer programs offered students academic support and opportunities to explore careers, as well as interventions to raise awareness about responsible sexuality and drug abuse prevention. Embedded in some of the goals were objectives that involved emotional well-being and social responsibility. Goethe is reputed to have said "thinking brings forth only thought, while feeling is with living fraught," a couplet that, for me, translates into the interactive nature of thought and feeling: feelings can be shaped by thoughts and thoughts influenced by feelings. Both are necessary. What did these ideas have to offer the SYTE students, then aged twelve and thirteen, at the beginning stages of forming their identities? Most of the youth could be described as impulsive, volatile, and highly physical. While there certainly was variation within the group, in general their teachers felt and the staff concurred that these children knew little about their own feelings and did not see thinking, and more particularly words, as a way to solve social conflicts.

For the boys, athletic stamina and agility, especially in boxing, was the goal. Parents taught children the axiom, "If someone hits you, you hit back." The street taught that drugs and violence were the pathways to success and local power. If you talk problems out, this logic concluded, you become prey—a faggot. Machismo dictated the rules of the game. The program, in contrast, offered SYTE students opportunities to expand their concepts of self by virtue of the education they could attain. The program's message affirmed a direction opposite to the values of the street—as one student expressed it, "what the program wanted me to do went against the grain in my neighborhood." SYTE signaled that education offers the one best hope for getting out of poverty. Hope can act as a powerful motivator to imagine and work toward a better future. The program endeavored to create at least a temporary community that collectively would support members' aspirations.

Central to the possibility was not only believing that one had a future, but that the road toward that desired state would require a change in values—values that affirm self-worth; values that comprise nonviolent solutions to problems and frustrations. Carl Husemoller Nightingale in his book, *On the Edge: A History of Poor Black Children and Their American Dreams* (1993), concludes that education must be supplemented by guidance in "emotional self-awareness." He asserts:

> The ability to name painful emotion, locate its origins, and develop nonviolent ways of expressing it should be part of our educational curricula and an especially important part of the national upbringing of inner-city children. (p. 193)

For some students—like Terrance, who described the destructive nature of his mother's addiction, awareness is riveted into his consciousness. He named and located the sources of his pain and, as his writing displays, he could find nonviolent methods of expressing these hurtful memories. Other students were less able to express their distress. While SYTE did not offer courses to promote emotional literacy, through retreats, individual conversations with staff and sponsors and, when necessary, through therapists, the program attempted to reduce "social isolation" and give students alternatives to violence.

The First Funeral

Despite our efforts, sometimes acts of violence demonstrated that our students could become victims of adults and peers who felt they had no other recourse. Then the norms of their environment that relied on violent acts took over, and children had little capacity to prevent tragedy. Dan's murder was such a case. Dan, or Danny as his friends called him affectionately, was a cheerful, pleasant, twelve-year-old. Dr. Harris, who knew him very well, thought he was "a nice child." His parents were divorced. While his mother had custody, she was seldom at home. Addicted to crack cocaine, her time was spent strung out on drugs or desperately trying to find enough cash for her next fix. Danny befriended a neighbor, an older man named Robert who was a short-order cook. Robert often took him to work with him on weekends, and Danny helped out by washing dishes and pots. He was a frequent guest at Robert's apartment and often spent the night. One night after he fell asleep, he heard Robert argue loudly with another man, who claimed Robert owed him ten dollars from a drug deal. When the argument turned into a heated fight, Danny crawled out of Robert's room and hid in a small room one flight up. In a fit of rage, the intruder shot Robert dead and pursued Danny to the next floor. He broke open the latched door and shot Danny thirteen times.

When Randall and I heard of Danny's murder, we visited his grandmother to offer our condolences. At nightfall, we climbed the stairs to her row home and rang the bell. A neighbor let us into the darkened house. One bare light burned brightly on the dining room table where Danny's elderly grandmother and two neighbors sat quietly. Randall and I expressed our sympathy for her loss and asked when the funeral would be held and its location. Danny's grandmother said: "We don't got money for a proper funeral. His mother has stolen any money that she could find in this house and even stole clothes and furniture that she sold to buy drugs. I'm wiped out." Randall explained that Danny might be entitled to some money the city's Department of Public Welfare set aside for paupers' funerals. I said the program would pay for a head-stone. The grandmother begged us not to give any money to her daughter, because she would only use it to feed her habit. We agreed that money we offered would go directly to the funeral director.

The Weisses hardly knew Danny. But they were shocked and pained at this senseless loss. Diane visited Sulzberger the day before the funeral to talk with Danny's friends and offer whatever comfort she could. The Weisses decided they would not attend the funeral; they feared their presence would turn the somber occasion into a media event. Instead, they arranged to meet the family at the funeral home that night to pay their respects.

The next morning, I met Randall and a large group of SYTE children at the church where Danny's funeral would be held. The service began with the singing of hymns and readings from Scriptures. Then the minister, dressed in a black robe with maroon velvet trim, started his fiery eulogy. His message reproached the mourners with a fearsome jeremiad about Danny being in the wrong place at the wrong time, a victim of circumstances. And he hammered away at the evils of drug dealing and drug using that were corroding family life in the neighborhood. The allusions hit home. He made it clear that only those people who truly accepted Jesus could be saved from the fate that befell Danny. And he called upon the youth in the church to come forward and testify that they wanted to be saved by Christ. Several SYTE students raised their hands slowly, rose and walked to the altar to profess their desire to be saved. The minister urged the children to write their names in his note-book so that he could follow up with them at a later time. While the children were recording their names and addresses, I asked Randall how the minister might follow up. He replied, "This is a poor church. He wants to help, but he doesn't have any staff or funds. Maybe he'll meet with our kids once or twice, but not much will happen." When the last SYTE student completed writing her name in the minister's notebook, final hymns were sung and the last flash camera photographed Danny's outstretched body, dressed in a white shirt and black trousers with a bright red button imprinted 'Say Yes to Education' pinned to his shirt. The Say Yes button signified hope for Danny's future, a hope unfulfilled.

Danny's funeral presaged four more that marked the passing of SYTE students killed violently. Kenny, age fifteen, was estranged from his mother, who asked the courts to find him incorrigible and commit him to a group home. One night he and three friends stole a car. Police pursued them in a chase that ended when Kenny crashed into a wall. Nasir, age sixteen, killed a rival drug dealer and, the next night, was murdered in revenge. Tyree, age seventeen, an active drug dealer, claimed in his suicide note that he had no means to pay for an apartment to care for his pregnant girlfriend. And Aaron, age twenty-five, a long-term drug addict and high school dropout, who had stopped using, had married, and held down two jobs—died when a man Aaron's wife had fought with earlier that day broke into their apartment and killed him. The five students who died over the span of the Belmont program's existence were either victims of drug-related crimes or involved in selling; four of the five were classified as learning disabled. A sixth died of natural causes.

Chapter 3, next, provides case studies of SYTE students who did not complete high school, and the factors that seemed to make a difference in how they were able to use the gift.

Dropping the Ball

Dropouts

"I experienced life on life's terms, without education"

—Shamira

Students whose lives are focused on being "street"—chronicled in this chapter—join drug gangs, drop out of school, and solve problems violently. A review of the six case studies highlighted in this chapter, none of whom complete high school, reveals the impact of being labeled learning disabled, the influence of the drug trade, and the prevalence of emotional instability among some inner-city youth. This chapter identifies a strong association between poverty, being learning disabled, dropping out, becoming an adjudicated delinquent, and eventually being convicted as an adult felon. After telling the stories of six students who did not finish high school, I'll examine some of the commonalties and differences between these life stories, which illuminate how dropouts lost interest in school, how they managed their lives after leaving school, and what meaning the scholarship had for them.

University City High School

Classified as learning disabled, 39 percent of the SYTE group was enrolled in special education classes. These students attended University

City High School, which served two thousand students. SYTE sponsors and staff were concerned that the prognosis for these students' school completion would not be good if they took the standard special education curriculum. The dominant instructional strategy was to ask students to complete worksheets. There was little active learning, no hands-on experience in applying academic learning to work settings, and little, if any, evaluation of the effectiveness of these strategies in producing positive student outcomes. Typically, only a small percentage was mainstreamed into regular education. Of those who had remained in special education throughout high school, an equally small percentage completed a special education program. A significant percentage, discouraged by being retained in grade and not sensing that they were making academic progress, dropped out in frustration and in the belief that school would not help them master skills that would make them competitive in the workforce.

I discussed these conditions with the superintendent of schools, Constance Clayton, who recommended that I start planning with the special education faculty to see if a better program could be designed for all ninth grade students. Intensive conversations ensued involving all relevant faculty, the principal, several parents, supervisors, and directors from the central office of special education. After five months of planning, a proposal for funding was written that substantially restructured the special education program so that work experience was at the center of the curriculum, with academics taught in relation to specific skills required by the workplace. The proposal emphasized the work ethic, problem solving, conflict resolution with coworkers, and close monitoring of the curriculum every six weeks to determine students' mastery of skills and concepts.

The president of the University of Pennsylvania secured a promise of $1 million to field test the new special education program at University City High School. However, the more direct and explicit discussions of this proposal became, the more resistant the faculty became, because the proposal required basic shifts in personnel, relocation of activities, and changes in instructional strategies. The faculty finally rejected the proposal they helped shape, but devised a compromise solution that required that the least successful SYTE special education students be released from University City High School to attend Randolph Skill Center, a vocational school. This solution left the University City High School program intact and provided a weak support system for students slated for the vocational school. Predictably, these students did not do well in this setting, nor did the students who remained in the comprehensive high school. Only twelve out of fifty-three (23 percent) SYTE special education students graduated. In the comparison group, the results were four out of twenty-four (17 percent). Thirty-nine SYTE students eventually dropped out—fifteen females and twenty-four males. Thirty of the thirty-nine dropouts were in special education.

Some special education students thrived at the Skill Center. Monica learned how to bake, gaining her a job in a bakery. Taylor found some success in carpentry, which motivated him to find a job as a carpenter's assistant. Kara ran the switchboard for the entire school, giving her some of the skills required of a receptionist. But the Skill Center faculty was not experienced in teaching special needs students. They were accustomed to students who had mastered basic skills and displayed social competence. The lower end of the Say Yes special education population consisted of students who were reading at a second through fourth grade level. These students were not the population Skill Center teachers had taught previously. Some teachers had difficulty adapting, but made an effort; others refused to change their teaching routines to accommodate these students. Higher functioning special education students were assigned to University City's main building and fifteen attended Bartram Human Services.

This chapter presents the following risk factors that contributed to students' dropping out: lack of success in progressing beyond a rudimentary education, stressful and unstable family relations, teenage parenting, histories of aggressive behavior as young children that persisted into adolescence, and the lure of fast money earned through the drug trade. All these risk factors are illustrated in six case studies of Cory, Anthony, Tyree, Monica, Shamira, and Tasha, selected from among those students who dropped out and did not complete high school. There is variation within this group and some similarity in projecting their life courses. Tasha was not involved either in using or selling drugs. Neither was she involved in crime. And unlike the other five students in this sample, Tyree was in regular education.

The Stories

CORY

A short, slight young man with an outgoing personality, Cory earned a reputation among his teachers in elementary and middle school for being a persistent talker in class and distracting students from their class work. Teachers viewed his irrepressible need to say whatever he was thinking without regard to class rules as a sign of social immaturity. By fourth grade, his teachers recommended him for special education placement in hopes that a smaller class size would give Cory the structure he needed to mature, and provide the kind of instruction that would allow him to advance academically. Three years later, in seventh grade, Cory's test scores revealed that he was reading at a fourth grade level, while his math scores were those of a fifth grader. His mother and teachers alike felt that he constantly needed to be pushed to work up to his ability. Sports, in contrast, did hold his attention, especially basketball. He also sustained various after-school jobs to earn extra money.

Cory's academic work was erratic. His progress was dependent on his attending classes regularly and his ability to control his disruptive behavior. But as he grew older, he became even more rebellious and defiant. His mother found him hard to control. By ninth grade, he was feeling alienated and depressed. The coordinators' annual report records that in August 1991, he swallowed the contents of a bottle of acetaminophen in a suicide attempt. He spent two weeks in the psychiatric adolescent wing of a hospital. Later that fall, he gave a teacher in his high school a note saying he was a failure and that he felt badly for letting down his mother and others who had supported him. He stated in the letter that he felt like committing suicide. Subsequently, he admitted himself to another psychiatric hospital. He was released after two weeks. Cory saw this as a painful time in his life. "I felt bad about myself," he reflected two years later. In the hospital, he accepted that he needed help and gained some perspective on his problems by understanding that he "was not the only one who felt like this." He claimed he learned "how to deal with certain situations" and how to cope with his anger. Foremost, he learned about his values: "What I got to live for. Who I got to live for. My future." His psychiatrist told him he would "always have problems, like everyone else." What he needed to learn was how to deal with his problems.

His family life was complicated. His mother, his sister, and his grandmother were all people he trusted. He said about his mother that, "No matter what I do, whatever happens, she's always going to be there. She's always going to take care of me." That statement turned out not to be completely true, which becomes apparent as Cory's story unfolds. Absent from his life was a father figure. Randall Sims thought that since his biological father had abandoned him when he was three years old and his stepfather was always beating him, perhaps a healthier relationship with a male might be beneficial. He assigned Cory a mentor, Mr. Sansom, who maintained a relationship with him for three years, from seventh through ninth grade. Cory describes their relationship as full of "fun." "He was like a big brother," he recalled affectionately:

> We used to take the train down to Baltimore. We used to go on a sailboat. He's constantly staying in a nice little condo in South Philly. We used to go to movies. He inspired me a lot. He also tutored me and helped me read. He was trying to teach me the values of life. Structure of families. He tried to teach me how important school was and how you gotta. . . . He taught me a lot of things, but at sixteen I was a knucklehead. If he had caught me when I was nineteen or twenty and had a little more wisdom I would have came out better. But it was just that I was young and I was between that and the streets. The streets caught me; they sucked me in. That's when me and Mr. Sansom kinda parted our ways.

I asked Cory if he had told Mr. Sansom about his life on the streets. He said, "No. I never told him. I still wish he'd call sometime." Cory recalled that their relationship ended when he ". . . was running the streets. He couldn't catch up to me. He was trying. But it wasn't on him. It was my fault. On Christmas he dropped off a model of a Lamborghini. I still have it to this day. Nobody messes with it. It's in a glass case. That's the only thing I have to remember him by." Then he remembered one other memento. "I have a picture of me and Mr. Sansom on my graduation day from middle school. I still have that picture."

By tenth grade and sixteen-years-old, Cory had had enough of school. He had fathered a daughter and was looking for work. He also was reunited with his biological father, the first meeting in thirteen years. School seemed irrelevant. He felt that his special education status hindered him from real learning. Placement in special education, he insisted, was his greatest obstacle to making progress in school. "Special ed classes didn't help like they're supposed to. They keep going over the same thing again and again. I don't learn anything new so I could advance to a higher skill. It was kind of frustrating," he said in exasperation. Cory rarely attended classes in tenth grade, received no credit, and consequently was retained in that grade for a second year. Retention was the final insult to Cory's sense of justice; he felt it was a hollow message: "So when I was held back in tenth grade, it really didn't mean anything, because I didn't want to go to eleventh grade because a lot of the people in eleventh grade don't know nothing," he said contemptuously. In a more contemplative moment, Cory had an insight about his lack of success in school:

> I've always had a problem with discipline. I couldn't discipline myself. I know it was wrong, but I'd do it anyway, because I didn't have any discipline at all. I'd get distracted right off. Instead of sticking to it and disciplining myself, no matter what, no matter what it looked like or feel like. Just disciplining and I know I'd be all right. And, I could never discipline myself so long to go far enough to see the light that way. I never made it. If I think I had discipline I'd probably end up better off.

School was not a place where Cory knew how to succeed. He remembered teachers and his mother's exhortations to "sit still, or pay attention, finish your work, stop playing." He could not sustain focus. His attention flitted aimlessly from one impulse to the next. He tried four different high schools: two comprehensive high schools, one vocational school and a school that permitted students to work at their own pace. When Cory turned twenty, he informed Randall that he wanted to prepare to take the test for the General Equivalency Diploma (GED). Randall hired a special education teacher to work one-on-one with him. Over a three-year period, his attendance was sporadic, interrupted by his need for court appearances and a stint in jail. When he finally took the test, he passed the math and science sections, but failed reading, English, and social studies.

If school was his nadir in learning basic academic skills, there were two places in Cory's life where he felt competent: an after-school job at his mother's place of work and on the streets where he participated in a large drug ring. He lived two lives: the hourly worker at a conventional job and the drug dealer. In some sense, the first job was a kind of cover for the drug business. During the time he sold dope, he advanced in his job at a wholesale furniture factory. From age sixteen until he was twenty-two years old, he rose through the ranks. His first job in the factory was as a housekeeper. After two years, he was promoted to switchboard operator. By the time he dropped out of high school, he had advanced to the position of truck dispatcher, earning fifteen dollars an hour with full medical benefits. While he was working at the factory in a legitimate job, he started out in the drug business:

> I was working in the factory and sold drugs too. I started out as a runner delivering drugs for people. Later I hooked up with a group of guys that was selling. I was into girls, sex, drinking, and partying. I got arrested for selling and I spent thirteen months in a work release program. That was a big lesson; I don't want to go back there again. But I didn't learn yet, because I'm still hanging around the same guys that got me there and I'm in trouble now. They got me. Actually I was with somebody that was selling that I should not have been hanging with.

When I asked him to describe the police charge, he said in a matter of fact tone: "conspiracy to drug trafficking, and things like that, it was a federal indictment." He explained that he was part of an "organization, twenty-five guys. In the hood, we're called "a team." And that team is made up of my homies, my niggers, or my dogs. What we were doing was all about making money, fast money, people that couldn't wait around to get it." The deeper Cory dug into the drug world the more stressed he felt with his family:

> My mom, she knew what was going down, didn't agree with it; she didn't approve it. And that caused a communication between us. I moved out and don't call. It's hard for her to sleep at night. My grandma had a birthday party with family members and I never showed up. And then when I did show up, I showed up with fancy cars and everybody in the family asked my Mom what I'm doing and so she feels bad about it. So I don't show up the next time; I don't want to be bothered. My mom said she didn't want to see me if I was selling drugs. She moved to another state, gave the house to my sister and me. I had everything, did everything and messed it all up.

I reminded Cory that he also had a scholarship and asked what having that opportunity meant to him. He waxed philosophical, commenting on what he has observed in his neighborhood as a drug dealer. He concluded his comments with feelings of regret at having wasted a once in a lifetime chance:

That's like, in my opinion, the scholarship is the most blessed thing, because I've seen all types of people and I know what a lot of people go through. I sold drugs and I see. I sell to people I went to school with, to their mothers too. And you see everything. So I know how it's hard for a lot of people that get the scholarship to go to school. So if I was able to give it to somebody else that really deserves it, I would. Because I, people gotta work two jobs just to go to school and struggle. A lot of people out there needs a lot of special opportunities and there ain't too many out there and I was blessed to have that. And sometimes I'm ashamed to tell people that I have a scholarship because they think "Are you crazy? You're supposed to be graduating from a university this year or last year." And I know these things and I don't try to make myself feel bad, but it happened and I can't take it back. I have to deal with it. It was special to have a scholarship. I was very proud I got it. I was bragging about it.

I interjected: "You felt proud to have the scholarship but that didn't necessarily change your . . ." Cory understood my question before I fully stated it:

No. It didn't change. . . . I don't know what went wrong. I think I wanted attention when I was younger and I chose the wrong way to get it. I wanted attention and I chose to hang around drug dealers and sell drugs, and get that attention. Instead, I could've taken advantage of my scholarship, and graduated, and went to school, and got that attention. I made the wrong choice somewhere and now I'm paying for it. If anyone want to learn about the hard way, they can ask me. I can tell people how easy it is to lose control of your life fast. You have to put it together, and then it takes thirty seconds to throw it all away.

Cory longed for attention, recognition that he was somebody to reckon with. Selling drugs gave him notoriety, status, and all the material trappings. His factory job, in contrast, offered him a steady income and the potential for limited advancements, but it could not compete with the rush, the glamour, and the "fast money" of being a drug dealer. Not getting attention was the road to depression. He didn't want to be an ordinary person. "I'm not the kind of person that can accept that." But then he quickly mitigated his position. "Not that I couldn't accept that, but I never chose to accept it. I always wanted attention. And today," he said with bravado, "I'm a popular person out in the streets. I'm very popular." He paused, his mood changed; he lowered his voice. "But it don't even pay off. Don't give you nothing. All the people I know, all the friends? It's like I don't really have friends. All the good friends, all friends going the right way." He despaired that his "friends" were leaving him behind as they found more conventional ways to live. Poignantly he claimed:

> They're burning my bridges out. They say, "What Cory doing lately? That kid, he playing around." After a while, people tend to wash their hands with you. Some people don't look at it that way, but I know. They don't want to be bothered by a kid who's going the wrong way. You have to come their way sometimes.

Adolescence is prime time for drug selling for inner-city youth living in poverty; but, by their late twenties, most understand that that economy is a dead end, if not a personal death. Those who continue in the business become the bosses of the organizations and increasingly link up with other forms of crime. "To come their way," Cory must figure out how to live a conventional life. At the time of this interview, in September 1999, Cory was twenty-four; in addition to his daughter, he was also the father of a one-year-old son. After months of court appearances, he overcame his legal problems and was again thinking about finishing a GED and moving on to a postsecondary degree. His father had introduced him to a friend involved in television production. Cory attended an open house of a local college that grants an associate's degree in TV production, and offers support in GED preparation prior to entering the college program. Cory did not enroll. Periodically, he would call the SYTE office asking for help in preparing to take the sections of the test he failed previously. His pattern was consistent: he called for help, attended a few tutoring sessions, missed several appointments, then disappeared.

ANTHONY

At age thirteen, when I first met Anthony, he looked older than most of his peers. He was tall and muscular and, on the surface, had a pleasant, engaging personality. His home life had been disrupted two years earlier by the death of his mother, who had sent him to live with his father shortly before she died. This change in homes was hard for

Anthony. His mother was easy to talk with and he felt comfortable sharing with her. His father, a maintenance worker at an area hospital, was taciturn and believed in setting strict rules for Anthony's behavior. As an adult in his mid-twenties, he reflected that communication with his father had never been good. "We just don't communicate, not because of me, but because of the way he is. I'll see him on the streets and he'll say, 'What's up?' "And I'll say, 'What's up?' And that's it."

Married for the past five years to the woman he has lived with for ten years, Rhonda, Anthony and his wife have three children. Anthony wants his children to have a different childhood than he had. "I will really be there with my kids," he said emphatically:

> I will sit down and talk to my kids. I want to make sure my kids go to school and get a good education. Make sure they don't run the streets. I'll make it possible for their friends to come over to our place. I help my daughter with her homework every day. In the morning time, after she eats breakfast, I go over it with her just to be sure she knows it, make sure she didn't forget it. My daughter's real smart. I think she's going to an artist. She's just turned five.

Anthony's hopeful depiction of his daughter was sharply different from his experiences at that age. Anthony had gained a reputation as a fighter in first grade. By third grade his aggressive behavior could no longer be managed in a regular education classroom. He was placed in special education, designated learning disabled and retained in third grade. In seventh grade, when he became a participant in Say Yes, his reading and math scores and his behavior improved sufficiently so that he was able to take regular education classes with the added support of a resource room backup. These changes were short-lived. He became defiant at home, refusing to abide by the curfew his father set. In school, he was disruptive in class and constantly fighting. A meeting was called to discuss his behavior. The principal, the counselor, Anthony, and his father attended. The principal made it clear that he could no longer stay at this school. His father advocated his assignment to a disciplinary school. "When I was Anthony's age," his father said, "I was popping off too. They put me in a disciplinary school and I got straightened out." Most of the participants at the meeting disagreed and recommended that Anthony try another middle school in the area, and he agreed to attend. But he never did. Instead, he moved out of his father's house and never returned to school. He had dropped out in eighth grade.

Anthony complained that his father kept him on a short, tight tether. "If I go out, he wants me to come back in every half hour, or come back every hour, and I had to come in at 8:00 P.M. That was too much for me. I was a big boy. I moved in with my brothers and I didn't have to come in at 8:00 or nothing like that." His father tried to have him placed in a residential facility for his incorrigible behavior. Anthony refused to appear at the court hearing, but continued to live a loose, unsupervised life with his three brothers. Living with his brothers made dropping out easy. In 1993, when Anthony was eighteen-years-old, Randall asked him how he decided to drop out. "I ain't really decided that long," Anthony said. "I just wouldn't go one day and then I wouldn't go the next day, then I wouldn't go the next day. I ain't never made up my mind that I ain't going back to school. I just wouldn't go." It had nothing to do with decision making in his mind. Rather, each day he did not attend school established a habit of not going. In the end, Anthony was a dropout.

Six years later, when he was twenty-five-years old, I pressed to learn if there were contextual reasons for dropping out. Anthony gave a familiar answer:

> I wasn't really comfortable going to school, because it was a fashion thing of the time, and everyone was wearing new stuff, and my family wasn't buying the new stuff: the new sneaks, the big shirts, the designer stuff. So I tried to get the stuff myself by doing what they was doing—selling drugs. And trying to get stuff to make me feel comfortable with going to school, and my whole intentions was to get dressed, and get some money in my pocket so that I can get to school. And once I started getting that money everything changed up. The streets got me.

In *On the Edge*, Carl H. Nightingale (1993) chronicled the lives of a small group of preadolescent black children living in West Philadelphia in the late 1980s. He emphasizes the all-encompassing effect of American consumerism on black children living in poverty. The advertising industry targets this market using larger-than-life images of prominent African-Americans to sell expensive products on television, films, and billboards. The standard-bearer of the latest fashions in inner-city neighborhoods often is the drug dealer, sporting high-priced sneakers, gold jewelry, designer sweatsuits, leather jackets and trousers, and a baseball cap turned backwards.

Anthony craved these symbols of power and status. His father was neither willing nor able to buy those things for him. Anthony felt embarrassed to be seen in school with ordinary clothing. Like Cory, he reached for the attention he felt he deserved. Wearing the right "uniform" gained Anthony acceptance by the culture the drug dealer's wardrobe represented. The clothing he sought helped him conceal the humiliation of living in poverty. Several additional factors beyond not having hip clothing made Anthony's school leaving certain: his oppositional behavior with teachers and his father, academic difficulties, aggressive behavior with peers, and a body that felt oversized for a school environment. Those factors combined with the growing habit of not attending school made early school leaving inevitable.

By age fifteen, Anthony earned $5,000 a day, sported a fancy car, and owned a house. School could not possibly compete with the excitement and instant rewards of his drug business. He vividly described what it meant to inhabit that way of life:

> I was making all this money, and I could get, do anything I want. Open me up a couple of bank accounts. Get any girl I want. When I bought me some jewelry, I was the first one walking around with gold teeth. I wasn't thinking of anything else but getting me that money, messing with girls, shopping and driving fast cars. It was cool.

But the streets also demanded their due recompense. A rival drug dealer shot him several times, leaving him seriously wounded. A few days after he left the hospital, he was pistol-whipped and returned to the hospital with multiple head injuries. Each time Anthony suffered a setback on the streets, he considered going back to school. In 1990, with the superintendent's support, SYTE organized "Project Fresh Start" for our more difficult-to-place special needs students. The project was located within the Skills Center. In addition to the vocational specialists, I requested from the superintendent that a special education teacher be appointed to teach reading and math, especially as these subjects relate to the skills needed to perform various vocational tasks. Out of school for two years, Anthony agreed to enroll in project Fresh Start. He liked the informality of the Skills Center.

> It wasn't like you had to sit down in class and do all the stuff with a same group of people. At that school, you teach yourself, like almost. They tell you what to do and they watch you do it. And

then they'll see if you're doing it right. And if you don't do it right, they'll tell you what your mistake was and make you do it all over again till you get it right.

He contrasted this hands-on mastery learning approach with the regular classroom instruction he experienced.

In regular school they ain't really give you a chance. They'll tell you what to do, then you have to do it. And then they'll give you a grade on it. So if you did it wrong, then you did it wrong. And if you did it right, then you did it right. But at the Skills Center, they made sure you did it right.

He studied cooking and received a commendation for good work. But after three months, he dropped out. "I just couldn't concentrate," he said. But cooking continued to be a strong interest, partly because of his experience at the Skills Center and also through the influence of his older brother, who is a chef. When he dropped out of the Skills Center program, he disappeared for almost two years, only to reappear at the SYTE office destitute and homeless. Randall helped him make contact with the Department of Human Services and began conversations about returning to school. Shortly thereafter, he disappeared once more and picked up his life on the streets.

This pattern repeated itself several times. He would enroll in a skill-training program, stay a few months, then leave. Often he would get into a fight with other students and that would make it awkward for him to continue. Once he claimed a student in the class called him stupid for not being able to respond to a question the teacher asked. That fight led to his expulsion. Other times, the school would ask him to leave because his attendance was poor.

Being a dealer began to lose its attraction after two of his best friends were murdered in drug-related crimes. Shortly after his friends' murders, Anthony was incarcerated for drug trafficking. When he was released from prison, his wife convinced him to get out of the drug business for good, so he ended his career as a major dealer. But if he was broke, he still knew many people "in the game." They would give him a small amount to sell. "I'd get rid of it," he said casually, "and get some money like that." Then he countered with an explanation for his easy access on his terms: "Because, I still know a lot of people in the game, or whatever. Because I still get a lot of respect even though I'm not doing it any more."

After his release from prison, Anthony worked for a moving company for thirteen dollars an hour. "I'm just living. I still live in the hood. I work every day. Come home every day to an apartment that ain't worth paying for. Our living expenses is nine hundred a month. And between my wife's salary and mine, it's hard. Barely living." I asked him if he thought Say Yes had helped him in any way. His candid response was:

> I didn't let Say Yes help me. I can look around at those that went to college and say I should have done it too. But I didn't do it. So I have this block thing going on. I look and I be like, dag, I could've did that, then I block it right out. I do think about it and say, damn, I should've, but then the block comes. Even though I didn't take advantage of the scholarship, I do want to shake your hand and thank you. Sitting here and thinking about it, I wish I really did do it. But hey, I just put the block now.

The "block" anesthetizes Anthony's consciousness to the pain of lost opportunities to shape a better life for himself and his family. But the block does not wipe out his appreciation for the gift that was his.

TYREE

Tyree committed suicide during the summer of 1996. He was a profoundly angry, aggressive child and this behavior worsened as he became a young adult. Tyree was a well-known enigma in the program. He was retained in seventh grade, but did much better the second time through the grade. Based on his academic improvement, staff convinced Dr. Harris, principal of Sulzberger Junior High, to skip Tyree to ninth grade so that he could be with his peers. This proved to be a good decision. He continued to show satisfactory progress into tenth grade. His school failures were not a function of ability; he had a keen intellect. However, he was frequently suspended for starting fights in school. Teachers reported him for insubordination and an overall bad attitude toward school. He was easily influenced by peers and needed to prove himself to them by acting out in outrageous, defiant ways.

In high school, Tyree attended Bartram School for Human Services. This was not the typical impersonal school setting where students were often nameless faces. Teachers knew Tyree. They tried unsuccessfully to respond to his academic and social exigencies. Repeatedly, the Say Yes staff reached out to him. He knew we cared about him. I once asked him why he showed up at our office in response to frequent phone calls, but failed to follow any of the suggestions we offered him. He said wryly, "If I don't come see you, you won't stop bothering me."

In the winter of 1993, he mysteriously dropped out of school in the eleventh grade. He was not failing any subjects at the time, although he needed to make up two subjects he had failed the previous year. If he had successfully completed eleventh grade by taking seven subjects, and attended summer school to make up for previous failures, he would have attained a high school diploma. Instead, he dropped out precipitously and refused to consider re-enrolling. At the same time, he became a father. The child's mother left Tyree's home and did not take the baby with her. Tyree took on the responsibility of raising the child.

With few marketable skills in the legal economy, he earned money by selling drugs. At the time of his death, he lived in his mother's house with his girlfriend, reputed to be pregnant with his child. Tyree's suicide note said that he despaired over getting enough money together so that he and his girlfriend could move into their own apartment. Getting a job never seemed to be an option for him. He couldn't stand people telling him what to do. While he had a winning smile, he seldom shared it. He often looked angry and tense.

Shantih, his mother, was a heavyset woman with dreamy eyes often clouded by drugs. Her deep husky voice, honeyed by years of smoking, rolls over the listener like a gentle wave. When Tyree was thirteen, we matched him up with a mentor, an accomplished black male professional. After the first meeting between Tyree, his mentor, and his mother, Shantih asked the program's project coordinator if she could date her son's mentor. The coordinator said that would not be appropriate. When Tyree was sixteen, he found his mother in bed with his best friend. Tyree was devastated.

Shantih's public presentation of herself, in contrast, often was constructive and beneficial to the Say Yes community. Whenever Say Yes organized parents' meetings, Shantih would attend. She was an active participant and contributed her time generously. In appreciation for her efforts, her peers elected her vice-president of the SYTE parents' social activities committee. In June 1996, three years after Tyree dropped out of school and one month before his suicide, Shantih attended a parents' meeting. Coming to meetings at this point in her life appeared to be her way of fulfilling a ritual that in some vague way she hoped might help her son or herself.

In July 1996 at Tyree's funeral, the sponsor of the Say Yes program, George Weiss, addressed Tyree's corpse outstretched in his coffin: "What you did was stupid. Why were you so unbearably stubborn? Why didn't you let us in? Why didn't you let us help you?" The questions trailed off as the mourners wailed in disbelief and grief. Those who tried to help Tyree were left without immediate solutions that might have prevented his suicide. There seemed to be no meaningful way of stemming the assault of negative crises in his life. No single life event precipitated his suicide. Rather, a complex set of stress factors seemed to make life meaningless for him. He was a profoundly angry person who suffered from depression. His relationship with his mother contributed to his rage. When George Weiss visited his home and spoke candidly with Tyree and his mother, urging them to seek family counseling, they agreed to see a therapist, but failed to make an appointment.

While Tyree's home contributed to his despair, his neighborhood and schools failed him too. Tyree's neighborhood was rough. Drug traffic and gunfights were commonplace. Tyree sold drugs and ran the streets with a violent group of homies. The drug economy provided him with the instant gratification he needed, absent the possibility of finding decent work.

The gift of a scholarship, from Tyree's perspective, was a vague abstraction. There was nothing in the scholarship program that could change the concrete conditions of his daily life. Substandard housing and other consequences of intense poverty did not change because a student had the promise of a scholarship. Say Yes was about a "dream deferred" in the present. Samaj, another SYTE student who finished high school and college, offered a particularly compelling metaphor when explaining his feelings about the scholarship opportunity. Even for him, a successful student, a scholarship offered at the end of sixth grade was an abstraction some children learned to turn into a reality while others were never able to fully grasp.

But we were children. What are children supposed to do? Are we supposed to go out there and . . . we're supposed to have fun. You know, hey, we got a gift, everyone kept telling us about this gift. And we said, hey, let's tear the package open, let's tear it open and see what's inside. And when we saw it, it was like what's this you know, I mean, Say Yes kept telling us it's a good thing, you gotta treat it right and we were like, uh, whatever. We put it on the shelf, we played with it when we wanted to and now a lot of people paying for it. A lot of people paying for it.

The program encouraged students to imagine and work hard to achieve a better future. Those who were able to buy into the program believed that their investment in education would eventually pay off with an escape from poverty. Tyree gave up on education as a possible solution to his problems. His circumstances did not give him the freedom to imagine a better future. He was locked into a miserable present and saw no hope. Howard Stevenson (1998) would describe Tyree's condition as "hopelostness" (p. 5). Much of my work over the years has been to help children who live in poverty act as if they have control over their destinies. I say "as if," because it is not clear how much autonomy they actually have. They have to learn how to stem the onslaught of chaos so that they can shape their lives in a positive direction. Unfortunately, few of the adults in their neighborhoods offer protective guidance. Half of the Say Yes students' parents were addicted to drugs while they raised children. In communities where adults have given up hope of achieving economic security, their children are largely raising themselves, inventing their lives as best they can. E. Anderson's (1999) point is confirmed—that the "old heads," men and women who acted as positive neighborhood role models, are gone. What replaced them are the drug lords who introduce the values of a youth-dominated society, extolling the virtues of fast money and violence.

MONICA

Amanda, Monica's mother, gave birth to her when she was seventeen-years-old. She dropped out of school in twelfth grade in order to take care of her baby. Active in community politics, she spoke passionately about the injustices that abounded in her neighborhood. In her late thirties she went back to school to prepare for the General Equivalency Diploma (GED), which would give her access to better quality vocational training schools. She succeeded in attaining a GED and then achieved a barbering and hairdressing certification at a local school. She was intensely ambitious for her own development as well as her daughter's.

She had high hopes for Monica's future and advocated for her when she felt the school system was not responding to her needs. Amanda was instrumental in placing Monica in a junior high that had a slightly better reputation than did Sulzberger. She enrolled Monica in Shoemaker Junior High School rather than Sulzberger so that she could pursue her interest in running track. A natural runner, her mother supported Monica's interest in the sport. Track brought Monica a sense of accomplishment. She rattled off her history as a runner with pride:

> I came in as most valuable player my first year at Shoemaker. I ran in the Penn relays two years in a row. I had a private trainer for two years. And I won trophies for high jump, 100 yard meter dash, 4x1 medley relay, and I have a pendent for shot put.

The confidence and competence Monica felt as a runner did not transfer to her academic work. Lack of progress in reading led her teachers to recommend that she be placed in a special education class in fourth grade. She was retained in fifth grade and again in ninth. Her reading ability entering junior high school was at a third-grade level.

Finding little success in school, she dropped out at the end of ninth grade. Soon after, Monica hooked up with a drug gang. She portrayed this period of her life as a nightmare of excesses: "That's when I thought I had everything. I was at the top of my life, you know . . . 'cause I was making a lot of money. I had two cars boughten for me." Like Cory and Anthony, she coveted fancy cars and faddish clothes, all bought with drug money. In a reflective moment she explained why she got into the drug business:

> 'Cause I had all the things I dreamed of having. 'Cause I was being snotty-nosed and I didn't want to listen to nobody. I thought I knew somethin' and I didn't and I was smelling my own piss, and didn't. . . . You know, I couldn't do nothin' right. In one year got arrested four times.

This phase of her fast life was interrupted temporarily when the State Police arrested her in Backbay, Maryland. Her current boyfriend had murdered a man. The police wanted Monica for questioning because she witnessed the murder. A court case resulted and she was sentenced to three years' probation. Attending school was stipulated in the judge's order. Once the danger of further prosecution was over, she returned to the streets and selling drugs.

Simultaneously, she broke away from the Say Yes staff and did not return to school. Because she gave evidence against her old boyfriend, she was ostracized by the local drug dealers, who barred her from her main source of income. Cut off from support, she soon found herself destitute and homeless. "I was in and out of shelters and juvenile facilities. I lived on the streets for a while, I took care of myself." Pregnant, she moved back to her mother's home where she delivered her first child. Living with her mother fomented frequent conflicts and a war of wills often ensued. Because of the tension between them, Monica moved frequently in and out of her mother's house. A place of refuge in times of despair, it was also the scene of heated mutual criticism.

While Monica resided in her mother's house, staff recruited her for the baking program at the Randolph Skills Center. She thrived at the school, especially when she was learning the practical tasks of baking. However, the school was not organized so that she could work at mastering baking every day. Two full days each week, the school scheduled basic skills instruction. Those days Monica dreaded. She began to cut the basic skills days and attended only when she could bake. After three months, she dropped out, saying that she could not find childcare and needed to stay at home. But baking, and later cooking, were marketable skills she was able to use when she looked for work. With just three months' worth of baking skills, she was able to land a job at a local bakery. The work required that she rise at 5:00 A.M. so that she could start work at 6:00 A.M. During the time she worked at the bakery, she became pregnant with her second child. By the end of her fifth month, she could no longer meet the demands of the job and quit.

Two entries in Randall's monthly reports, about a year apart, describe the ongoing issues Monica faced for several years:

> 4/23/99. Monica's mother, Amanda, called me to inquire about Monica getting enrolled in a cooking school. She found a school, B & Z Caterers, that would train her and give her help with her GED. Amanda asked me to take her down to the school to enroll her. I replied, "I don't do that for students any more. They have to get themselves enrolled in school." I told her I would be available to provide assistance if she had any problems getting into school. I called two days later to see what progress Monica had made. Amanda informed me that she had taken a job with Dwight Southern Barbecue.

Randall made an important point in this first entry when he said he would not take Monica to the school to enroll her. He was reinforcing a program policy designed to wean students from a dependent relationship with staff. He wanted Monica to assert some independence and take responsibility for her education. In this instance, Monica did take initiative in finding a job. But for the time being she abandoned plans to pursue a GED. Ten months later, as she continued work in various low-level jobs, she also enrolled in a GED class.

> 2/22/00. Monica enrolled in a GED program. She works at Big George's, a restaurant at 52nd Street, as a cook and food server. Prior to that she was employed as a cook/food server at Kentucky Fried Chicken earning $5.50 per hour, working from 3:00 to 11:00 A.M. six days a week. To get to work she had to travel on two buses to get to South Philadelphia. This long commute on public transportation did not allow her to get home until 1:00 A.M. She had to abandon the house she got through one of the city's rental assistance programs because it was unfit for habitation. Monica is not lazy. She is willing to work hard. However, the money she earns does not free her from needing public assistance for her children.

Randall's entries note that Monica was pursuing a GED preparatory program. She realized that finding employment that pays a living wage was directly related to her ability to improve her basic skills and to show that she had mastered the skills required to function effectively in a workplace. This reality was driven home to her when she realized that "Even Kentucky Fried Chicken wants you to have a high school diploma or a GED." Her realization strengthened her resolve, but also made her feel anxious. She was so traumatized by her school failures that she became very skittish about preparation programs. Like Cory, she made some progress when working one-on-one with a special education teacher Say Yes hired. But she frustrated easily, got discouraged, and soon withdrew. She understood her learning disability this way:

> I had a reading disability that jeopardized it and stopped me from doing things I wanted to do. It made me scared to go out and face the world. I have a, it's not a phobia, it's just a cop-out I've used for a long time. It stopped me from achieving a lot of things in life that I could have been a lot further, if I hadn't let it overcome me, rather than me overcome it. It was some type of Dyslexia. But, now, I've overcome it. I read constantly. I buy books. It takes me

a while to finish them. I'm not going to let anything take hold of my life, because my life is mines, and I'm never in my life willing to let anything take it from me again.

Monica has a strong will, a stubborn determination to succeed. She would spin out business plans for a clothing store or a restaurant she'd like to open: she would scope out a site, identify the equipment needed, cost out expenses and look for partners to help her with the down payment. At eighteen, she described her plans for a clothing store this way:

> Yeah, I'm going to open my store, hopefully by September. I been saving my lunch money and my carfare, and I been going back and forth to school, and my little extra spending money, and puttin' it in the bank. I priced the store four weeks ago—it's $1,000 a month rent. But it's eight hundred square feet of store. I have my own cooling system, my own alarm system, two business offices. . . . You know, I have a stereo system all through the store. That was $1,000 a month. She says I can rent to buy. So you know that comes to—. I need another partner.

At age twenty-five, her business scheme shifted from women's clothing to finding a way to capitalize on her pleasure in cooking. She was investigating what it would take to open a restaurant. Her plan required these steps:

> I've been calling companies and finding out how much materials are and I've been calling real estate companies finding out if they have any stores that are already equipped with fryers and ventilation systems that were previously restaurants that closed down. I'm trying to find out what actually money I will need to start it. . . . I want a storefront place with apartments on top of it so I can rent out the apartments to pay for the restaurant to pay for the bills, the insurance and the water.

She was actively engaged in fantasizing about these plans. Unfortunately, she was not ready to take such big steps. She was trapped in situations that limited her potential. At age twenty-five she was the mother of five children. As she once said about Say Yes female students, "Some of us had babies too early." The plans for businesses that she saw as liberating her from low-paying jobs and public assistance were too grandiose to realize. At some level she knew this when she said, "If I'm going to own a business, I'm going to need to improve my reading and my math." Ambitions of opening a business or preparing to take the GED prompted a call to the Say Yes office. For short periods a few months at a time, Say Yes became important in her life. Despite her impulsiveness, she could be reflective about the scholarship and her understanding of the opportunity was out of sync with the way she lived:

> You were expected to go to college, be on a straight path from here on out to the year 2000. And life does not work like that. It just does not work like that. You have your downfalls and your good and your bad. Life is only what you can make out of it. It's not a straight line, it's not a rope you tie around someone and say: "This is the straight path you're supposed to follow." It's not that. It's life. It has its twists and turns like a road and you never know where it's going to lead you, and where you're going to end up at. As an older adult I can sit, and see that I could have achieved a lot more in my life if I really put more effort and try to walk the straight path that was laid for me. Since I didn't, I'm not angry and I'm not hurt. It's just a lesson that was taught. So it makes things a little harder when it didn't have to be, but it'll be OK. And I'll still go on. But if I do succeed before June 2000, I'd thank Mr. Weiss a hell of a lot. And if I don't, I'd still thank him a hell of a lot because he has given me a hell of a lot, and he has helped me, and this program has helped me a lot. We've been together so long that we've become more like family than friends.

Eloquent about her life's story, she searched for lessons to pass onto her children. She loves her children and has dreams for their future: "I say to them, 'I do want you to go to college. But if you choose not to go, I'm not going to be upset. I'm not going to love you any less. But a high school diploma is a must. You have to give me that.' " She spoke more directly to me then: "Because when I get mines, it's theirs. It's going on the wall for them." Then she reconsidered her demand that her children must graduate from high school and argued ambivalently: "Until I get mines, I can't, well I can, because I'm their mother. I am their parent, be strong, but how can I ask a child for something I don't have myself?"

SHAMIRA

The first time staff visited Shamira's home, the interview took place standing. There was no place to sit; the living room was full of trash and debris. Shamira's mother claimed they were trying to fix up the house. Randall Sims and Robin Wall Hill wondered if the house was legally habitable. It certainly did not provide an environment in which Shamira could study, let alone offer shelter for two brothers, a sister, and a stepsister. In seventh grade at Sulzberger Junior High School, Shamira did not pass any of her courses and was absent frequently. By the end of the second report period, she had been absent sixty-four times and late twenty-four times. When at school, she often instigated fights. This pattern of excessive school absences and fighting with other children had already been established in elementary school. Shamira had devised a system for avoiding aspects of school that she felt might put her on the spot. She explained: "I only went to school on certain days: like Monday, because you get homework, Wednesday because of the quiz and Fridays because of a test." Tuesdays and Thursdays were the only two days she could avoid academic pressure. But there was no guarantee that school would attract her attention any day of the week. Often she spent the entire week hanging out with friends. Her mother felt these friends were a bad influence. Shamira attended three different elementary schools before she was admitted to Belmont. The psychologist at Martha Washington Elementary School certified her for special education based on low reading scores and lack of emotional control. She was expelled from Martha Washington for starting fights and transferred to Belmont's special education program.

By the time she moved on from Belmont to Sulzberger Junior High School, she was an experienced user of ". . . marijuana, crack, cocaine, and alcohol." She claimed in a nonchalant manner, "My first experiences at smoking weed, snorting crack and drinking started when I was around thirteen." Shamira not only used drugs, she also sold them, which provided money to her sister and stepsister, several cousins, and herself. Her mother, an alcoholic, sought help for Shamira's drug abuse problem. She committed her to a rehab center where she lived for a month. When she returned home she made a pass at going to school, but soon she was back on the streets. Her mother, frustrated by her inability to control her behavior, took Shamira to court. Shamira summarized her account of the hearing this way: "My mom went to court with me and told this lady to keep me." The court decided that she needed to be in a residential correctional center for adolescent delinquents. The judge assigned her to Sleighton Farms. Initially Shamira felt betrayed by her mother when she told the judge that she could no longer handle her at home. Later, when her mother failed to visit her, she also felt abandoned and hurt. Shamira remained at Sleighton Farms for six months and then was transferred to Lourdsmont, another residential school about a ninety-minute drive west of Philadelphia. Lourdsmont, managed by an order of nuns, felt like a more caring institution to Shamira. Little niceties made a difference to her:

> They would take you out and give you an allowance, and take you clothes shopping. I liked that. The teachers would be right there to help. They didn't have thirty kids in one class where they wouldn't have time for each of them. They had like ten kids in each class and they had time for each of them.

She regretted that she did not stay longer than four months before she left the school permanently. Her boyfriend, also at Lourdsmont, was being released. He begged her to complete her term at Lourdsmont, but she could not bear being separated. Reflecting several years later, she saw this decision as a crucial error and believed that if she had stayed at Lourdsmont she would have been able to attend college. Normally, her failure in seventh grade would have been grounds for retaining her in grade. However, since she had been retained twice in elementary school, she was overage for her grade. When she returned from Lourdsmont to Sulzberger Junior High School, rather than retain her, the principal sent her on to University City High School based on social promotion. However, in ninth grade, she persisted in being absent frequently and acted inappropriately with regard to the school's social norms. If her teachers did not respond to her requests for help immediately, she became angry. She justified her impatience:

> They say, "Wait a minute," but you never get no help. So, I feel neglected and I leave the class. If the teachers be straight up and help me, I want teachers to help me. Not just write me off when I raise my hand, and wave me off, and then the period's over. That makes me mad. This one math class I had, I gave the teacher my homework, she graded it, it was an "A" or something. But every time I asked her help in math, she probably think I know it. I just want someone to understand me; that's all I ask for.

At University City High School, she continued selling drugs. School was irrelevant to her way of life. Dropping out was not a conscious decision. It simply happened as a result of seeing the streets as a place that gave some meaning to her life. She explained stoically,

"I experienced life on life's terms, without an education." She joined a Jamaican club, where, in a scuffle with some girls, she was stabbed in her lower back and seriously injured. As soon as she recovered, she was back on the streets selling drugs and "hanging out with the drug boys down in Olney." She was insightful about the cycle of despair drugs brought her:

> I wanted to fit in. Always trying to fit in. I should have been fitting in with education, but I was fitting in with the other stuff. The stuff that don't get you nowhere but three places: jail, death, or an institution. I've been in jail a few times. The last time they caught me for prostitution. That's when I was stabbed and almost died.

The theme of caring was a generative metaphor for her life. She saw Say Yes as a real opportunity to improve her life's chances and she was self critical for wasting the gift. "These people care," she reasoned:

> They wouldn't have done this if they didn't care for us. I don't know. I don't know. I had a chance to go to college free and I wasted all their time and patience. They had tutors and everything. People there to help us, and I said the H with them, and went about my merry way. Which y'all saw right there. Maybe I was saying to myself, "these people don't care about me." I didn't believe it.

Shamira understood at one level that the program was about reaching out to students. However, she had a hard time trusting in the staff's caring for her. Memories of how people had cared for her in the past merged with more recent experience. Her train of thought shifted from feelings of guilt for not using the program's help, to remembering the day her mother abandoned her and sent her off to Sleighton Farms. She tried to make sense of that painful moment:

> How can somebody care and just send you away like that. But that was caring though. I didn't understand that then. And my mom was right there and she said, "Send her away." I was like, "Mom, you just met him, and you sending me away." But I agreed to go. I agreed to go.

Arriving at a more adult appreciation of caring, she resented her mother's decision to send her to a correctional school, while conceding that sending her away was a way of trying to rescue her from the vortex of drugs and prostitution.

At twenty-six years of age, Shamira developed more constructive ways of coping with her anger. She learned to walk away from a potential fight and was trying to find people in her life to help her move in a more positive direction. Her changes were tentative and uncertain and she was still living on welfare. "I'm getting all the free money I can get," she said in exaggerated joy. Then, changing her mood she noted in a teasing tone: "I don't have to. I can go to school and y'all give me an allowance for going to school. But I choose welfare over going to school."

If Shamira questioned the Say Yes staff's reliability and commitment to her needs, the staff also had reason to wonder if she was serious about pursuing her education. She gave double messages: on the one hand she would like to achieve a GED, but on the other hand she missed many appointments for tutoring and failed to show up for special preparatory classes.

At the end of this interview, I asked if she had anything else she wished to say. This is the dialogue that ensued:

Shamira: Nice meeting you again.

Interviewer: What did you think about this interview?

Shamira: You get to free your mind and feel good about yourself. I need to talk.

Interviewer: You seemed willing to talk.

Shamira: Because you're trying to help me.

Interviewer: I'd like to, if we can.

Shamira: If I don't run away no more.

Interviewer: I hope you won't.

Shamira: I don't need to run away. I'm tired.

Interviewer: I believe you.

Shamira: After twelve years, I'm tired.

Interviewer: Enough.

Shamira: Enough.

TASHA

Tasha Sullivan comes from a family of ten children. When she turned eight-years-old, her twenty-four-year-old sister, Leslie, became her legal guardian. Tasha moved between her mother's and her older sister's houses, but increasingly spent more time at her sister's. "I wasn't getting what I wanted at my mom's house. I couldn't. Too many kids. It was dirty." Her mother didn't work. She suffered from bouts of acute alcoholism that necessarily affected her ability to maintain a household. Leslie put more structure into Tasha's life. She had to clean her own room, do household chores, and be in bed by 9:30 P.M. However, the one area Leslie had limited influence over was the irregularity of Tasha's school attendance. Pat Sanahan, chair of the special education department at Sulzberger Junior High School, had tried to work with several of the Sullivan children. His assessment was pessimistic: "The Sullivan kids do not come to school. It's a family trait." He was particularly concerned with Tasha's poor attendance. "She's a really nice kid, pleasant and cooperative when she's in class. I think she has the ability to advance to resource room status, if she'd only come to school." Her reading and math scores placed her at a fourth grade level entering ninth grade.

Tasha's mom moved into Leslie's house with her five children when she lost her own house because the rent collector was involved in a drug scam and never gave the money he received to the owner of the house. The crowded household increased tensions among family members that exploded into violence. Tasha complained that:

> My whole family is violent. Every time we get together we got to fight each other or somebody else. It's the little kids that starts it. If they be yelling, one person will go and tell their mom and then everybody gets into it. I be wanting to leave sometime.

But it was not only the children who precipitated fights. Strained relationships between adults would burst out into uncontrollable anger that resulted in violence. Leslie and her husband Jake argued frequently. Jake became physically abusive to her and also threatened Tasha. Once, their altercation reached the pitch of rage. Leslie reacted to Jake's abuse by firing a bullet at him. Their marriage of ten years ended with that shot: Jake was forbidden to enter the house by court order, although he could visit with his children outside the house. And Leslie, for her part in the fight, faced a four to eight month sentence at correctional facility.

Tasha felt surrounded by violence: within her family, on the street and in her high school. She was afraid to walk out the door for fear that something awful would happen to her. Her fears, while somewhat extreme, were not unfounded. The following example makes her point about the arbitrariness of violence: "You be hearing kids coming to school with guns. That scares me too, 'cause you don't know if you argue with somebody, if they're going to pull out a gun and shoot you." At a more personal level she was robbed near her home. She related this harrowing experience:

> I was walking down the street, and a girl came up to me, a real big girl, put a knife to my neck and told me to give her all my stuff. She put this fear in me, "I'm going to be looking, watching you and stuff, and you better not tell nobody." So that had me scared, I just was nervous. My sister always talked to me and said: "She's not gonna bother you, go out there and do what you have to do." She always told me to go ahead and I'll take you to school.

These fears paralyzed her. She was terrified of being hurt, and dealt with these fears by staying at home. The street robbery gave her yet another reason to feel phobic about going to school. Leslie's offer to accompany her was little comfort. Whatever the reason for not attending school—real, imagined or family tradition—the juvenile court finally determined that Leslie had the legal responsibility of insisting that Tasha attend school. The court backed up its decision by imposing a heavy fine on Leslie and instituted a monitoring system to insure that Tasha did in fact attend school regularly. The court's interference was effective in changing Tasha's pattern of attendance. And with more routine attendance, she was able to improve some of her academic skills. Her consistent effort earned her the right to be moved out of special education into a regular English class. Unfortunately, these gains were short-lived. The following year, in tenth grade, her attendance again deteriorated. This regression happened at the time of the bitter fighting between Leslie and Jake. It was apparent to Tasha that Leslie needed her help taking care of her children.

In eleventh grade, Tasha was in the process of dropping out. She'd go to school every other day, then skip a week; return to school for a couple of days, realize that she had fallen behind in her work, stay out for another week, then stop going entirely. George Weiss tried to get her to reconsider her decision. He visited Leslie and Tasha at their home. Both promised him that she would start school again. They also agreed to go into joint therapy to see if they could work out some of the underlying reasons for Tasha's reluctance to attend school. They did attend therapy for a while, but Tasha's attendance did not improve. She was upset with herself and felt conflicted. Staying at home was boring. At home there was nothing for her to do besides helping her sister with childcare. However, attending school provoked fear and anxiety that she might be harmed physically or psychologically. Even when she made some genuine progress in her studies, as she did in ninth grade, school was the place where she felt "stupid" and unsuccessful. Because she did not accomplish any of the work for her grade, she was retained in eleventh grade. Tasha never returned to high school.

She had dreams and aspirations for the future. By age twenty-four, she was able to move out of Leslie's house and into her own place. She lived with her own two children, another sister and her child, and a younger sister, age thirteen, who attended middle school. Tasha's mom was in a shelter so taking care of one of her children seemed like the right thing to do. She was proud that her younger sister liked school and felt successful, "bringing home report cards with all As and Bs." Tasha felt that helping her family was a way to give back to others who need support. But she wanted to do more than offer a home to family members in need. She wanted to be a role model for them: "So I want to get out of here and show them that they have to do something to get up in life. After I got my own place and had my kids, I had to look at them and say it's time for me to get on out of here."

Discussions with her grandmother helped Tasha focus on a job that would capitalize on her ability to care for others. She described the process she used for finding work: "I found the job in childcare on my own, looking through the papers every day. I made out an application for it. And when they called me I was so happy." She worked at a preschool called Tots Earn to Learn, based on the Montessori method of educating young children. At the time of the interview, she had held this job for seven months. "I'm so glad I got something to do every day," she said with pride.

> I'm trying to show my kids how by getting up every morning, I'm showing them that you have to work. You have to get out there and go to school and get your education. So I think by me getting up every morning and telling them that mommy's going to work,

they have that in their head, because when you sit around and the kids see that, they follow you. I hope I'm doing the right thing for them to have a successful life.

Tasha modeled for her children work habits that would help them be successful in school and later when they start work. But reliable attendance is only one component of the skills one needs to succeed at work. She knew that she would access higher-paying job options if she passed the GED examination. Like Monica she feared failure on this exam and so avoided taking it or even attending tutoring sessions that would prepare her to take the test. She had a long history of asking for help from Randall Sims. He would offer ways of assisting her, but at the appointed time she would not show up. She was aware of her unreliable behavior with Randall and she described how her previous encounters had failed. She also claimed that this time the results would be more constructive:

> I'm the type person that let's say, I'm going to come to the Say Yes office to see Sims and then he calls and I'm not there and stuff like that. But now I'm gonna be there, because I really want it. Yeah, I know I'm never reliable, but I'm willing to do it now.

I pressed her to test her commitment. I suggested the following hypothetical situation to consider: "What's going to happen when you have an appointment with Mr. Sims, and a voice in your head says, 'come on, I've got better things to do.'" She responded cautiously: "I guess I'll have to ignore that voice. Unless it's something real important that he'll understand, but if it ain't important then I'm right here."

Conclusion

In the six lives presented here, a cluster of interactive forces within school, at home, and on the street influenced the final outcome of dropping out. As the lives I've described suggest, there is no single reason students drop out. William Julius Wilson believes that the corrosive effects of dysfunctional communities make "normal" development impossible (1987). Wilson states that the high rates of joblessness among adults in the inner-city alienate students from school. They see no point to an education that does not lead to gainful employment. A vicious cycle of frustration and despair "is perpetuated through the family, through the school, and through the community" (1987, 57). For J. Fishkin, personality is an irrelevant category (1983). Environment shapes the life course. In his book, *Justice, Equal Opportunity, and the Family* (1983), Fishkin summarizes his research this way:

> Children who grow up in homes plagued by these disadvantages— low income, crime-ridden neighborhoods, broken homes, inadequate housing, and poor education . . . are more likely to be denied an equal chance in life, because the development of their aspirations and talents is hindered in their environment. (p. 17)

In the concluding section of the chapter, I bring together themes across the six profiles and discuss the program's limitations in meeting all their needs. I return to the organizing questions that I mentioned at the start of the chapter, and use them to summarize the crosscutting issues.

Dropping Out and Special Education

Dropping out is an end point in a lengthy process often starting as early as first grade (Brooks-Gunn & Guo 1993). For example, Anthony and Shamira had been identified in early elementary school as aggressive and poorly socialized to school. Some researchers find that aggressive behavior at the beginning of the elementary grades is predictive of who will later drop out of school (Kellum & Hunter 1990). The environmental stresses within family, neighborhood, and school create a set of negative interactive forces that lead these children into reactive aggressive behavior. Their situations seem to preclude their learning positive coping strategies (Spencer 1995, 1997).

Five of the six students profiled were labeled "learning disabled" and placed in special education classrooms, which are supposed to provide the educational and social supports that will help the student progress. Yet Cory is bitter about the inability of special education teachers to help him. From his perspective, teachers keep reviewing the same material, so that it becomes impossible to master advanced subject matter. His teachers might counter that Cory attended class so sporadically that mastery of new material was impossible.

Of the thirty-nine SYTE students who dropped out, thirty were designated as learning disabled. Should we conclude that being so labeled and therefore placed in special education in the inner city was a prerequisite for three-quarters of the total number of SYTE dropouts to leave school? Mainstream social scientists would disconfirm that hypothesis by bringing IQ tests, subject area tests, attendance records, and psychological tests to show that these students did not have the ability or the habits of mind to succeed; therefore they could not benefit from schooling. Critical educational researchers like H. Varenne and R. McDermott in their book *Successful School Failure* (1998) would ask us instead to interrogate the school, its system of testing, its need for competitive rank ordering of students, and its all too limited understanding of how children learn. After such an investigation, I suspect that the least we could say is that, for the SYTE student, being learning disabled and placed in special education did not improve their chances of completing high school.

If schools failed to educate SYTE's students in special education, life on the streets substituted a different form of schooling. The drug economy caught the dropouts' attention by satisfying their need for money and respect. At the peak of our students' involvement in drug dealing, George Weiss and Randall Sims knocked on the doors of the families whose children were drug dealers, sat down with the students and their parents, and threatened to remove them from the program. Students who were in regular education classes listened and stopped drug dealing. But even in this group, the cessation often was short-lived, with fitful stops and starts based on financial need and the lure of friends in the business. In contrast, those labeled as special education students often saw no other options than joining the drug culture or some other form of criminal activity. As mentioned previously, thirty of the thirty-nine dropouts were designated as learning disabled when they attended school. Twenty-four of the dropouts were adjudicated delinquents. Out of a total of twenty adult felons who served prison sentences, seventeen were learning disabled. Three served long prison sentences, six or more years, for their involvement in capital crimes. Thus, there seems to be a strong association among these conditions: poverty, being learning disabled, dropping out, becoming an adjudicated delinquent, and eventually being convicted as an adult felon. My research suggests that the combination of poverty and a learning disability places youth at greater risk of moving toward a life of antisocial behavior. An analysis of recent research on the factors identified here confirms clear connections. First, recent demographic studies have found a growing relationship between poverty and risk for disability (Fujiura &

Yamaki, 2000; Kaye, La-Plante, Carlson, & Wenger, 1996). Among children with disabilities aged three to twenty-one in the United States, 28 percent are living in poor families. By contrast, among the children without disabilities in the same age range, only 16 percent are living in poverty (Fujiura & Yamaki, 2000). Second, once a child is referred to special education, juvenile delinquency is much more likely. A conservative, preliminary estimate of the prevalence of youth with disabling conditions in juvenile corrections is 32 percent. This finding is notably higher than the prevalence of disabilities among school-age children in the United States, which is about 9 percent (U.S. Department of Education 2000). Finally, numerous studies find that individuals with long and serious juvenile criminal careers are likely to have equally serious criminal activity in their adult lives (Wolfgang, Thornberry, & Figlio, 1987).

There simply are too few options available for this population, which feels condemned to a low-level existence. The drug world, all too familiar to these youth, offers a quick way out of their dilemma. However, it would be incorrect to assume that all SYTE students, who were at one time designated for special education services, eventually dropped out. That is not the case. Twelve students originally assigned to special education were eventually fully mainstreamed into regular education. Of those twelve, four matriculated to four-year colleges and attained bachelor's degrees; two attained associate's degrees from two-year colleges. Three graduated from high school with special education diplomas and then completed trade certificates at accredited vocational schools. One student attained a trade certificate without graduating high school. And two students graduated high school with special education diplomas but did not pursue additional education. While the proportion of high school graduates from SYTE's special education population (26 percent) is not statistically significant, it is modestly higher than that of the comparison group.

Female dropouts shared some of the same characteristics as their male counterparts: several sold drugs, had police records, lived the fast life, and had ongoing difficulty in mastering school subjects and skills. Having children complicated their lives. Among some SYTE females, childbearing isolated them from the world as they retreated into their households. For others, childbearing became an escape, a way to avoid the need to finish education. Dropping out was a way of stopping the humiliation of repeated school failure.

Four of the six students presented in this chapter feel appreciation for the gift that was given to them. However, in retrospect, their appreciation is tempered by guilt that they may have wasted a valuable chance to escape poverty. Cory recalled how proud he was to be a recipient of the gift. He knew that others less fortunate than he was would have had to struggle to pay for college. He was ashamed to say that he had this opportunity and wasted the chance to use it.

Anthony said directly, "I didn't let Say Yes help me." He was grateful that he was given the opportunity but pained by the knowledge that he didn't use it. He protected himself from this pain by blocking out the experience. But the "block" did not always work and he felt regret. Tyree never said explicitly how he felt about the gift. Monica valued the gift and the gift giver, George Weiss. She believed that she benefited from her association with the program regardless of the fact that she might not use the gift. But she was also critical of how people in authority—such as parents, teachers, and perhaps SYTE— think about education. She said, ". . . life is not a straight line, it's not a rope you tie around someone and say, 'This is the straight path you're supposed to follow.' It's not that. It's life. It has its twists and turns and you never know where it's going to lead you, and where you're going to end up at." She asked that people acknowledge the vicissitudes of daily living; especially in the context of her life, traveling the straight path is a fiction. But she also blamed herself for not exerting greater effort to walk the path that was available to her. Shamira felt guilty about wasting the opportunity and blamed herself for losing this chance. Then she protected her feelings by insisting that the program did not care about her; she had a hard time believing that anyone could care for her. Tasha was trying to invent a new life for herself and her children. She knew she has a history of avoiding school. But she wanted to model for her children that it's important to get up in the morning, go to work or school, and be productive. Having broken many appointments she set up with Randall Sims, she wondered if he'll believe she is committed to finishing her education.

Most students, including the dropouts, believed that the gift and the interventions implemented to help SYTE students make use of it were, in Cory's words, "a blessed thing." Some dropouts felt guilt and shame for not using it, but seemed to possess too few resources to move out of a dead-end situation. The Say Yes dropouts' stories underscore the complexity of the assistance they needed. While the staff tried continuously to respond to the dropouts' needs, the magnitude of the interventions they required pushed far beyond the scope of the resources and expertise the program could offer. If students in special education, who comprised 75 percent of the dropouts, are to succeed in high school, faculties and administrators must become open to the kind of restructuring I described at the beginning of this chapter. Researchers have established that while the purpose of special education is to benefit students, this is rarely the case. D. K. Lipsky and A. Gartner find that for many students, referral to these programs is a one-way ticket (1989). In addition to improving special education for those who are not succeeding in regular classrooms, interventions in reading and social development from preschool through third grade are more likely to avert long-term academic problems. It is far better to prevent educational problems before they jeopardize a school career. The title of this chapter, "Dropping the ball," is an allusion to the football Diane Weiss threw to the sixth grade class graduating from Belmont. Some dropouts caught and dropped the ball over and over again. Others never caught the ball; it was out of sight. A postsecondary school scholarship was a gift they could not use.

CHAPTER 4

Making It

High School

Transitions from elementary to middle and from middle to high school can be fraught with danger. For students with academic difficulties, the move to an unfamiliar environment with different expectations for which they have not been prepared aggravates already existing problems (Newberg 1991; Eccles and Midgley 1989). For SYTE students, each of these school-level transitions was a disastrous experience: 25 percent were retained in seventh grade, 30 percent in ninth grade. However, both statistics were lower than the citywide averages. For example, at Bartram and University City, two of the high schools SYTE students attended, 35 percent and 52 percent, respectively, of all ninth graders were retained (School District of Philadelphia 1990b). There is some evidence suggesting that the cause of these precipitous drops in achievement may be associated with the structure and organization of school levels, which puts large numbers of students at risk (Fine 1994; Eccles et al. 1993). Four of the six students presented in this chapter, and most of the college-bound students, attended Bartram School for Human Services. In order to place the stories of the high school graduates in a larger context, I first provide quantitative outcome data comparing SYTE outcomes six years after the start of the program to a comparable group of public school students not in the program. I next describe SYTE's association with Bartram School for Human Services in some depth, and then offer six portraits of students who graduated from high school.

Quantitative Research Data: The Outcomes

Little quantitative research has been reported about tuition-guarantee programs and the affects on those who participate (U. S. General Accounting Office 1990). Of the data that have been reported, none, to our knowledge, have shown their results in relation to a comparison group. I present the following data to redress that omission.

By August 1993, forty-four SYTE students had graduated from School District of Philadelphia high schools. An additional five students received high school diplomas or Graduate Equivalency Diplomas from private or out-of-state schools. Three students were deceased. One hundred eligible SYTE students were compared with a group of eighty

Figure 4.1

Comparison and SYTE Students Six Years after
Leaving Elementary School (August 1993)

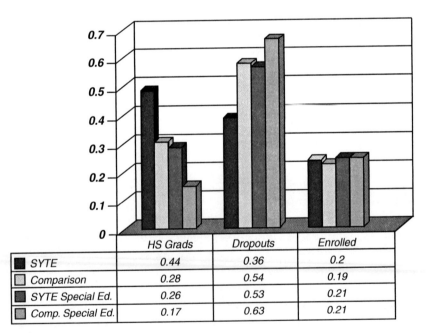

	HS Grads	Dropouts	Enrolled
SYTE	0.44	0.36	0.2
Comparison	0.28	0.54	0.19
SYTE Special Ed.	0.26	0.53	0.21
Comp. Special Ed.	0.17	0.63	0.21

(Full data table available in Appendix A)

Source: Schlesinger, M. 1993. A study of a tuition guarantee program. Unpublished doctoral dissertation, Temple University, Philadelphia, PA.

students similar in background. The results indicate that 44 percent (forty-four students) in the SYTE group and 28 percent (twenty-two students) in the comparison group completed high school. The difference is significant at the $p < .05$ level.

Comparing the graduation rates of all male students in SYTE with those of a comparison group, the results were 46 percent and 22 percent respectively ($p < .05$); for females it was 43 percent compared to 34 percent. These data show that SYTE male students did significantly better than did the comparison group's, but there was no significant difference for females.

If we consider the regular education students separately from the special education students, we find that 60 percent of SYTE and 32 percent of the comparison group graduated ($p < .01$). Again looking at the group as a whole, the dropout rates for the two groups also differ: 36 percent for SYTE and 54 percent for the comparison group (as cited in Newberg & Sims 1996, 156). For regular education students, the dropout rate was 21 percent for SYTE and 50 percent for the comparison group ($p < .01$).

Despite the daunting conditions many SYTE students encountered, by 1996, sixty-nine (62 percent) of the Belmont 112 had graduated high school and fifty had experienced one or more years of postsecondary schooling. No records exist documenting the graduation rates for the comparison group after 1993. However, since that group did not have ongoing support, it seems likely that SYTE's graduation rate is higher.

High school graduation was an essential goal that SYTE students had to attain if they were going to access the Weiss' gift. The next hurdle would require them to score competitively on the college entrance exam, the SAT. Say Yes scores on the SAT, despite a lengthy preparation course provided by the Say Yes program to familiarize students with the content and form of the test, ranged from 450 to 1050. Only one student of the thirty-three who took the test scored above the national mean of 1011. Three other students scored at or above 900. Seven students scored at or below 500, placing their performance in the bottom 10 percent nationally. The average SAT score among the SYTE students was 656, 350 points below the national mean and 41 points below the average for the city.

While schools like Penn Bartram School for Human Services and University City's Motivation program in Philadelphia were nurturing and academically challenging, their standards did not compare with those of prestigious magnet schools such as Engineering and Science, the school Richard attended. Richard scored 1050 on the SAT—the highest score among Say Yes students and the only score above the national mean. Richard enrolled in the University of Pennsylvania and began his program without remediation. Most SYTE students entering less competitive colleges were required to take one or more remediation courses before they could matriculate at the college level.

By September 1993, forty-five were enrolled in two-year or four-year colleges: twenty-one in two-year and twenty-four in four-year colleges. Two students attended trade schools. Postsecondary data about the comparison group is not available, since the school district only reported graduates who made applications to two and four-year colleges, not the number who were actually accepted and enrolled. In chapter six, I will summarize the degree or certificate attainment outcomes for those students who completed a postsecondary program. These outcomes will be compared with census tract data and completion rates for a comparable program in Philadelphia, Tell Them We Are Rising.

Penn Bartram School for Human Services

Generally, students disperse to a variety of settings for high school. The SYTE leadership felt that it would be helpful to concentrate a substantial proportion of their students in a small, caring school so that academic and social development could be supported. In 1973, I had helped create Bartram School for Human Services, a small satellite of the larger comprehensive high school. Human Services had the reputation for knowing how to shepherd a class of students through high school. However, the school only included students from grades ten through twelve and had no provision for special education. The program's sponsors and I convinced the school district to include ninth grade; they invited SYTE to form the first freshman class. To mark the reorganization of the school, George Weiss insisted that the school be linked to the University of Pennsylvania. The school was renamed Penn Bartram School for Human Services to reflect the change.

The size of Human Services, 250 students, made it easier for teachers to take a personal interest in students and more difficult to hide academic or social problems. Bill Hanson, a history teacher, remarked that "the small size of the school translates into more attention to student needs." The individual efforts of teachers contributed to its caring and nurturing environment. Bill Hanson credited the director of the school, Charlotte Little, with setting the tone. She did not tolerate fighting in the school and said without hesitation, "The first one to throw a punch is out." She continued, "Students seem less likely to fight in this school. They know they can go some place or to someone in the school to resolve the problem." Teachers extended themselves to help students succeed in academic work. The school's size and the educational philosophy that each student's needs should be addressed "holistically" shaped teachers' ways of interacting with students.

Human Services derived its name from the many human service vocations and professions that mushroomed in the 1970s. As American companies relocated their factories to Asian countries where labor was inexpensive, cities were left with empty factories where blue-collar workers once earned a living. Their jobs were replaced in an economy that provided services. The School for Human Services acknowledged this shift by exposing students to human service jobs in the sophomore and junior years. Students attended school in the morning and, four afternoons a week, apprenticed in schools, government offices, health clinics, and daycare centers, assisting professionals in their work. Once each week, teachers debriefed students about their work, and analyzed their experiences in terms of the kinds of skills were required to perform the tasks.

However, by the time our students were ready to participate in this aspect of the program, the quality of the placements had deteriorated and students were no longer challenged by the work. SYTE staff, Diane Weiss and an outside community organizer revamped the placements so that students had more choice and better supervision. For example, Melvin planned to become a men's fashion designer; Diane found him a position in an upscale men's clothing store, where he learned how to sell a line of new male fashions. Christina expressed interest in becoming a lawyer; Diane convinced a prominent councilwoman to allow Christina to intern in her office. The following year, we secured the services of a woman who specialized in creating volunteer work opportunities; she expanded these improved career explorations so that they became available to all the students

SYTE staff and sponsors were instrumental in supporting the faculty and, whenever possible, in improving the quality of services to all students. SAT preparation was a case in point. I noticed that the coursework seemed superficial and did not allow sufficient time for students to master the content and the style in which test questions were presented. SYTE hired an outside expert to provide SAT prep to all students in the eleventh grade class. Instead of a minicourse consisting of eight sessions, students met twice each week over a three-month period.

It was during SAT prep that I became aware of the students' poor performance in vocabulary understanding and usage. In one session, students were asked to define and use in a sentence the word "concede." No student in the eleventh grade prep class knew this word. Ironically, the word had been featured in the newspapers when former President George W. H. Bush conceded the presidential election to Clinton in 1992. The staff and I found this knowledge gap alarming. I approached the director of the school with my concern and suggested that she consider introducing opportunities for vocabulary building across the curriculum. Ms. Little, defensive at first, accepted the suggestion and discussed the problem with her faculty, explaining that not hearing a variety of vocabulary at home limits students' access to higher academic discourse. She wanted her students to feel that they had choices in their use of language. She remarked: "We're trying to create an environment in which 'big words' are going to be comfortable. You see, up to a point, a kid will strictly ridicule the use of big words . . . and we're trying to create an environment so kids won't be ridiculed and that big words, at some point, will simply become part of the vocabulary." As a result of these meetings, teachers agreed to emphasize vocabulary building across the curriculum. Vocabulary lists were distributed in each classroom. After each morning's announcements, students introduced new words over the public address system. Teachers made students more aware of new words in reading assignments and made those words a part of classroom discourse. The vocabulary campaign was helpful, but did not significantly change the results in the verbal section of the SAT test.

Another intervention SYTE sponsored in support of Human Service's academic program provided tutors, one hundred recruited from the student body at the University of Pennsylvania, who worked one-on-one with students at Human Services and University City. At Human Services, the tutoring program was particularly successful. Teachers noted that students took advantage of tutoring both during the school day and after school. Don Masters, a highly regarded math teacher at Human Services, used tutors consistently in his classroom to support instruction. He remarked, ". . . the connection with Penn meant that students could receive individualized attention." Sally Cantor, the special education teacher at the school, was also an enthusiastic proponent of tutoring. She reported that:

> It made a big difference having tutors, because some kids are lost in class and they really want to do well. I'd assign a tutor to work with those students that were having difficulty. And the tutor often could help them catch up, as opposed to waiting till they failed the test and then go back and review.

Thus, SYTE became a program that attempted to change the context of school and the odds that defeat inner-city students' success. In a sense, the program was much more than a gift that changed the opportunity structure for students from low-income families. The program made a critical point: without transforming relationships and widening the sense of possibility, students would not be able to take advantage of a better opportunity (Newberg and Sims 1996).

Students enter high school expectant. Physically, they continue to cope with puberty and rapid growth spurts. In their cognitive development many, but not all, are able to think more abstractly. They begin to consider ideas. Increasingly, they make connections between themselves and a larger world. Adolescents are preoccupied with who they are and imagine, dimly at first, who they want to become. Erik H. Erikson (1950) labeled this stage, "identity formation." H. Markus and P. Nurius (1986) defined the period as the opportunity to imagine "possible selves." Trying on possible selves for fit starts tentatively in high school and continues into postsecondary schooling and the world of work.

SYTE introduced its students to a variety of ways to create possible selves through career exploration, internships, and association with mentors and staff. The gift of an all expenses paid scholarship to a postsecondary school was a source of motivation for some to explore and try out possible selves. For others, it was only background noise, as they lived their lives on the street rather than the classroom. However, being able to use the scholarship was not solely a function of intellectual ability and personal ambition, it was also a function of environmental circumstances that sometimes disadvantaged students unfairly. As Monica said in the previous chapter, life, "has its twists and turns like a road and you never know where it's going to lead you, and where you're going to end up at." These stories are further illustrations of her point.

The Stories

This section explores what made a difference in six students' lives and extrapolates the range of conditions, circumstances, and opportunities that moves a population in a positive direction. Are there particular sets of factors that appear to predict success? How do students operate in certain circumstances? How does contact with affirming or disconfirming people (parents, friends, teachers, SYTE staff) make a difference? Why do some people give up in difficult circumstances, while others do not?

In presenting these students, I kept Monica's analysis in mind by detailing "the twists and turns" in their lives. Over the high school experience, some students became goal-oriented; they developed a sense of focus that helped them deal with distractions as they pursued a high school diploma and the possibility of gaining admission to some form of postsecondary schooling. Other students appeared buffeted by external forces over which they had little or no control. This group, paraphrasing Monica, never knew where the road they were on might take them. They seemed victimized by an external force called "life." Of course there are variations between these extreme characterizations; they, too, are represented in this sample.

The six portraits are of students derived from the larger SYTE sample. Two introduced in chapter 2, Christina and Richard, took opposite sides regarding the SYTE group's behavior during a popcorn fight at a Fellowship Farm retreat. Only 25 percent of the total sample, including Richard, lived with their mother and father. The remaining five profiled here lived in female-headed households. Derrick, Roger, Michelle, and Ebony come from severely stressed homes where one parent was addicted to drugs or alcohol. Roger and Christina were retained in grade once, and Michelle twice. Each of these young people represents a type of student who graduated from high school and entered a postsecondary school. Five of the six were accepted by and attended a college. One attended a vocational school.

Students' statements were verified by cross checking with parents, teachers, other students or program staff, and school records. In the analysis, the sample was stratified not only by student characteristics, but also by the social contexts of their lives (continuity in the home and school, access to positive, caring adults, exposure to abuse, selling and/ or using drugs).

The contrasting stories illustrate how lives are reciprocally affected and, as such, move beyond a record of individual defeat or success. In utilizing a social context and an institutional approach, we hope to contribute to the recent thinking of M. B. Spencer (1995), M. B. Spencer, D. P. Swanson and M. Cunningham (1991), D. P. Swanson and M. B. Spencer (1991), L. F. Winfield (1991), and M. Rutter (1987) about how resilience operates in the lives of inner-city students. We argue that resilience must be more than an idiosyncratic quality of individuals. Rather, resilience is a function of the interaction of individuals and their social contexts—home, school and community institutions. Following the portraits, I present a counseling session in which students examine the pressures and stresses they feel as they try to live up to the expectations of the SYTE mission.

Derrick

Derrick is the oldest of four children. His little brother is twelve years younger than he is; his sisters are one and nine years his junior. His mother, who worked as a bar waitress, did not finish high school. His father completed high school and entered college on a football scholarship, but dropped out after one year. None of his aunts or uncles completed high school. Derrick felt that he and his father might share an important status in the family: both would be high school graduates. Derrick held out the hope for himself that, one day, he would become a college graduate as well.

Growing up in a family with both parents employed, he felt he was "a spoilt child" who got everything he wanted. In addition to material gifts, he also managed to convince his mother when he would or would not attend school. He seemed to be making adult decisions before he was ready to understand the consequences of his behavior. His teachers praised him for his intelligence, but cautioned that he was missing too many days of class and often came late to school.

His parents separated when he was in ninth grade; Derrick felt his world crumble around him. Bills didn't get paid. At one point the electricity was shut off. In the winter the gas was shut off. As Christmas neared, his father paid an outstanding gas bill of $2,000 so they would have heat. The hard times reached a crisis when his mother started to drink heavily. And because mortgage payments were not paid for months, their home fell into foreclosure. Derrick pointed to the period between ninth and tenth grade as the most difficult time in his life.

Some teenagers do not have the luxury of a leisurely adolescence. Circumstances at home may require that students pick up adult responsibilities. Derrick is a case in point. He explained that when his parents separated, his mother was often inebriated, leaving family responsibilities in his hands. He was no longer the "spoilt child."

> I worried how my little brothers and sisters were doing. My attention went to were they eating, being dressed properly, and going to school every day. After I got them all set, I felt tired. I didn't feel like going to school any more. If I didn't have to deal with my family, I would've been in school more often, and my grades would've been better, because I wouldn't have anything else to worry about. My head would've been in the books. I was fighting with myself, saying to myself, "Look, this would be a stupid opportunity for you to give up, drop out [a reference to the scholarship]." But I was also saying, "I got to look out for my family." Some days I didn't come to school. Then some days I came, but was late. And often I had teachers telling me: "We hear you're a very bright and intelligent man. So what's going wrong?" I tried to tell them. But they still didn't get the picture. And then I got frustrated.

Freshman and sophomore years were full of upheaval. Derrick's family moved from his father's to his grandmother's to his aunt's houses. His life was unstable and school expected him to perform as if his home life were orderly. While he complained that teachers did not understand the magnitude of his situation, individual teachers at Penn Bartram School for Human Services were understanding of his situation and tried to help him cope with his studies. He was allowed to make up tests. His math teacher gave him special help so that he survived a challenging Elementary Functions class. One of his aunts rescued his family and gave them the shelter and structure that allowed Derrick to pay attention to schoolwork.

George Weiss, who had purchased a seat on the Philadelphia Stock Exchange, was able to offer a few students paid summer internships; Derrick was selected by the SYTE staff to be one of the interns. He spent three summers learning and performing various support service tasks. One summer, his job entailed sorting stocks, matching stock numbers, and checking to see that the right amount of money was written on the check for the purchase of a particular stock. He also packaged stocks for transfer to various companies for pick up.

He felt that he was a quick study and an avid learner, inquisitive about the work in other departments. Eventually, after a college education, he hoped to become a stockbroker serving clients and making his own investments. He recognized that he was trying to move his potential career along the path George traveled. But he also considered that his education might lead him into managing a business. He liked direct contact with people and felt he has a talent for conversation and salesmanship.

He worried that his underachievement in academic subjects would not represent the true potential he and several of his teachers felt he had. He was particularly upset by his poor performance on the SATs: he scored 260 on the Verbal and 310 on the Math exams, for a combined score of 570 out of a perfect score of 1600. He submitted five applications to colleges and was rejected by them all. On the essay for one of the colleges that eventually rejected him, he tried to represent how his family troubles had compromised his ability to achieve at a higher level.

> During my days in junior high school, I could never make it to school on time. Because of this I wanted to attend a high school close to home. However, my freshman year at Penn Bartram School for Human Services was the worst of my life. I missed forty or more days of school and was late every day I attended. Personal problems at home such as my mother's addiction to alcohol had a negative effect on me. I still continued to struggle with problems at home over the next two years and was forced to move several times. Fortunately, my father, aunt and Say Yes advisors helped me through this very rough period. I give credit to them for leading me in the right direction and turning my attitude around. They made me see positive things about life and school. Now I'm rising to the top and going for the gold. I feel more motivated than I ever have about school and about entering a college. If accepted, I feel I will do well. I can overcome almost any obstacle. I won't be satisfied until I reach my goals.

His initial college choices were unrealistic. Later, staff helped him apply to Virginia State, which did not consider SAT scores as a part of the admission process. He also applied to the University of Hartford's

Hillyard College of Basic Studies, which offers a two-year associates degree as a terminal degree, or as recognition that the student would be accepted for matriculation at the four-year college. Both schools accepted him, much to his delight. He chose to attend the University of Hartford, where George would be close by.

In the spring prior to high school graduation, the staff arranged for students to attend individual and small group counseling to discuss separation anxieties and managing the transition to a more independent life at college. In an individual session with one of the counselors, Derrick reflected candidly on his pattern of handling stress. "Derrick admitted that he is afraid of failing and that he sabotages himself when he gets frustrated with his home situation or his schoolwork."

ROGER

Roger's family comprises an older brother, a younger brother, and a sister. His father graduated from high school and served in the armed services. His mother did not complete high school and, for most of Roger's school age years, was unemployed and received welfare assistance. His father died when Roger was four-years-old. In sixth grade, his mother developed a crack dependency. He remembers that "things in the house started disappearing and living conditions were horrible." His mother abdicated her authority to set and enforce limits. "She started to become less of a parent," he recalls, "and more of a sister, like a friend or something. Because she wasn't like forcing us to come to school; it was optional." Discipline was lax or nonexistent; bed times and wake-ups were his decision. If he got into trouble at school, his mother would not hit him, which for him would have been an expression of concern. By seventh grade, he was five foot six and growing, while his mother was five foot five. Perhaps, he conjectured, she feared he might return the slap. He maintains that he would not.

Roger was quick tempered and resorted to fist fighting with little provocation. Mostly he fought peers, but he had several altercations with teachers and administrators; he was capable of more extreme violence. In a fight over a girl with a rival male, he cut the other boy and the girl with a knife. That incident took him to court several times; eventually the charges were dropped. When asked why he carried a knife, he told us that his mother advised him to carry one and be quick to use it if someone jumped him. He acted on that advice.

In seventh grade, Roger moved at least four times and attended four different schools. Family members and friends offered housing to him and his family, but invariably a conflict soon developed and they were forced to move. At one point they lived in a public shelter. Each of these moves was punctuated by a violent episode at school, which necessitated a transfer to a different school. Roger described seventh grade as:

> Hard, because I was into fighting everybody for no good reason. And my life changed big, big during seventh grade. That was when I left home for a month and hung out with some friends. And then when I came back to school I got left back. I had to take seventh grade over again.

In an end-of-the-year report, the staff said:

> We are trying to find Roger's address so that we can get him into a stable tutoring program and offer other support. He needs social and academic services interventions very badly. It's obvious that his mother cannot manage him. She appears to have personal problems [an allusion to her addiction] which make it impossible for her to supervise his school work.

From the shelter, his mother reconnected with her closest childhood friends, Nicole and Cherrell Ryan, who lived in a house with their mother, Lillian Ryan, who became Roger's adopted grandmother. Her daughters, each of whom had a son his age and were also part of the Say Yes program, became his adopted aunts and cousins. Gradually, Roger increased his stay at grandmother Lillian's house and finally moved in and became a part of the extended family. In some ways, this was a positive step, because he didn't have to worry about finding food or a place to sleep. But because his mother was not living in the house, he was not treated like the other children. His adopted aunts treated ". . . their kids better than they treated me," he complained. He felt "lower than these people in this house in a way," but inside he felt he wasn't. "So in a way," he realized, "that feeling inside me was what kept me feeling up."

One of Miss Ryan's daughters, whom Roger called Aunt Nicole, was a teacher's aid at a local school. She offered to use her influence to get him into her school where she could watch over his behavior. But she made it clear to him that he ". . . wasn't coming there to mess up her reputation. And that if he showed off, she would be the one to handle it." She reinforced her promise when Roger misbehaved in school by hitting him with a ruler while other students watched. By this time he had also been told by the school district that the next time he was expelled for fighting he would be placed in a disciplinary boarding school.

The principal of this latest school noticed Roger's potential to do academic work, but also understood his need for close supervision. The next time Roger got into a fight with a teacher, he did not make an official report of the incident. Rather, he put him in a special education class. Roger received daily assignments from his regular teacher, but was required to do the work in the special education class and have it checked by his regular teacher at the end of the day. He thrived in the small class of ten students and soon was helping the teacher by tutoring the other students. The special education teacher got him involved in after-school swimming and skating classes. Roger appreciated these activities as strategies for keeping him out of trouble.

Once he started to respond positively to offers of support in school, Roger's Aunt Nicole decided to expand his network. She contacted a SYTE program coordinator and told him that Roger was attending school regularly and she hoped the program would get involved with him. Roger graduated from eighth grade as class valedictorian with a straight B average. Program staff renewed contact with him and convinced him to attend the annual summer program, which presented a preview of courses he would encounter in ninth grade and an introduction to the Human Services faculty who would teach SYTE students in the fall. Roger explained his experience of this transition: "I got to know a lot of teachers and when I started high school . . . they treated me different 'cause they already knew me. It wasn't like I was a new freshman, they knew what type of person I was, they knew what kind of work I could do."

Roger enjoyed the summer program and understood its purpose. But once he entered Human Services without his aunt's watchful eye and the highly personalized attention he got from the special education teacher, he reverted to some of his old behaviors. He did not attend consistently. When he did attend, occasionally he could be seen walking the halls or shooting baskets in the gym. If asked why he wasn't in class he would say, "I'm not here today." He often drank beer and sometimes hard liquor before coming to school. He did not adjust well to the relative freedom of even a small high school setting. His first report card recorded four failures and one passing grade. When he brought his report card home, no comments were made. He understood more clearly than ever before that he was ". . . on my own. If I want to do better, I gotta make my own effort to do it." By year's end he made a slight improvement by passing some subjects with Ds.

Human Services prides itself in paying close attention to students' academic progress. If a student fails two subjects, as Roger did, he or she is required to meet with the faculty to discuss whether the student can stay at the school and under what terms. The faculty agreed to let Roger stay, provided his grades and attendance improved. But he recalled that they also asked ". . . a biology teacher, Ms. Vaddy, to represent me. So that anything I did wrong in the school came back to her. Teachers sent daily reports to her about my work. And she started signing me up for stuff. She taught an after-school science club. And I had to take that." Ms. Vaddy was no pushover; she demanded that Roger work up to capacity. He responded to her call for discipline and hard work:

> She's always been hard on me. If you try to get away with it real easy, she will not let it go. If she feels you can do the work, she'll make you do it. And a person who doesn't want to do anything, she'll talk to you and say you're not giving up. She'll tutor me next fall and give me an independent study on advanced biology.

In addition to demands for academic responsibility, the faculty figured out a way for Roger to be thoughtful about disruptive behavior in the school and, by extension, his own behavior began to change:

> I remember like in the beginning of the tenth grade, they had this thing called the Disciplinary Society—it was like all the kids that was in trouble in school had to go before this panel . . . the teachers elected a student to be the head of the panel. So they elected me and a couple days later I was chosen as sophomore class president and so I started to get active in, like, making the school better, trying to teach the Human Services spirit.

In October 1990, we took Roger and several other Say Yes students to Hartford to spend the weekend with the Weisses. George introduced Roger to one of his business partners, Mike Christiani, who casually encouraged him to call if he ever needed someone to talk to. Roger accepted Mike's offer. They struck up a friendship, discovering that they shared common interests in basketball, pizza, and hunting. Mike made an agreement with Roger: if Roger made the honor roll in the first marking period, he could come to Hartford and spend the weekend with Mike and his family. Roger was intrigued by the offer and the person who made it:

> Mike told me, he said, "You do your best and don't worry about what other people say." He said, "Sometimes it's hard, so you just take advantage of every opportunity you have and get the work done." I wanted to be the same type of person that Mike is. . . . And I wanted to be like him. He got a nice wife, and a nice house, and I want the same thing.

Roger also said: "People make role models, they don't just have role models." Mike is a self-made success and was showing Roger how to do it for himself. The incentive produced the desired result. Roger made honor roll each marking period. He visited with Mike and his family several times that year ". . . hanging out, going for hikes, helping him in his office." Roger believed that Mike and he developed "a father-son relationship."

Roger has demonstrated a knack for latching onto people who could help him. George Weiss gave him his 800 number as he did with many Say Yes students. Roger, however, was one of the few who called him on a regular basis, sometimes two or three times a week. Increasingly, SYTE became his surrogate family. Program coordinators served as father, mother, and sister: "Sims, I'll tell him everything; he knows me and what I've been through. I trust him." The older female coordinator, Robin Wall-Hill, he thought of as a mother:

> I never had that kind of relationship with my mom. Like places my mother is supposed to accompany me, Robin is always there. She's always taking me places and telling me right from wrong. And then Leanne, she's like a big sister—a little sister 'cause she's short. She helped me select different colleges, told me what to look for in a college. She helped me out with the applications.

Roger mastered the ability to communicate with people, taking advantage of opportunities given to him. He was not ashamed to ask for help or to offer it, and he was developing a sense of reciprocity with fellow students in need: "I don't want to regret not calling anybody, if somebody was in trouble or needed someone to talk to. I would call them because I don't want them to have to go through it alone. Try to be their friend."

I asked Roger to reflect on reasons some SYTE students have dropped out, and to expand on how his analysis might be relevant to himself:

> Like one of the cases where a student dropped out of school, it was like a financial thing. He needed money and he needed it bad. . . . They say with a long-term education, it pays off in the end. . . . But the person I'm talking about didn't see it that way. He needed money now. So he dropped out of school and started selling drugs and he's still selling. That guy could have been me. . . . But, I mean, money isn't everything. Since I changed my life, I know I'll make honest money. There's a lot of people, Ms. Vaddy, Mr. Sims, they all educated and make money. Mr. Weiss wasn't always rich. He went to college and now he's making lots of money.

Roger had made a connection between getting a college education and the ability to make money. He was also developing a sense of the need for delayed gratification—seeing education as a necessary step toward building the kind of life he wants. He said somewhat grandly: "I'll go to school the rest of my life." His plans ranged from becoming a doctor to becoming a physical therapist. The shift to physical therapy came during his internship in the summer of 1993 with a University of Pennsylvania scientist. He tried out his career goals with the scientist, who gave him a clearer sense of how he might pursue a variety of career paths in allied medical fields. Roger adjusted his goal to one he thought was more realistic, given his good, but not outstanding, school performance. His freshman year had been a disaster, with two failing grades in English and science. But in tenth grade, he achieved all Bs in his majors, and in eleventh and twelfth grades, Bs and As. His SAT scores, however, were weak, with 240 Verbal and 250 in Math making a combined score of 490. He was admitted provisionally to the University of Hartford.

RICHARD

The reader met Richard in chapter 2; in the aftermath of the popcorn fight, he was one of a few students who accepted responsibility for the disorder the fight caused. Richard came to the retreat dressed in pressed slacks, a white starched shirt, and a conservative tie. Dressing formally was a mark of appropriate behavior for members of Richard's church. For Richard, talking about goals for the future was serious business. He wore the "right" uniform for the occasion. The staff, like the rest of the students, dressed informally. When Randall confronted students for starting the dining hall popcorn fight, Richard accepted that he was "his brother's keeper" and felt guilty that he did not try to stop the melee.

Richard was one of the taller students among the Belmont 112; therefore, he was seated at the back of the stage on graduation day, June 17, 1987. The unique opportunity that Diane Weiss offered that day flew over the heads of the even the taller boys in the back row. Richard recalled:

> When Ms. Weiss was speaking, I was speaking with one of my friends on stage. So I wasn't listening. . . . I wasn't really paying attention. I wasn't expecting anything like that. Suddenly everybody start clapping and roaring and standing up. So everybody on stage stood up. And I started clapping. And I didn't know what I was clapping for until it was over and then I found out what happened.

At Belmont Elementary school, Richard was one of two students identified as mentally gifted (MG). Teachers appreciated his disciplined approach to his studies. His MG status was a factor in his gaining admission to an academically competitive middle school. He participated in SYTE's after-school tutoring program in seventh grade not so much because he needed help, but because it was held in a quiet place.

His mother had joined Jehovah's Witness in 1981 when Richard was six years old. Richard accompanied his mother to Kingdom Hall regularly and gradually began to see himself as serving within his religion. His father, who worked at a bank and had completed an accounting program at a community college, was opposed to the Jehovah's Witness religion. The divided family's religious allegiances resulted in household tension that persisted throughout Richard's high school years. The differences between his parents also made it awkward for SYTE staff to help Richard pursue a college preparatory program. Diane Weiss wanted Richard to experience education at a rigorous college prep school. She convinced The Haverford School, a suburban private school, to offer Richard a scholarship to attend a special summer program between seventh and eighth grades. The Haverford staff was so impressed with his performance that they offered him a full scholarship for high school. However, after intense debate among Richard, his parents, the staff, and the sponsors, Richard declined the offer.

In eighth grade, at SYTE staff's urging, he applied to one of the city's most prestigious academic high schools, the School of Engineering and Sciences. His application was accepted. But he was also accepted at a vocational high school that he decided, surprisingly, to attend. The staff was ambivalent about advocating for a college preparatory program, in light of his mother's wish for him to attend Bible College. We searched for strategies that might help Richard see that it might be possible for him to be loyal to his religion's dictates and also complete a college education. At one point, Randall found two Penn employees who were college graduates and practicing members of Jehovah's Witness and arranged for Richard to meet with them. The meeting was a positive experience for Richard, but it did not change his opinion about attending college. After many conversations with Randall and his parents, Richard conceded that he would like to attend the public college prep school, Engineering and Sciences, to which he had initially gained acceptance.

Richard made the adjustment to high school without too much difficulty, maintaining a B average. Between ninth and tenth grades he met his first girlfriend and fell in love. The relationship was consuming. His grades in school plummeted and, for the first time, Ds and Fs appeared on his report card. "I kinda forgot about religion and college. I was just focusing on her." His relationship with his girlfriend was part of a defense Richard constructed so that he would fail in a rigorous academic program. He attended the public college prep school halfheartedly. And when he understood that this school was designed to assist him in gaining acceptance at competitive colleges, he asserted, "I wanted to do what I could to be certain that I didn't get into college."

He continued to sabotage his chances to be an exemplary student until a fellow student forced him to reevaluate his priorities. Richard attended the SYTE summer program between tenth and eleventh grades. During a geometry class, he faced a moment of truth that redirected his thinking about his studies. The math teacher asked a question that no one but Richard could answer. Derrick observed that unique moment and was amazed at Richard's grasp of the subject. After class he approached Richard and said, "You really know that work. You must have straight As, or at least As and Bs or something. You must be on the honor roll." Richard felt embarrassed. He didn't tell his classmate that he was earning Ds and even Fs.

That exchange with Derrick prompted a period of introspection. He wondered why he didn't earn more As. He probed more deeply and asked himself what was "bringing him down." He asked, "Did I really want to waste the gift I had? I didn't want to be one of those people who in the future would say, 'I could have done that.' If I knew the work, why was I getting these bad grades?" The answer became clear to him, and so was the remedy. He broke off his relationship with his girlfriend, changed the way he acted at home, made up missing work at school, and maintained a regimen of studying after school, rather than playing basketball with friends in the neighborhood. Previously, he dressed casually for school, but his reformed self-image required a more disciplined, deliberate "look." He relied on an old standby, the traditional uniform that identified members of Kingdom Hall: pressed dark colored slacks, a starched white shirt, and a conservative dark tie. If he was going to take his studies seriously, he would have to dress the part.

Once he decided to change, Richard became goal-oriented. He wanted to "dominate everyone else" with his academic prowess. With a sense of sadness he remarked: "Hurting people was the hardest thing I had to overcome. Letting them go. They didn't understand and thought that I was stuck up or something." He was aware that some of his friends thought he worked too hard and was constantly worried about grades. But being totally absorbed in an academic race was exhilarating to him. He felt that his singleness of purpose was ". . . what changed me around." He asserted that he had hit his stride and was not going to stop. In academics and athletics, he wanted to dominate the field. He wanted people to fear and respect him. He sums up his mission this way: "If I try hard, I don't want to be second; I want to be first."

At the end of eleventh grade, when he took the SAT exam, he scored 1050, the highest score of the Belmont 112. Richard achieved first place among his Say Yes peers. His transformation was not limited to subject mastery; rather it opened up new possibilities for achieving excellence. He entered a Shakespeare declamation contest at his high school. His presentation of Mark Anthony's speech after Caesar's death was a showstopper. His description captures his moment of triumph:

> There were juniors and seniors that filled the whole auditorium. The whole school was in the auditorium. And there was maybe

fifteen contestants huddled behind the curtains. Then one person would come out and say their names and do their presentation. And I was number eight or something. And then when I came out it was like a roar or something. And everybody stood up and was clapping, and I just stood there calm. Then I said my name is Richard and I went about my presentation. Then I finished it off and stopped. And everybody just roared. And afterwards the secretaries came out of the office and said, "We heard the cheering from the office." And I just felt so good.

In the summer between eleventh and twelfth grades, Say Yes organized paid internships so that students could get the feel of various work opportunities. Richard was given a job at a prominent center city bank. His superiors were so impressed with his work ethic they invited him to work after school during his senior year and even suggested that he should consider a career in the bank after he completed college.

It appeared that his father's career aspirations influenced his decision to attend college. His father had hoped to become a Certified Public Accountant, but he finished only two years of a four-year college program and did not qualify to sit for the exam. But Richard had the potential to live out his father's dream. Richard's refound success in academics and his work at the bank gave him confidence that he could succeed in business. He applied to the University of Pennsylvania and was accepted into Wharton, one of the nation's most prestigious business schools. His interest in business was also tied to a sense of social responsibility. It would be unseemly to be in business only to make money; his religious upbringing would not allow such a utilitarian goal. "What I want to do in the future is start my own chain of businesses." His vision for the future spoke to his need to give back to his community. "Maybe daycare centers, or supermarkets, or something in the community to help the community out." His motive for wanting to start neighborhood businesses was motivated by his observation that the businessmen in his neighborhood were white or Asian. He felt exploited by the high prices they charged and their lack of commitment to his neighborhood:

When I go to a store, I give people money that don't care about me. They charge ridiculous prices. It's not that I wouldn't be in it for a profit, but I would lower prices and be reasonable. If we had more businesses run by African-Americans, they would create jobs in the community. If you own a lot of stores in the community, then you have a certain amount of power in the community. So you can go to your neighborhood councilperson, and get your legislator to listen to the people to see if they want this or don't want this. And since you'll have the power, that'll be power among the people cos you're a businessman, and you will have a say in the situation.

Ultimately Richard saw himself emulating George Weiss' gift-giving: "And if I'm able to, I'd like to start something like Say Yes. If ever I become rich, I know that's what, down the road, I'd like to do."

In June 1993, Richard received a call from Brenda Artwell, the principal at Belmont Elementary School, inviting him to be the guest speaker at Belmont's closing exercises. Richard was thrilled to have a chance to say something inspirational to students who sat where he had six years earlier. His theme was "Heal the World and the year 2000." He explained that the reference to the year 2000 honored the time this class would graduate from high school.

Richard was an outlier among his peers. He had two parents who cared about education. Perhaps the strongest influence was his religion, which gave each day a sense of purpose and an orientation to his future. Richard admitted that while he lived in a poor neighborhood, he did not have nearly the challenges his peers faced: "single parents on drugs. I have both my parents here. And they both loved and supported me" (Mezzaccappa, 1993).

EBONY

Both Ebony's mother and father had graduated from high school. Her mother attended George Washington University for one year while living in Washington D.C. with Ebony's father. She worked as an executive secretary. Her father then moved to North Carolina, where he completed college and engineering school. While he kept in touch with Ebony throughout her life, he made it clear that she may not live with him. Her early childhood was marked by transience. Her mother moved with her several times from Philadelphia to Washington and back. These moves were burdensome for Ebony. She explained:

> It was like every year: One year we'd stay in Washington, the next year we'd stay here (Philadelphia). It was kind of confusing because you have to go through all these schools. And every time you have to start all over again. It was hard. It's like I'm never in one spot.

Not only did we move from city to city, but from house to house moving in with different people. It made it hard to have friends. And I didn't get along with my Mom because I'm always moving from one place to another.

Finally, Ebony's mother settled in Philadelphia to attend to Ebony's grandfather, who was seriously ill. Ebony lived with her mother, her aunt, grandmother, and grandfather in a small West Philadelphia row house.

Unlike most of the Belmont 112, Ebony entered Belmont in fifth grade. Like her peers on that sultry June graduation day, she did not comprehend the commotion that ensued when Diane made her announcement. Only after she returned home did she understand that she had won a scholarship to college. Prior to the scholarship announcement, she claimed, she ". . . hadn't even heard of college. I thought you went till twelfth grade and then you were done. It was time to get a job."

I asked her about her experience at junior high school. She was emphatic that junior high was a washout. From her point of view those years were "horrible." Her distress was not connected to school, but more to unhappy relations with girlfriends who constantly undermined her self-confidence. The irony of this situation was that Ebony triumphed over the petty humiliations. Her grades consistently averaged around B. In eighth grade, her counselor recommended she apply to two magnet high schools. One of these schools accepted her application, but she declined the offer, deciding to attend Penn Bartram Human Services, the school that about half the SYTE student body would attend. In tenth grade, her mother died after a protracted illness. Without older siblings, she felt alone and distraught. She describes how traumatized she felt, but also her wish not to succumb to despair:

> There were many times when I felt I wanted to break down, that I didn't want to do nothing anymore. Just give up everything. Not that I ever had a lot. But even the little that I got, I wanted to just throw it away and not think about anything. But that's not who I am. There's no hope in that. And that's not who hopefully I am.

As a result of her mother's death, she felt adrift. She was even uncertain about where she might live. She traveled to North Carolina and visited her father at his home, but after a couple of weeks returned to Philadelphia. Her grandmother took her in. However, the generational differences between Ebony and her grandmother caused tension and arguments. These arguments often ended with Ebony moving to live with another aunt and then, after a cooling off period, returning to her grandmother's house. But in spite of her troubles, she managed to pass tenth grade. Randall called her a "real survivor."

While she kept her personal feelings to herself, she seemed quite willing to seek help if she were having difficulty with schoolwork: "Sometimes if a teacher explains something and I can't see it, then I ask. Some people feel stupid doing that, but I don't see it like that. I don't care. I still ask. I know not asking will hurt me in the long run."

Her self-assessment seemed accurate. When she was failing Algebra II in the final semester of her senior year, she sought the teacher's help. He worked with her over several weeks and she gained enough proficiency to pass the course.

Asking for academic help was relatively easy. But asking for help with a personal problem may have evoked unresolved issues with her family that she did not want to revisit. She thought of Say Yes as "one big family," her surrogate family. "We all get on each other's nerves, but we always come back to each other. And we always be there for each other." Ebony substituted an idealized version of Say Yes for the family that she felt was not "there for her." Perhaps that may explain her response to the Weiss' divorce:

> George and Diane care about every one of us. They listen and they call you and they ask you to write to them. I was mad at Mr. Weiss and Mrs. Weiss because they were going to divorce. . . . It just makes them like . . . I know we screw up, but when they screwed up, I broke up. Like half of me was with him and half of me was with her. I cried. I cried for real. Why didn't they talk to me about it? I didn't want them to break up and I miss them. Mrs. Weiss used to take me to the bookstore and buy me books. She got me five books. I got two more to read. Mr. Weiss took me out to dinner when I got good grades. And everything . . . I enjoyed their company.

Ebony's reaction reflected the intense personal association some students felt for the Weisses. In Ebony's eyes, they were perfect, not subject to human foibles. She accepted that she and her peers screw up, but not the Weisses. Perhaps her most poignant response was her expression of regret that the Weisses had not sought her advice before deciding to divorce. If she could not help them with their problems, she imagined that if she could have told them the painful effect their divorce would have on her, perhaps they might have reconsidered their decision.

When I asked Ebony to recount her strengths, without hesitation she said: "I write and I talk." Her writing first gained her recognition in fifth grade when she entered a contest in which students were to give the President of the United States advice on how to solve the drug problem in America. In junior high school, she was awarded a prize for an anti-graffiti essay. She said repeatedly that she loved writing, but she was contemptuous of the artificial writing assignments teachers force on their students. "I hate writing when a teacher tells you to write about a stupid topic," she said. But her imagination fired up when she considered "something creative." She sat back in her chair and mused, "I love to just sit there and think about stuff, and everything." Then quietly, but with certainty she asserted, "I'm going to write a book about my life. I will, yes. I love writing." Returning to her statement that what she does best is write and talk, she summarized, "Writing helps me get my thoughts on paper. It's like the feeling you get when you're able to get all your troubles on paper. And with talk, it's like letting all those feelings come out, everything that you feel."

Given her love of communication, I imagined she might be interested in a career in which she could exercise her talents. I was surprised to learn that she was considering majoring in nursing in college. "I was going into communications," she explained:

> But everybody keeps saying that communications is going to be harder to find a job. And that's for everything really. But at least with nursing, you know that's not going to run out, because everybody needs that kind of help—medical assistance. So that's why I changed to that. But I could always go back, or take a double major in nursing and communications.

I asked her what she would like to be doing five years into the future. In her response, she didn't link her professed college majors to future work. Rather she stated: "So, in five years I'm going to be working, living in my own house, and paying my bills. Hopefully I would also be engaged or whatever. Yeah, I'd like that now. To be living on my own and working and everything. But I can't do that now." She understood that she must provide her own support, to free herself from dependence; but she also knew that without marketable skills, that would not be possible. By April of her senior year, Ebony was accepted by Virginia State College, Lincoln University and Community College of Philadelphia. She chose Virginia State as soon as she received her letter of acceptance. The SYTE college advisor noted:

> Ebony took great interest in the application process, and thought honestly and realistically about her chances of getting into each school. Her SATs (310 Verbal, 310 Math) with a combined score of 620 were within the average range for those that took the test. But a low B average in her majors and outstanding recommendations and extracurricular activities were enough to get her a positive response from Virginia State.

CHRISTINA

Christina lived with her younger stepsister, her sister's child, her brother, and her mother in a cramped house located near the main business district in the Belmont area, on Lancaster Avenue. Her father was dead. Most of her peers attended Sulzburger Junior High School. Christina could not adjust to the school and her mother transferred her to Shoemaker Junior High School, where her adjustment was easier.

At the Fellowship Farm retreat, Christina demonstrated that she had no compunction about stating her views, especially if the issue might impinge on her rights. Diane Weiss, during the retreat, identified her as a "leader" and urged her to call if she needed help. The Weisses encouraged all SYTE students to call them, but Christina was one of the few who called frequently. For a few years she ignored SYTE staff, preferring direct contact with the Weisses. She claimed that she felt comfortable expressing her needs or concerns to George or Diane. Sidestepping the staff she asserted: "That way they know what my problems are, if I tell them my thoughts." She participated in SYTE activities infrequently. By age thirteen, she had set up a beauty salon in her living room and over the next few years earned enough money to help with the family's expenses. Her mother worked sporadically as a store manager for several years, but due to illness, she finally went on disability to make ends meet. When her health improved, she returned to work on a regular basis.

Christina displayed a talent for cosmetology, but defined that vocation as a temporary backup to her interest in becoming a lawyer or a psychiatrist. Her view of the amount of time she would need to attend school to become a lawyer was misinformed. She said: "I want to go to law school, right? But then I don't want to do as many years in law school as required." I mentioned the number of years of college a law degree would require, stating that first she must complete a four-year Bachelor's degree, followed by an additional three years of law school. As if she believed she could pick and choose the number of college years that met her timetable for becoming a lawyer she responded:

> Yeah. So I'll take those three years, and then instead of going out and being hired, I want to go ahead and take the bar exam. Then I'll get into a firm, and I'll settle for being a public defender, or something like that for a little while and then I'll go higher.

Her wish to become a lawyer seemed associated with her comfort in speaking persuasively in arguments with teachers and peers. In junior high and through ninth grade at Bartram Human Services, she was often praised for her leadership. She was convinced she would be able to go to college, despite a lackluster career in school. In junior high school and high school her teachers and the SYTE staff characterized her as boisterous and talkative, and seemingly unwilling to concentrate on schoolwork. There seemed to be a disconnect between the grandiosity of her verbal ability and her disdain to do the follow-up work that would substantiate the ability teachers and SYTE staff believed was hers (see Fordham 1993).

In reviewing Say Yes staff entries about Christina's academic progress, a pattern emerged from seventh through eleventh grade, when she dropped out of school. During each school year, her grades tended to hover between Cs and Ds. Periodically, they would fall to failure, rising again to a C or D. Her teachers and the Say Yes staff recognized Christina's intelligence, but despaired over her lack of discipline and respect for authority, and her inability to conform to conventional requirements for school attendance. For example, in eleventh grade she was absent fifty times; she claimed that she was experiencing emotional problems and could not endure the pressures she felt at school. Another time she said her mother was sick and she needed to take care of her. By tenth grade, students at Human Services became distrustful of her leadership. In earlier grades she had been popular with her peers; her willingness to confront authority had established her as a leader. Increasingly, however, she seemed to be at the center of fights with other Say Yes students. Her popularity waned and she became isolated at school.

George, Diane, and Randall tried repeatedly to convince her to take her studies seriously, but without success. As a result of excessive absences combined with poor grades, Penn Bartram School for Human Services retained her in eleventh grade and recommended that she be transferred to University City High School. Christina could not accept her situation and gradually stopped coming to school.

When she dropped out, she railed against the system that she felt miseducated her. She claimed that school bored her, because teachers were constantly reviewing old material. Relieved of school work and the expectations she felt others placed on her, she enjoyed the release of not feeling stressed:

> At home everybody left me alone. They stopped pushing me. That way I had time for myself, time to figure out that I am doing this for myself. I'm getting my diploma, right? Like before I was think-ing I was doing this for my mom, and my grandma and somebody 'cause they was always pressing me. Or I was doing it for the Weisses. Then I felt like I'm doing it for me. That's why I feel better for doing it. I feel I work better without all that pressure on me.

After a few months at home, she returned to high school and, because her grades were satisfactory at the end of the first semester, was advanced to twelfth grade. Retention had been humiliating, but it also gave her time to assess her priorities. Because public schools did not teach important basic skills, she felt, college was going to be harder for her to grasp. She was contemptuous of the poor teaching she experi-enced. Speaking about her former teachers, "They don't worry about what you learn," she concluded by saying the reason those teachers were ineffective had something to do with their "style." She wanted them to have more "street smarts, more connection to the real world." Then she drove her argument home, showing the enormity of the failure to communicate across class and, perhaps, racial lines: ". . . they [teachers] talk to me and I don't understand them and then they look at me like I am illiterate, because I don't speak like them. Like what she talking about?"

By June 1993, a majority of her SYTE peers graduated high school. Christina, however, needed four additional subjects before she could advance to twelfth grade. Randall arranged for her to attend

Rittenhouse Academy, a proprietary high school, so that she could complete her course work at her own pace. Christina had been critical of the public high schools she attended, but Rittenhouse Academy offered her a fresh approach to learning. She thrived in a program that was intensive and challenging:

> Every day we learn something different. Like in English we got two workbooks that we got to work out of, plus we have to turn in an essay every Friday. So you always work. You always got work. You can't just be getting the same work you got last week and you hand it in to the instructor, or you don't. Or you get lazy and then, you don't work. So if you just keep working every day like that, it keeps you up.

She seemed engaged in her studies, and attributed her success to the fact that she wrote about topics that connected to her life:

> I wrote about violence, violence against children. I wrote about sexual abuse. I turned in three different articles: one about the mother who used her two little daughters to get drugs, and the other was about the day a homosexual man was killed because he was a homosexual; and the last was about the woman that was raped in Queens Village.

Christina felt gratified that her writing earned her good grades. But even at Rittenhouse Academy, Christina was only able to pass two of the four courses she had failed in eleventh grade. University City High School allowed her to enter as a senior under the condition that she pass the two remaining subjects by going to night school at Rittenhouse. Attending school day and night, while also maintaining a lucrative business as a part-time hairdresser, returned her to the pressure she hated. She missed school frequently, but finally earned enough credits to graduate.

Immediately after high school graduation, she resolved that she would pursue a career in cosmetology and wanted to enter school so that she could become a licensed hairdresser. However, she did little to advance this plan. She took the entrance exam to one school, but failed to attend. Following that episode, she claimed she wanted a business school degree so that she would gain the skills to manage a beautician's shop. This plan required her to take the SATs. She failed to attend an SAT prep course but took the exam, earning 260 in the verbal test and

240 in the math section. Staff made arrangements for her to visit
Delaware State College. At the last minute, she decided not to attend.

Christina not only frustrated staff, sponsors, and teachers, but also
motivated them to work on her behalf. The results often ended in her
advocates feeling disappointed and confused by her behavior. Ms. Little,
the principal, had often extended herself to Christina, but to no avail:

> Now, one particular person I feel so disappointed about is no
> longer with us. That's Christina Johnson. I felt so disappointed
> with her, in fact, almost angry, but then you say, well, who are you
> angry at? Why are you angry? Because this was a student that I saw
> had so much potential. But it didn't matter what support, even the
> support that Say Yes gave wasn't enough. What we gave wasn't
> enough, so I really feel disappointed, but then I don't know who
> I feel disappointed at. So it turns somewhat to anger; I'm angry,
> how dare she do that (drop out of school).

Christina's science teacher was also disappointed in her inability
to use education productively. She explained her frustration this way:

> She is a disappointment because when I met her before in ninth
> grade, I said, wow, here's my girl. You know how you figure there's
> gonna be one who's really gonna achieve, that's really gonna do
> well, not even just to latch on, but I'm gonna read about her, she's
> gonna go places, you know. She might have to get this English
> language together, but once she does that, she's gonna fly, and she
> didn't fly and that really disappointed me. In tenth grade, she kind
> of did okay, and then I said, well, she's just not ready yet. By
> eleventh grade, that's when she's really gonna do well. And then
> she fell apart and I don't know, and I don't know what happened.

George Weiss was equally disappointed in Christina's failure to
rise to the expectations she herself set and that those working with her
believed were possible for her to achieve. He struggled to understand
her and ended his reflection by making a personal analogy:

> What really bothered me, and the focus of my attention, were the
> kids who haven't been successful, that still haven't got their act
> together. Christina not getting it done, that's pretty sad. Maybe we
> could be faulted. Maybe my having so much confidence in her and
> the staff because of her leadership, etc.—that may have put too

much pressure on her. Maybe the expectations were too great and it's like having a kid wanting to be an athlete. People have always told her that she's good. It's a good thing I didn't have sons. Maybe that kind of pressure I [would have] put on a son I put on Christina.

Christina was a fiercely independent young woman who resisted other people's expectations for her future. She had to find her own way. Rather than agreeing with those who say she disappointed them, a more accurate reflection might allow her to determine her own future. For now, hers is a story of "not yet . . ."

MICHELLE

Michelle is the second of seven children. Her mother was nineteen when Michelle was born. Neither parent finished high school. Her mother dropped out in eleventh grade, but her father did complete a General Education Degree. Her parents separated when she was seven. The family income is below the poverty line and her mother, who has a long history of drug dependency, receives welfare assistance. Michelle said that, at her birth, her dad said to her mother that she was no longer his "first girl." That remark seems to have engendered jealousy and hostility between Michelle and her mother that persisted through her adolescence. They fought frequently. She believed her mother hated her and wished that she were never born. Throughout her years growing up, until she turned eighteen, her mother beat her ". . . with ironing cords or whatever she could pick up." Sometimes she hit her with her fists.

Michelle's family moved several times in her early childhood, causing her to miss school. She claimed that she was retained in first grade ". . . because we moved so many times." From June 1987 to June 1993, she lived with three different family units: her mother for two years, and her grandmother for three years. For one year, she lived with an uncle and an aunt to help take care of their mentally disabled child. Each of these households was crowded with younger cousins and various members of an extended family. For the first three years of the SYTE program, staff made frequent attempts to visit Michelle's mother at her home. Each time, staff was told that she was unavailable. Contact with Michelle was limited to school or on the street. Although she often promised Randall Sims that she would attend program activities, she rarely did.

In reviewing her school records, staff learned that she had performed below grade level in reading in fourth grade and was recommended for a special reading class that used programmed instruction on a computer. As a reward for completing work successfully, she was allowed to play computer games for the remainder of the class period. Within one month, her reading teacher noticed that she was reading at grade level; therefore, she was no longer allowed to work on the computer. She reported that she "cried hard" when she lost that access.

Throughout middle school, Michelle's grades were below average, but passing. It was apparent to teachers and program staff that she had the ability to do better, but lacked the motivation to do so. In June 1990, she announced that she would not go to a regular high school; she wanted to attend a vocational school to major in architecture. The staff tried repeatedly to convince her to attend a comprehensive high school so she could take college preparatory subjects. She refused to listen. By October of that year, she regretted her decision and transferred to University City High School, where she took an academic track curriculum. None of her voc-ed courses were transferable; she spent the entire year catching up. When it became apparent that she would fail three major subjects, she stopped working and frequently played hookey with her cousin. Ironically, she passed both Algebra I and Physical Science in summer school with ease.

In tenth grade, her attendance was sporadic. Even though she failed one subject that year, she was recommended for a special program for students who had the potential to attend college, but were underachievers. The Motivation Program, as it was called, was a small school within University City High School, with a faculty that worked with a cohort of students for three years. In such an intimate environment, students were seen and heard, and the anonymity of the larger school was significantly reduced. The smaller organization also made advocacy for Michelle by SYTE staff simpler. If we requested a roster change, it did not require a flurry of paper marched through the bureaucracy to effect the change; one conversation sufficed. That summer, SYTE staff found Michelle a paid internship in an office using a computer. She was elated. Her excellent performance earned her the opportunity to continue this work part time during the school year. However, without much explanation, she did not return to work that fall.

Staff noted that ". . . Michelle got into frequent fist fights with peers and seemed unperturbed if she was suspended. She looked angry. Her home situation continued to frustrate her, especially when her mother moved back into her grandmother's home." The staff decided to hire a therapist who initially worked with a group of students including Michelle, and eventually scheduled individual sessions with those students in greatest need. By the winter of 1992, when she was in eleventh grade, Michelle accepted that she did have problems. Her academic performance was poor and it was clear that she would be retained in grade. She wanted help. She also wanted to go to college. She said of the counselor: "It seemed like I was talking to my best friend. I could tell him anything, and he would help me out." Concurrently, her grades improved. Previously, she had achieved mostly Ds and Cs, and had at least one failure. Now she was consistently making As and Bs. In the summer of 1993, she took a college-level course in data processing and achieved a B as a final grade.

Michelle made some basic changes in her life and became more trusting of caring adults, such as her supervisor. Therapy helped change Michelle's attitude toward her brothers and sisters; previously she had used them as a target for her anger against her mother. She said: "It wasn't that I was angry at them. It's just that they was there at the time when I was angry, so I took it out on them. But now my attitude has changed towards them. I don't holler at them at all like I used to. But if I do, I always end up apologizing to them."

Her English teacher, Mr. Muller, got her interested in books and reading. She admired him because he made her think. She appreciated the reach for excellence he demanded of students. "He pushes students to do the best that they can do," she remarked. "Then he pushes them to do better. Most teachers are different: if you don't want to work, they leave you alone. But Mr. Muller, if he sees that you don't want to work, he will find out what the problem is, why you don't want to work, and will try to help you out."

Slowly, Michelle understood the value of supportive guidance. And she appreciated the pressure and expectations that motivated her to excel. She used writing as a way to make sense of her experience. Her English teacher encouraged her to write an essay for a contest on the importance of getting an education. She described how she came to believe that she could strive to compete:

> And we had to write a paper about education and I just wrote how I felt because my teacher has taught me a lot, when my counselor wasn't around, I needed somebody to talk to. So I talked to my teacher . . . and he helped me out a lot. He was like a friend

to me too. And he always pushed me to do better and kept telling me don't let this get you and don't let that get you. And I started taking his advice, and after that, my counselor's advice. And it changed the way I started thinking about things and that's what I wrote about in my paper.

Michelle won first place in the contest and received a plaque to commemorate the occasion.

Several times in high school, Michelle had been on the verge of dropping out and resisted being helped. SYTE staff understood that students move in and out of connection; the program did not give up on her. At some level, she had to learn the value of help and to trust the helper before she could accept it. She began experiencing success and saw, by contrast, the consequences for some of her classmates who have dropped out and shook her head.

We asked Michelle to reflect on why some SYTE students dropped out of school. Again, she raised the theme of pressure to excel. But by this time, she had understood that pressure must be internal:

> Maybe they [the dropouts] thought that it was too much of a struggle for them. . . . Maybe they're just used to doing things like if they think its okay, then that's just good enough. They're not used to pushing themselves, or somebody pushing them to do things. At first I didn't like being pushed 'cause my mom never pushed me or nothing. . . . And then I started getting used to it. Now it's helping a lot. The program had a major effect on my life because now I know if I really put my mind to it I can do something. Cause I just want to further my education and I really want to go to college and learn about computers. . . . If I went to a trade school, they won't teach you everything. They will probably try to teach you the basics but there's a lot of little things that you got to understand, too.

Michelle is the first one of her family who would go to college. Aunts and uncles in her family ". . . graduated from high school but they went into the service or a trade school." Looking for role models who would inspire her to attain college, she would not find them in her family. But SYTE bridged this gap in Michelle's experience through visits to many college campuses and by frequent contact with college tutors. Michelle became goal-oriented. "Getting a high school diploma," to her, "means that I have reached my goal, done what I had to do and that's just my reward for finishing what I had to do." She was able to take her goal-directedness and project it into the future. Five years after the interview, she imagined that she would have her ". . . own office, working in a big, big business building. Maybe a manager. 'Cause I'm into computers." She allowed that she might have a child and marry. When we asked if anything could interfere with her attaining her goal she said emphatically: "No, nothing at all. I want to live. See, I'm not a party person, so I don't be out that much, so I just stay in the house and do whatever I have to do."

Michelle's SAT scores were: Verbal 310, Math 420, with a combined score of 730. She was accepted in the regular program at the University of Hartford.

The Pressure to Live Up to SYTE's Expectations

Senior year in high school produced a rush of activity for those aiming for college: taking SAT tests, completing college applications and their required written essays, visiting colleges, filing for financial aid, and assessing their next steps as college letters of acceptance and rejection appeared in students' mailboxes. In addition to Robin Wall Hill and Randall Sims, project coordinators, Leanne Gorfinkle joined the staff as a full-time college application coordinator. Leanne, a former high school English teacher, conducted workshops on writing college essays, conferred with individual students on the development of their essays, and packaged and mailed their completed college applications. The program's fiscal manager, Rashida Holmes, did similar work with parents and students on submitting applications for financial aid packages.

However, for those who would not graduate, either because they had dropped out or been retained in grade and needed to repeat one or two years before they could finish on time, there was the stress of being left behind. Still others would graduate from high school, but knew they were unlikely to succeed in college even if they tried to compete. I felt that students needed help in coping with the stress of anticipating going to college, and for others, with the feelings of disappointment about being left behind to finish high school or dropping out of school entirely. Therefore, I engaged a counselor, Vance, who conducted group sessions in which students had a chance to express their concerns. What follows is a transcript of one of these sessions, illustrating how expectations, pressure, and stress affected the students as they approached graduation.

Marcus, a student who was retained in twelfth grade, opened the session by sharing his frustration poignantly:

> You know they help you try harder [a reference to the SYTE staff's work with students], but you try and you go in there and make a good effort and get good grades from the start, I mean that's what you are supposed to do and you're average and everybody else in your class gets higher than you, but I'm trying to do this so I can be like them. But I'm saying everyone wasn't born for this college thing and everyone wasn't born to be real smart and I mean if everyone was born to be smart, then everybody'd have a job and everybody'd be equal and everybody was born equal, but everybody not equal.

RANDALL: [*speaking to the whole group*] Um, who is under the impression that they be forced to go. . . . Let's dispel some myths first. Who is under the impression that they have to . . . ?

ERICA: You all making us feel like we gotta go. . . . We don't gotta go.

MARCUS: Yeah, yeah. We gotta go; we don't go, we gonna be nothin.

ERICA: It's not like you all force us, but it's like a way you all force us is pressure. It's like I'm going to college; you all wait for the dream; you all wait for this; you all wait for me.

MARCUS: And you all going to be statistics like, you know . . .

RANDALL: But is that realistic? So you're saying that . . .

MARCUS: No. I'm saying that my dad been to college; he been to college for two years and he in jail. My mom ain't gone out of tenth grade and she manages just fine. So now she ain't no statistic. My dad's a statistic and he went to college.

RANDALL: So your point is that anyone who don't want to go to college . . .

MARCUS: Don't have to go.

ERICA: Our expectations too high for ourselves.

MICHELLE: You either make it or you won't.

VANCE [*group facilitator*]: I think Marcus is making a really important point. I'm imagining that being a student in the Say Yes program, it really does bring with it a lot of pressure to succeed—

ERICA: It is [*agreeing with Vance's assessment*].

Marcus controlled this conversation by telling two compelling personal stories. In the first story, he explained that effort alone will not bring you success in academic subjects, if your abilities are only "average." He said he wasn't "born smart" and therefore, college was not a possibility. Then he gave a global critique of equity in society based on a sceptical, deterministic view of life. If you were not born smart, he claimed, you will not succeed. Marcus's second story tried to redirect the importance of college by pitting his father's failure, despite the fact that he completed two years of college, against his mother's success in life, even though she dropped out of high school. He summed up his position by noting that his mom did not turn into a statistic, while his dad, counterintuitively did. Becoming a statistic, a provocative metaphor for Marcus, meant adding to the percentages of inner-city youth who drop out of school, become teenage parents, sell or use drugs, and are incarcerated for criminal activity. He also used this term to heckle his peers by predicting that their futures would be bleak. In the following section, he shifts the focus to the media's treatment of Say Yes students. From his perspective, the press had been abusive and intrusive. His conclusion that the press robbed them of their identity by stealing their names hit a responsive chord in Ebony and Erica.

MARCUS: I'm saying they [*the media*] show all the really bad things that happen to the Say Yes—like some of us go to jail. Soon as you see the newspaper it read, "Say Yes student burns up scholarship and ends up in jail." You know what I mean? Say Yes kid this, Say Yes kid that. . . . It's embarrassing.

EBONY: Like we superstars.

Randall: Let's take a minute to address that. Everything Marcus said is true. I could get you the newspaper from today or yesterday or two weeks from now and there are stories about other people not in Say Yes who are in jail or dead.

MARCUS: But I ain't saying that. I'm saying the people you talk about they not in the program. Since we in the program, they forgot our names. And we're Say Yes kids.

ERICA: We are not individuals any more; we just all Say Yes. I'm a particular type person. I've been this type person and I can't be just a Say Yes kid all the time. And it's not like they force you to go to college, but in some ways they saying if you don't go to college you've got no chances, and we did all this for you and you can't do this. I mean there's just so much pressure you can take,

EBONY: It's like it's our last name. It's like we got no other people than Say Yes. You all help [*talking to the SYTE staff*]. It's not that you all's help's not needed. But you all push. And sometimes you all push us a little bit too far. You try to get our expectations a little bit too high, and then when we all by ourselves and it's hard. . . . As soon as you see your grandmother she say, "Don't throw that scholarship away. Haven't you got that free scholarship school?" They forgot our name. They don't even say, "How you been?" They say, "I know you going to do good. I know you all ready to go to college. Don't you graduate next Sunday?" All this and we ain't even graduated yet.

VANCE: Let me ask you a question. When the pressure starts feeling like it's too much, when the expectations are really high; do you feel you can bring those feelings to the staff?

EBONY: I'll tell anyone. I'll do the best I can. I'm not living for you, I'm living for me, and I'll do what I gotta do.

VANCE: Well OK. That's really important, because life has pressure no matter what. We all have to organize pressures and you have a very special form of pressure on you. And I guess the questions I have for you are: What kind of pressure is it? Is it the kind of pressure that gives you more choices in life or fewer choices in life?

MARCUS: Both.

EBONY: You know, you understand that everybody is giving you more advantage to do a lot of things. And you might complain about it, like I complain about everything, but I always be here every day to take advantage of everything they have to offer me 'cause it's helping me. It's helping me, I know, like if I'm doing volunteer work, ten years from now I can put that on my resume. You know it's not benefiting them [*the SYTE staff*]. You know they get the experience with us kids, but they understand what we feel: what things we like and what we don't like. So they can use what they learn from us with the next go round with different kids. So it's more, it's more help in the experience for us.

VANCE: So for you, even though sometimes it gets to be a hassle, and sometimes it's pressuring, that in the long run—it's worth it.

EBONY: I'd do it. I'd do it.

MICHELLE: It isn't really either of that. It's either you're going to make it, or you're not. Whether you're Say Yes or not, you've still got to take that chance. But by going to college it just helps you out a little bit more. You have a better chance of getting a good job and stuff.

EBONY: If it came down to, if you in the room with somebody who just graduated from high school, and you just got your Ph.D. in college, the Ph.D. is going to get that job before the high school student does— most likely they [*the employer*] going by your education and stuff.

VANCE: In some ways, being in Say Yes makes your life more complicated because it gives you more choices, but that's kind of a nice complication in your life—to have a few more choices.

Vance helped students to see that pressures are a part of living. Then he asked if the pressures of working with SYTE toward higher education goals gave them more choices or fewer. Marcus gave a one-word answer, claiming that the program's pressures have both increased his choices and limited them. Ebony, in contrast, seemed to understand that she would be better off if she succeeded in attaining a higher education. Those students who graduated from high school in June 1993 and entered college that summer were leaving one set of conditions where they understood the rules and roles of the game, and moving into an unknown set of circumstances. Say Yes offered an opportunity for motivated students to leave an environment that was unable to provide the chance to go to college, and enter one that could. Ebony and Marcus, in the last months before many SYTE students would graduate from high school, struggled to make it through a "status passage." B. G. Glasser and A. L. Strauss (1989) define "status passage" as "movement into a different social structure." These passages may be "desirable or undesirable," entailing a "loss or gain of privilege, influence or power" (p. 2).

Marcus felt the loss of status, as he rationalized the reasons he would not graduate with his class. Erica was also critical of the program for making her feel guilty when she slacked off. She learned that the gift comes at a price—accepting the discipline that higher expectations exact. Ebony, unlike Marcus, graduated on time. She was ambivalent about her ability to cope with the demands of a college, yet clearly wanted the rewards that a college degree might afford.

Not all SYTE students felt consumed by the program's high expectations. Samaj lived with his grandmother. He stated confidently that they knew how to manage their lives in Say Yes and at home:

> My grandmother has taken part when she's supposed to, and I take part when I can. And at home we take care of home. When we got to go to Say Yes, we take care of what we have to take care of at Say Yes. There's never been that pressure thing at home. Just all the excitement of getting ready to go.

Richard asserted that once he determined that he would attend college, he became single-minded in his commitment. He allowed no distractions to compromise his ability to achieve his objective. He wanted to dominate the field. He did not want to come in second best, when he knew that he was capable of being first.

Richard and Christina present somewhat different profiles. Christina seemed to have rejected the program and its attendant pressures, which she believed tried to transform her into someone she did not want to become. Christina is fiercely independent; her mother took pride in having raised her that way. She, too, was resilient, in that she did not give up when she failed. She reassessed her situation, used what assistance may be available and proceeded in the direction she charted for herself. Richard experienced a crisis involving his faith, family, and the opportunities SYTE presented to him. He was torn between his mother's dream for him and attending a secular university. While his crisis did not compare with the environmental hazards his peers faced, he nevertheless had to figure out how to shape an identity that could manage conflict so that he could benefit from the scholarship gift and also preserve a loving relationship with his family.

How SYTE students used the extraordinary gift needs to be filtered through their individual life histories, the stress and/or nurturance of living in their homes and neighborhoods, and the quality of instruction they received from kindergarten through twelfth grade. A student's success or failure in high school can not be explained by teacher-assigned marks or SAT scores alone. Neither can it be adequately explained by an individualistic concept that awards success to hardy personalities. Students live in an ecological system (Bronfenbrenner 1979). The effects of that system are disclosed by the quality of the interactions students experience with parents, peers, school, and community (Spencer and Youngblood 2002). The influence of these combined factors determines a student's capacity to succeed or fail.

PART 3

Paying Back

CHAPTER 5

Living the Gift

Postsecondary Education

Having chronicled the histories of six dropouts in chapter 3 and six students who became high school graduates in chapter 4, we now pick up the threads of the high school graduates' lives and examine the paths they chose to follow. The lives of those students who went on to postsecondary schools reflect the complex interactions between the students, their families, the SYTE staff and sponsors, and the institutions the students attended. These stories offer indications of why some students succeed and others fail.

Three questions organize these life histories. First, how did students attending a postsecondary school experience advanced education? Embedded in this question are concerns about their preparation for college, their ability to study and use supporting services, and their socialization to an academic environment. Second, how did racism affect their lives? At the integrated colleges SYTE students attended, racism was a factor. Most of our students lived in segregated neighborhoods and had attended all-black schools. Third, how did a postsecondary education help students clarify their career goals?

The last chapter provided comparative high school outcome data that allowed the reader to compare participants' success in the program to a similar population. The following sections present SYTE's postsecondary results compared to another tuition guarantee program also operating in Philadelphia, and to census tract data.

Comparisons across Programs

When considering high school completion, it is interesting to note that participants in Tell Them We Are Rising (TTWAR) and SYTE outperformed a comparison group of high school graduates by a 50 percent increase in graduation rates (See Schlesinger 1993; Sewell, DuCette and Shapiro 1995). Similar findings are also found in the I Have a Dream programs. Joseph Kahne and Kim Bailey (1999) studied two IHAD chapters in Chicago and found ". . . their high school graduation rates (71 percent and 69 percent) were roughly twice those of their respective comparison groups (37 percent and 34 percent)." Fundamental to producing these outcomes was the ". . . emphasis on developing strong relationships between youth workers and participants" (Kahne and Bailey 1999). If maintaining these caring, productive relationships improves high school graduation rates, why is there so little evidence that an equally intense monitoring and support of those students who move on to postsecondary schools would also yield a significant outcome?

The IHAD Foundation headquarters in New York City has available to researchers ten studies of various chapters. Four of the studies offer testimonial statements extolling the value of the programs, absent quantitative data. The remaining six studies do report the percentages of high school graduates and those who proceeded to college or vocational training. Only the Kahne and Bailey study mentions high school graduation rates in relation to a comparison group. None of these studies, however, report student outcomes as a result of attending postsecondary schools.

These studies reinforce the body of evidence that tuition guarantee programs like SYTE, IHAD, and TTWAR have had a significant impact on improving high school graduation rates and make an important contribution to improving the lot of youth at risk. But it seems that most could not demonstrate a sustained carryover of these effects into college or vocational training schools for the same population. The numbers show that SYTE did make a significant impact on the Belmont population beyond high school. The numbers tell part of the story.

Tell Them We Are Rising

In Philadelphia, a tuition guarantee program comparable to SYTE was founded in 1988, one year later than Say Yes. Dr. Ruth Hayre, former area superintendent and later school board president of the School District of Philadelphia founded Tell Them We Are Rising and used the School of Education at Temple University for educational support and management of the program. In a personal conversation, Dr. Joseph DuCette, the Associate Dean of Temple's School of Education, offered TTWAR's summative data (July 30, 2003), which the following table compares with SYTE's.

Figure 5.1
Comparative Outcomes
2003

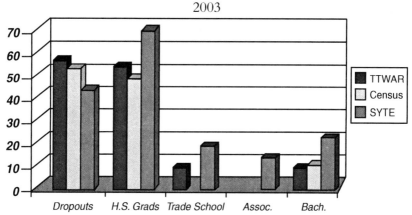

	Total Participants	Dropouts	High School	Trade School	Associate's	Bachelor's
TTWAR*	116	60 (51.7%)	56 (48.3%)	5 (4.3%)	NA	5 (4.3%)
SYTE**	106	39 (35.8%)	69**** (65.1%)	14 (13.2%)	10 (9.4%)	20 (18.9%)
Census***		48%	43%	NA	NA	6%

* Dr. Joseph DuCette, the Associate Dean of Temple's School of Education, offered TTWAR's summative data in a personal phone conversation (July 30, 2003).

** Annual program census, SYTE data.

*** 1990 U.S. Census Data for tracts 92, 104, 105, 106, 107, 108, 109, and 111 in West Philadelphia.

**** 65 students graduated with standard high school diplomas. Four received general equivalency diplomas (GEDs).

SYTE was able to increase the completion of four-year college programs significantly, even compared to a similar program: twenty SYTE students graduated from college (19 percent) compared to five TTWAR students (4 percent). Based on data from the census, SYTE increased college completion by sixteen percentage points over that in the census tract representing adults in the neighborhoods where SYTE students lived (19 percent vs. 6 percent).

What accounts for the significant gap between these comparable tuition guarantee programs? When I asked Dr. DuCette why so few students completed postsecondary schools in TTWAR, he hypothesized that "starting a college bound program at the beginning of seventh grade was too late. Too many deficits had accrued." This assessment is supported by research which finds that the beginning school transition and the early school years are critical (Alexander et. al. 1997). As patterns of performance solidify, children are quickly assessed and tracked. These in-school obstacles, compounded with social and economic factors outside of school, become predictive of later educational achievement. Dr. DuCette continued,

> The leadership involved with the group thought of the population's aspirations the same way middle-class families did. They believed that half the students would complete postsecondary school programs. The disappointing reality was that the students did not see the necessity of a postsecondary education.

While the TTWAR students were supported by mentors and a qualified project coordinator from seventh through twelfth grades, few of these supports continued when they entered postsecondary schools even though the scholarship funds continued to be available for eligible students. An important difference between these tuition guarantee programs appears to be the aggressive and sustained interventions by staff and sponsor on behalf of SYTE students attending postsecondary schools. In addition, SYTE staff and sponsors worked very hard to expand students' worldviews while at the same time allowing students to form their own definitions of success.

The Belmont 44: The College Experience

SYTE students scattered to integrated or historically black colleges distributed along the East Coast between Atlanta, Georgia, and Hartford, Connecticut. Their fields of study were diverse, and included business, psychology, aeronautical engineering, early childhood education, and high school biology teaching. Generally, only two or three students attended the same school, but the University of Hartford accepted nine students. Two were admitted to the regular four-year program immediately; the remaining seven students required a two-year stint in the University's Hillyard College of Basic Studies to remediate deficiencies or master study skills. Successful completion of Hillyard's program earned students an associate's degree and admission to the main college as juniors. Derrick and Roger attended Hillyard. This "batch placement" of students was not intentional; the University of Hartford offered Hillyard College, which provided a useful transitional program that remediated skills so that students could function as juniors in the regular college. That was an unusual arrangement at a university. However, the concentration of SYTE students at Hartford was beneficial, and has had great success elsewhere, notably with The Posse Foundation, headquartered in New York City. The Posse program identifies, recruits, and selects student leaders from public high schools to form teams they call "Posses." Posses are groups made up of ten students from diverse cultural and economic backgrounds who act as support teams and help to ensure that Posse Scholars succeed and graduate from college. It should be noted that, like ABC, and unlike SYTE, the Posse Foundation is highly selective about who they serve. This is also a likely factor in their success.

For SYTE students, matriculating at an integrated college required multiple adjustments. At Hartford, black students comprised 7 percent of the total population. Say Yes students had graduated from all black high schools; at Hartford they were suddenly relegated to minority status. The SYTE group was also disadvantaged academically as gauged by SAT scores. Half of Hartford's students had scored above 500 on each of the verbal and the math segments of the SAT (Peterson's Four Year Colleges 1996). In contrast, SYTE students attending the University of Hartford had combined verbal and math scores well below 700. This discrepancy in academic achievement was also typical of SYTE students attending other colleges. Few Say Yes students were as well prepared as their college peers, who were educated in suburban school districts or private schools.

The reader should be forewarned that graduation from high school was not the last hurdle. Most of the SYTE students struggled throughout their higher education careers. The first few years of college are for many a time of exploration and a first taste of freedom and independence. Many students struggled to complete coursework, distracted by a new social environment and exploration of the self. African-Americans who are the first in their families to attend college often experience feelings of incongruence and isolation, especially in their freshman year, and do not perform as well academically as their white peers. These obstacles to academic success were even more daunting for SYTE students, who were moving into a completely different world where students from a privileged middle-class background were largely sure that they would accomplish their academic goals and attain an undergraduate degree. SYTE students also had to adjust to a world in which not everyone was poor and black. The forty-four SYTE students who completed some form of postsecondary education had varied experiences. The stories in this chapter are intended to illustrate this range, reflecting the multiple obstacles faced and paths students took. Following the pattern established in the last chapter, Derrick, Roger, and Richard lead off, followed by Ebony, Christina, and Michelle. Derrick, Roger, Richard, Ebony, and Michelle attended colleges. Christina considered the idea of making an application to a two-year business college program, but soon dropped that possibility in preference for a school for cosmetologists. Their stories encompass the time period from 1993 through 1996, though some responses are also derived from the 1998–99 interviews. In the summer of 1993, twenty-eight high school graduates planned to attend four-year colleges, and twenty to attend two-year colleges.

DERRICK

> As far as this job interviewing process goes, it stinks. You guys give me a lot of feedback and encouragement and that feels good. It don't give me a job, but still feels good. Because Say Yes is not going to be there every time I fall. I gotta stop making excuses and take life seriously

Derrick attended Hillyard College of Basic Studies at the University of Hartford. Like some of his SYTE peers, his high school record and his SAT scores indicated to college admissions that he was not ready to matriculate in the four-year college. But he could attend Hillyard, and if he maintained a cumulative GPA of 2.0 he would gain admission to the four-year college. He produced a 2.0 GPA by the end of his first semester in the fall of 1993. His second semester in the spring of 1994 was slightly stronger, with a 2.5 GPA. That summer he spent working productively at the Philadelphia Stock Exchange. Senior Project Coordinator, Randall Sims, in his semiannual report on students' progress, noted that Derrick made a fairly successful transition to life as a college student. He made friends with his roommate and other students at Hartford. As the year progressed, however, his grades fell. Randall Sims reported in February 1995:

> (However) by the fall term of 1994, Derrick reported that he did poorly in his classes. Although he adjusted well at Hartford socially, he needs to work on his study habits. His GPA for fall 1994, was 1.16, and his overall cumulative average was 1.88. This below-average GPA put him on probation. He clearly needs to learn to use time better. He tends to procrastinate until two or three weeks before finals and pulls all-nighters to prepare for final exams. Staff has counseled him to get an earlier start preparing for finals and to develop a study schedule at the beginning of the semester.

In his freshman year at Hillyard, Derrick took several remedial courses that may explain the stronger GPA he attained and the weaker one in his sophomore year, when he took more typical college-level courses. By spring 1995, he had raised his GPA to a 2.0. He attended summer school and succeeded in his classes. His improved grades gained him admission to Hartford's Barney School of Business and Finance for the fall of 1995.

He claimed he did better in subjects he liked and that were necessary for his proposed career in business and finance. Consequently, he did poorly in biology, and writing papers felt labored and unproductive. When asked to explain his study habits, he noted that tape recording lectures helped him learn new material that seemed complex. He listened to these tapes again and again until he "got it." If that method failed, he would reread the textbook and answer the study questions at the end of the chapter. Only as a last resort would he call the professor for an appointment.

Like many students who fail a major exam, he found that very stressful. He worried that he may have disappointed the sponsor, George Weiss. Elliptically he says, "I don't want people, my sponsor to the program (SYTE), thinking that, you know, just that. . . . It's tough. It's very stressful." Then with a rededication to succeed, he maintained, "I try to bounce back. I try to leave it behind me and reassure myself by saying, "All right, I have a job to do. I'm here to do it. I'll talk to the professor, see if there's any make-up. And if there is any make-up, I'll try to work harder for the next time.' "

Derrick was determined to succeed, but did not show a critical or analytical understanding of the reasons he may have failed. He affirmed that he would try harder. But greater expenditure of effort without an understanding of his mistakes did not produce a better outcome. His answer to what he would do if he failed an exam is reminiscent of the way SYTE students at Fellowship Farm attacked the planning process for completing high school: "You put your head down and burrow your way through any obstacle." However, when describing his goal of becoming a stock trader, he indicated that he talked to professors about his interests. He expanded his network to include "professional workers and some portfolio managers." When he worked at the Philadelphia Stock Exchange, he displayed curiosity about how various workers performed their jobs. But because he could not see a connection between these subjects and his career goals, he had difficulty making a productive effort to improve.

Derrick lived with one foot in the world George Weiss and the SYTE staff encouraged him to join. But unsteady in his circumstances and his resolve, the other foot would drag him back into confusion and self-destructive behavior. Over the five and one half years he required to complete his bachelor's degree, he was twice on academic probation because his grade point average dropped below the 2.0 standard for continued matriculation.

George was his "idol," his role model. Derrick wanted to be a successful stockbroker like George. In a newspaper interview in 1994, George said he was exasperated by students who seemed to be abusing the privileged gift he had made possible for them. George felt that Say Yes had coddled the Belmont 112. He asked rhetorically, "How many times have these kids been given breaks? There's some point where the Derricks have to make it on their own." George's public disapproval of him written for all to see in the *Philadelphia Inquirer* embarrassed and hurt Derrick and forced him to reevaluate his relationship with George. He knew that George was a powerful presence who could influence Say Yes students. He remembered how George during Say Yes' high school years would commend students for doing well. "But if someone messes up, he'll come down, get into your house and see what's wrong."

Derrick respected George's commitment to be "real" with SYTE students. What infuriated him was George's public statement about him. "That was a slap on the face," he said. Derrick felt his trust in George had been betrayed. He found it incomprehensible that George would not speak to him privately about his displeasure with his academic performance. Part of Derrick's hurt was prompted by the indebtedness he feels toward George. He said,

> I went to him for a lot of things, a lot of favors like jobs and all, and I thank him dearly for that because the experience was great, and I loved it and needed it. But this hurts. To see a quote like "How many times have these kids been given breaks? There's some point where the Derricks have to make it on their own." What the hell is that supposed to mean? "Because you giving me a couple of jobs in the past year, I'm not doing for myself? What does that mean?"

Derrick rejected the notion that he is dependent on George's largesse to survive and tried to explain his situation, which he thinks is not unique. "Each kid in this program is fucked up, one way or another. I'm not pointing fingers, I'm not blaming." Still trying to make sense of George's criticism he said, "What does that mean, 'there's some point where the Derricks make it on their own.' Does that mean I can't find a job without you," as if speaking to George. He returned to his feelings of indebtedness, "I mean I thank you very much for the opportunity and all." Then he finished his tirade with muffled rage toward a gift giver he dare not confront. "But at the same time, you know, I'd say, fuck you. I don't know."

Six months out of college, Derrick had an epiphany. He realized that George did not inherit his wealth. He came from a family of modest means, and in order to acquire wealth, "he had to work hard to get to where he is. And um, it's funny I didn't really know what that meant, 'working hard to get what you want' until recently." His thoughts turned reflective:

> You know, most young people, we like to make excuses for ourselves. Excuses for why this or that didn't work out. Excuses for why we didn't do something. We take the easy way out. We don't, we didn't like to work hard. But at the same time we realize that if we don't work hard we won't get where we gotta be. A few

months before graduation I turned scared. Because Say Yes is there,
but now what I do depends on me.

He recalled the summer jobs he had in George Weiss' office
where he behaved inappropriately. "You know, I did stupid stuff, like
coming to work late and making excuses for it. Reassuring himself, he
said, "Work hard, don't make any excuses and I can get what I want."
Then his mood shifted sharply, "I'm not gonna have anything I want."
Derrick has had several job interviews, but no job was offered.

Class differences were apparent to Derrick. His mother was stuck
in a life of drug dependency and poverty. His father completed one
year of college, and escaped to a more middle-class lifestyle. Derrick
prided himself on being the first person on his mother's side to graduate from high school, let alone college. He was acutely aware of class
differences, whether produced by education or wealth. The following
scene illustrates how wealth develops tastes, sophistication, and cultural
distance from those who lack those experiences:

Because I was thinking about this lunch I had with Mr. Weiss.
And the funniest thing happened. A waitress came over to us and
she asked us what we wanted to drink. And I said, "May I have
some water please." And she said, "What kind of water?" And I
said, "Spring water." Then she named five different kinds of water.
And my face expression must have been so hilarious. Mr. Weiss
just started cracking up laughing. I just said, "Bring me some
regular, flat spring water." Having lots of money must be nice,
but let's keep things simple. Five different types of water, that's
ridiculous. And I was laughing at George. And it's like two different worlds.

Derrick saw the ludicrousness of elite consumption patterns. He
felt a closer affinity to his father's accomplishments. He ended this
scene by identifying with his father. "In short," he summarized, "I
don't think my life will be different from my father's. He's traveled a
lot, went to school and has a successful job in sales. I'll be happy with
that. He's very happy." Derrick had difficulty finding a job in finance.
After several disappointing rejections, he accepted an offer to work
with his uncle who sells sports memorabilia at major sports events
across the country. With the money he's saved, he invests in the stock
market and has purchased some real estate.

ROGER

> My image is, you know, even though I'm in school, I'm still the
> same person. But they don't see it that way.

Roger often said he wanted a profession in medicine, preferably
as a doctor. Rarely had he visited a doctor during his childhood.
However, lively fantasies stimulated by TV representations and what
he had read about the profession in books made doctors attractive.
Their prestige and the high regard in which they were held fed his
interest. He reasoned that he wanted to help people who were sick.
In addition to altruistic motivations, he saw medicine as a way to earn
a high salary. But his low scores on the SATs and uneven grades in
high school suggested that he might not be successful in a premed
program. Therefore, staff and mentors urged him to pursue an allied
health career like physical therapy, where he was more likely to succeed. And yet, as will be evident at the end of this case study, he never
quite gave up the dream of becoming a doctor. Resolved, at least for
the time being, to pursue a degree in physical therapy, he packed his
belongings, said his good-byes to his "adopted" family and boarded a
train headed for New England.

Roger's first semester at university was successful. He made lots of
friends, joined the swimming team and enjoyed the courses he selected.
In his first semester, his grade point average (GPA) was 2.7. He thought
it should have been higher. Despite his disappointment, and to his
credit, he took anatomy and physiology, a challenging four-point credit
course, and earned a B.

He soon learned that being a student in college was different from
his previous experience. In high school, SYTE staff, sponsors, and Human
Services teachers stood ready to encourage and guide Roger. If he
faltered, someone helped him mobilize his resources so that he could
move forward. But college was not like that. "In college, you have
nothing to rely on but yourself," he reminded me. "In college you have
to do it on your own." He continued, "Like in high school you do
what is required, but in college you have to put in more hours. And
then you have to break the requirements. You have to put your own
time into it, extra time. You can't just do what is required." He seemed
to understand the level of effort necessary to succeed in college level
work. It was his solid determination to focus on college that made it
possible for him to end his first semester with a sense of accomplishment.

But his success was marred by his neighborhood friends' rejection of what they perceived as his college persona.

He tried to live his newly crafted college identity, but found that the role of college student threatened his West Philadelphia homies. At college he made friends with a few white students and brought one home for a weekend. "I have white friends. I have friends of all kinds. And I bring them around with me. And I'm with them, and my old friends. And my old friends they kind of shaky about it. And they became my enemies because of the fact that I had white friends." He felt chastened by the realization that he could not bring his best friend Davis, who is white, to his neighborhood in Philadelphia.

> If I bring Davis to Philly, who's to know who's racist in a crowd. Who's going to begin a fist fight? The same is true for me up here. I see a guy looking at me, and I'm quite sure he saw I was looking at him. You may think all these people are your friends. But they may not be. You may think you know them, and believe that this person ain't gonna do nothing. But you don't know.

Having White friends made Roger suspect, someone who defied community social norms. But having White friends wasn't the only factor that turned his neighborhood peers into enemies. "It's almost as if they don't like you because you are in school." His Philadelphia friends felt he was separating from them and acting as if he were better than them. Going to college and talking about careers that require higher education builds a gap in the inner city between those who will stay and those who may escape the ghetto. Roger felt rejected by some of his neighborhood peers because he dared to be different. But some of his peers' suspicions about him reached back to who he was as a child.

> When I was young, I was wild and fought a lot. And people never got the chance to really know me. They hated me as a child. And as an adult, they hate me because they think I'm the same person. I don't present myself as being a real hard tough guy, because I'm not. If I could do it all over again, I would do it better. I don't hold myself responsible for it. I had no other choice. That was something I had to do.

Roger lived uneasily in two worlds: the ghetto kid who goes to college and comes back as a stranger and the ghetto's memory of him as a wild kid. An incident in early December of his freshman year started a downward spiral as he and his best buddy, Davis, were sucked into an altercation with another male student, Willy, and his girlfriend. Roger and Davis were walking through the student center when they noticed that Willy had made a muffled sound. Davis turned around sharply and moved close to the other student's face and asked: "Did you say something about us?" Willy responded with some "crazy shit," Roger recalled, and he and Davis burst out laughing, humiliating Willy in front of his girlfriend. As Roger and Davis walked away, Willy shouted he'd meet them up in their hallway and was bringing some friends. Shortly after Davis and Roger reached their rooms, Willy and his friends arrived looking for a fight. As Willy moved in, Roger picked up a metal baseball bat and holding it horizontally to protect himself, hit Willy in the head as Willy lunged forward. He fell to his knees from the impact. His buddy helped him to his feet. They left the area swearing they'd be back with more of their friends.

All four students ended up at the police station and gave evidence of how this fracas occurred. A disciplinary hearing recognized that Roger acted in self-defense, but that did not absolve him from serious sanctions because of his use of the baseball bat as a weapon. In addition to being put on probation, he was expelled from use of any university housing for the remainder of his college program. Being expelled from university housing meant Roger needed to live off campus, away from all the conveniences the college made available to students. Only one week after the hearing on the baseball bat fight, he and Davis were back in court standing in front of the same judge. They had joined a fight on campus. Davis was cited by police as the one who started the fight. Roger came along to court to see if he could help Davis. When the judge saw Roger, he pointed out to him that he should be in school, in class, or studying in his dorm room.

Roger found off-campus housing for spring semester 1995 using SYTE funding. After leaving campus housing, his grades deteriorated. He cited all the stress and anxiety resulting from the fight and the way he was treated by the university's Judiciary Board as the reason for his precipitous fall from a 2.7 in the fall semester to a .28 GPA in the spring. But succeeding semesters proved that he was constantly diverted from his studies. He barely managed to stay in school and would use summer school as the one time that he might achieve enough credit to recover from probation status. Over a four-year period, he was on probation five times. He blamed the baseball bat fight for part of his failure to establish a steady level of academic achievement. That incident and others that followed would set off a wave of emotional responses that took him away from his studies.

It was finally apparent to Roger that he could not return to college. SYTE, too, felt he was not able to discipline himself to benefit from a college education. Also it became clear that he had not developed the study skills that would give him a sense of mastery. He seemed preoccupied by activity peripheral to college. By 1998, when he realized SYTE would end in 2000, he accepted that he would not finish college at the program's expense. Adding complexity to his life, he fathered two children in 1995 and 1996. He had adult responsibilities and needed a marketable skill. He had been doing students' hair for some time. He made a quick shift by deciding to become certified as a hair stylist. He attended cosmetology school in Hartford and applied himself diligently. His attendance was reliable, his grades on exams were excellent, and he successfully completed the course. Necessity seemed to help him clarify his goals. To supplement his income, he managed a café in the evening at the University of Hartford and had a profitable business doing hair around campus. In addition, he and his adopted cousin designed a line of men's and women's clothing and were looking for investors to capitalize the venture. Even though he was successful in the different ways he earned a living, he remained wistful about his dream to pursue medicine. I saw him in 1999 at Michelle's wedding. He said to me, "Someday I will finish my degree and become a doctor."

RICHARD

> It's almost like a social depression that blankets the whole community and I want to be able, in the future, to develop an approach to the social question that depression in the inner city stems from poverty or unemployment. Or some other big social problem that deprives them from being able to see joy and the beauty of life and the power people can have over their own experiences.

In June 1993, I visited Belmont Elementary School to interview teachers who taught Say Yes students six years earlier. Ms. Reiley and Ms. Plunket, both veteran teachers at Belmont, remembered Richard and his family warmly. Ms. Reiley recalled that "the whole family was quite intellectual." She was impressed with Richard's writing. "He was forever writing," she said. She delighted in the quality of his stories. "I don't mean one line stories, but four to five pages. And he'd bring them to me every week to read. And they were kind of like science fiction stories, with a real plot. I'd take it to bed to read them. They were interesting." She asked me to confirm that Richard had a scholarship to Penn. I verified that he would attend Penn that summer. Mary Plunket wanted to know the major Richard would pursue at Penn. "Business," I answered. Ms. Reiley was proud that Richard returned to his former school as he was leaving high school to speak at the Belmont students' graduation. She reported that students received him warmly. "Now they all want to go to the University of Pennsylvania, like Richard's gone."

In the fall of 1993, he entered his freshman year at the University of Pennsylvania's prestigious Wharton School of Business and Finance. He thought he wanted to study accounting, a subject his father recommended would help him earn a good living. In accepting his advice, he followed his father's career choice. His father had completed two years of college while majoring in accounting. Richard's freshman year was reasonably successful. He earned three Bs and a D in Economics. In the second semester his grades improved. He took Calculus 1 and landed a B, in Economics a C, an A– in Writing about Poetry and in Spanish a B–. However, as long as Richard was enrolled in business courses, his GPA fell below a 3.0. By the fall of 1995, he understood that he might be asked to leave Wharton. He searched for alternatives to his business major, exploring humanities programs ranging from religious studies to English.

The slump in grades could not be solely attributed to the mismatch between Richard's aptitudes in the Humanities and the demands of the business school's curriculum. He complained about feeling preoccupied and unable to focus on his studies. In addition to the alienation he had felt attending Wharton, he also trapped himself in consumer debt. He purchased a new refrigerator for his mother, borrowed money to pay an overdue dental bill and bought a large stereo system. To pay these debts, he worked thirty hours a week, which significantly reduced his study time. When he received a rebate from a government grant, instead of returning it to the Say Yes office, which was program policy, he spent the money on personal items.

Randall and I felt that Richard was in a crisis; we needed to call his parents to a meeting to clarify Richard's situation. The meeting was cooperative though painful. An agreement was reached that Richard would forgo a meal plan the following semester to compensate the program for the check he had cashed. He would also reduce his work hours. Randall and I sensed that he might benefit from seeing a therapist. His parents encouraged him to take advantage of this opportunity, and Richard agreed to try it for a few weeks. It was during a session with his therapist that he realized that he might want to become a psychologist. He remembered that in high school he "really liked psychology and did well in it." He noted, "I could really see myself doing it, because it's not teaching per se. But in a way you are teaching someone either about their problems or how to solve their problems. It just seemed like something I'd be good at, and that I'd love to do."

He began to notice how other talents he possessed might relate to his potential success in psychology. Through journal and poetry writing, he had always been reflective about his life. Being personally reflective "at Wharton would be considered a distraction." He realized that he might be stereotyping business students. But he also believed that expressing feelings was not typical of what was expected in a business school. He wanted to write and explore human motivations. In the midst of his crisis, he was writing a play called, *A Mile in My Moccasins*. He explained, "It's about not being judgmental. And how that really can have detrimental effects on relationships." This was Richard's first play. In the past he had written stories and poems. He never imagined he could write a play and feel so satisfied with the results. He realized that he was effective in expressing himself in writing, and also in public speaking. He was the keynote speaker at the Belmont graduation. This event happened the same day as his graduation from high school. While sitting on the stage waiting to be called to the podium, he searched for his speech in his coat pocket. He was horrified to find that it was not there. He had no choice but to ad lib. "Being raised in my church, I had lots of experience speaking before crowds." Those were training experiences he could rely on when he needed them in other contexts.

I asked him if he felt that his high school had prepared him for the academic challenges of college. Without hesitation he answered, "No." He felt that college course work wasn't his problem. Instead he felt he lacked strong study habits. It was the pace of a course in a semester,

> . . . that was so much faster. And the competition was real great.
> So, coming from Engineering and Science High School, it was a

competitive school relative to other schools in Philadelphia. But compared to Penn, and the students that come to Penn, mostly from private schools, the competition wasn't there, just the raw education. I can't say they didn't prepare me academically. I don't think I came in here behind anyone academically. But I wasn't ready. I wasn't used to it.

While he felt somewhat battered by the Wharton experience, he also felt the demands made him into a better student. In retrospect he realized that he had not been a disciplined student. "Whereas now I study four hours a day, at least. Over the past semester, I was studying; I was really studying. In my freshman year, I didn't really study. I had papers. I did research. I crammed. But I didn't study on a constant everyday basis." Richard was in training: his study habits were more disciplined; he saw a connection between his current studies and his future; an undergraduate degree became a beginning, rather than an end. He had set his sights on attaining a doctorate in psychology and imagined himself in the future as influential in the field.

He intended to continue writing plays as well as books about psychology. Life options, once limited by the rules of his religion, widened: "I plan to be an author, to travel, to talk to people about my work." In scanning a book about contemporary influential psychologists, he was struck by the absence of black psychologists. He sensed that there would be room for him to make his mark. "And that's important, because I really want to leave a legacy, to leave a mark somewhere."

By August 1999, some of his thoughts about his career had sharpened. His interest in psychology had focused on becoming a clinical psychologist working primarily with depressed clients. "Depression," he averred, "is not only an individual problem, it can be a communal issue." Richard has become intensely aware of the effects of social settings on an individual or group's development.

> Just like growing up in West Philly and making that change to Penn, and just seeing the huge difference and the biggest difference I saw was expectations, what people expect in a salary, what you expect from society, what you expect from your government, The difference was just huge. It's like one group really didn't expect, they were lucky to have a good day. And the other groups expected success in just about everything they went about.

Richard wanted to find a way to give back to his community and also raise expectations for its children. First, he talked to Randall Sims, then to me, and finally to George about a way to motivate the June 1998 graduating class from Belmont Elementary School. It felt like déjà vu as we sat in the Belmont auditorium looking at the graduating class and waiting for Richard to speak. The principal introduced him as one of the Belmont 112 who had sat where today's class was sitting and had recently graduated from the University of Pennsylvania. Richard, calm and self-assured, walked to the podium and with his head turned toward the graduates urged them to set their sights on a college education. He said he was confident that they were willing to work hard to achieve that goal. But he also knew that they might need financial support. Turning toward the audience of parents and friends, he said that he wanted to raise $10,000 over the next six years so that he could award ten $1,000 grants. Toward that end he promised to match any funds the community raised. George beamed with pride realizing that Richard had understood the purpose of Say Yes, "to make a difference in your life and to make a difference in other peoples' lives" (Mezzacappa 1999b).

EBONY

> They made me better because they made me realize it's not just me. . . . I got to make a life for us. [My kids] make me more serious about me and my education. I think my kids are my most [important] influence.

Ebony's college experience did not follow a direct path; her situation as a young mother of two children with limited family support necessitated a less immediate route through higher education. Despite the intense responsibility of supporting two children as well as herself, Ebony remained resolute in her educational and professional ambitions. As her story unfolded, Ebony demonstrated keen insight into her desires, motivations, and educational and professional goals, and provided a poignant social critique of the world around her. Her resiliency, determination and perceptive awareness drove her toward her own definition of success; "I got that flame, but it's just not turning into a fire yet."

As planned, Ebony began her college career the fall after her graduation in 1993 from Bartram Human Services High School. She pursued a nursing degree from Virginia State University but quickly found she did not enjoy Virginia State and was not interested in the field of nursing. Ebony discovered that she was pregnant and did not return to Virginia State after the midterm of her first semester. At the time of our 1996 interview, she had two children, ages two and one, and was in the second semester of an associate's degree program at Harcum College, a two-year college in Philadelphia.

Since leaving Virginia State and having her children, Ebony found she was able to more clearly define her educational/professional goals and needs. She has learned that she must pursue a career and educational preparation that interests her, despite pressures from family and friends to pursue a practical profession with job stability and stable income. She stated:

> People will try to talk me out of what I want to do and stuff like that. I mean, like friends and family and stuff. . . . I'd rather do something that I like than to do something that I don't. And I'm not going to pretend. I don't care how much money you being a doctor and all that makes. . . . Nobody can change my mind.

She enjoyed writing, public speaking, and debating political issues effecting society; she thought a career in Communications would make her happy. She was aware that while her current education did not directly prepare her for this field, it was preparation for completing liberal arts courses and then specializing once she transferred to a four-year university. With this understanding, Ebony remained focused and did quite well at Harcum College, with an average just slightly below a B.

Ebony became more aware of the conditions in a learning environment that most suited her learning style. For example, she articulated that the small, personal learning context at Harcum was desirable and necessary for her to promote her sense of involvement and understanding of the material. In reference to pursing her education at a large school like Temple University, Ebony stated:

> . . . I just don't think I would make it. I need something small. . . . I think it would just throw me off track. I do, because Harcum is like so small, and it's like everybody helps you. It's even better than Community College to me, because at Harcum College, there are peers. You got professors, they hug you, any time . . . they understand when you have problems and stuff like that . . . they help

you find jobs, you know, help you set your resume up . . . do coops and stuff like that. And I think just going into a big school for me. . . . I don't think my heart would be into it.

Ebony contended that her high school education had not prepared her for the caliber of work at college. More generally, she felt that high schools and teachers at schools such as the one she attended that serve low-income black students did not hold high enough expectations or present educational challenges that were necessary for success at college. Hence, students like herself found themselves without the required skills and not sufficiently prepared for the rigor of college. She maintained:

> The work is totally different . . . because the things you do in high school . . . it's not being operated as a school. It's just like a play-ground for people . . . the education system is more, they're not preparing them kids for what is going to be out there, not at all . . . they ought to know how to take notes and stuff like that. They should have . . . a real college professor coming in and maybe doing an after-school program or something. You know, just to let them know what it is really like . . . [In reference to teachers] I think some of them are doing a good job but they just need to be harder.

Ebony also reflected on the various ways her children have influenced her life and the ways she views herself and her education more specifically. She explored the conflicting modes by which having children has both helped make her a more focused and better student while making it difficult for her to complete her education in a direct and timely manner. Ebony's perspective on the connection of parent-hood to educational motivation challenges earlier research, which interprets teenage parenthood as a factor in limiting educational attainment. After completing her associate's degree at Harcum, Ebony transferred to Weidner University. While this transition helped her define a career path, she faced additional challenges. Ebony explained that soon after transferring, she discovered the social work profession. She did not have knowledge of this career prior to beginning her education at Weidner, but after learning about social work, she found that it ideally met her goals of communication and helping others. Ebony realized that her desire to enter the communication field came from a motivation to help and that social work was an even better option for her.

She spoke eloquently about her desire to work specifically with women and children, particularly women who had been victims of domestic violence. She used social work terminology as she described her vision for assisting women through the "empowerment strengths perspective" in her role as a "case manager." At the time of the 1998 interview, Ebony had only completed one semester in her social work major, yet already had internalized and was able to articulate how to assist women and children in a social work framework. Ebony verbalized the ways in which both higher education, in exposing her to this career option, and education through her life experiences had prepared her for this field. She contended,

> I'm gonna always want to help people. It's like you know, it's like everything has influenced my life. Like I said, from things that I've seen through my friends. From just guys that I know. . . . Like seeing people getting killed. . . . I know I can't do it all by myself. But it's a start, and I just see a lot of things that I know need to be changed.

Ebony faced challenges at Weidner that she did not predict. After completing her associate's degree, Ebony lost the childcare benefits that she was receiving from public assistance. Based on the welfare reform law of 1996, she was deemed job ready and, hence, public assistance would not provide these additional benefits. Without subsidized daycare, Ebony scrambled to find babysitters, but due to the timing of her required classes was frequently unable to coordinate childcare assistance with her class schedule. As a result, Ebony missed many classes and, even though she completed all assignments, her grades were based on class participation. Ebony sought out her professors and explained her situation, which enabled them to support her as much as possible. She expressed the difficulties of maintaining her educational requirements without familial or state support to assist her with childcare responsibilities. The new welfare law forced her to withdraw from college and enter the workforce. Had she completed her bachelor's degree she would have been more likely to provide better conditions for raising her children.

CHRISTINA

> And I think that I'm very ambitious. I like to do things for myself. So I'm kind of independent, because I learn more that way. I appreciate things when I work hard for them, than when they're just given to me.

A public high school could neither contain nor nurture Christina on her terms. She was contemptuous of the poor quality of her schooling. "They didn't teach us nothing," she complained. "It was like the same thing over and over from middle school all the way up to twelfth grade. How am I supposed to do something when the highest math level I went to was Algebra 2?"

Christina felt unprepared for college. Her mother consistently thought she should become a lawyer. Initially optimistic about a law career, Christina became resistant. She knew that having a "big mouth and being able to speak my mind," as she described herself, would not transform her into a lawyer. Cosmetology was an area where she felt "naturally" successful. From age thirteen she had set up shop in her mother's living room to do hair. She was good at it and wanted to become more expert. Her first attempt at finding the right school took her to North Carolina, where she enrolled as a student at the Dudley University of Cosmetology. Very quickly the staff saw Christina's talent and put her to work coaching less able students. The school offered her a contract to teach once she obtained her certification.

She and several students from Dudley traveled to Tennessee to attend a major gospel show. The headliner was Kirk Franklin, a highly successful gospel star, whose singing had earned him a platinum album. Christina won the coveted prize of giving Kirk Franklin a haircut. Initially, she felt flattered by the attention and praise for her work, but soon she felt used. She had enrolled at Dudley as a student, but after a few months it became clear that this school had little to teach her.

Wiser about how to choose a school and how to present herself as a student, she returned to Philadelphia where she soon found a school that challenged her, the Jean Madeline School of Beauty. She presented herself there in a modest manner: "I kind of didn't show them what I can do. I let them feel their way through knowing me. That way I wasn't allowing myself to be used again." Her immediate goal was to secure a license to practice. But she was ambitious for more advanced training. In particular, she wanted to become a platform hair stylist, which would permit her to train other cosmetologists at a more advanced level. I asked her to explain her interest in this career. Without hesitation she said,

> Cause I'm my own boss and I get to use my creativity. And it's good money. And it goes with my personality. I'm into fashion.

And I like to talk people into things so that I can help them look better. I have the gift to talk people into change. But I'm using it in a positive way to help them keep up with fashion and help them look better.

I wondered if she would need additional education in her line of work. She agreed, "There's always something to learn." She illustrated her point by indicating that there were fourteen different levels in cosmetology. She had a clear sense of how additional education leads to more complex skills and higher remuneration. She described the ladder of competitive skills she expected to climb. "Like I'm a hair stylist. But I can go back to school to take up hair coloring. Then I'll be a master hair colorer, then a master hair weaver. If go up all fourteen levels, I can give seminars and I can charge $900 for three days presenting to fifty people in a classroom."

I was struck by her maturity and how much she had grown since her days in high school, where she was often ". . . very angry, ready for a fight, wanting to be center stage all the time and upset when people didn't follow . . ." her lead. And then in frustration she'd throw up her hands in disgust, and say. ". . . the hell with all of you. I'm out of here." Christina didn't see any contradiction in her behavior. She claimed she always knew who she was. She acknowledged she knew how to put up a good front. With a wry smile she reinforced her point, "I could be a hell of an actress if I wanted to. And one thing was being who my parents wanted me to be. They wanted me to be like them. That's what I was fighting. That was my real fight."

She saw her life unlike her mother's. Christina attributed her success in achieving her goals to the fact that she didn't have any children getting in the way. She said she learned from her mother's mistakes. Her mother had two children by the age of seventeen; Christina refused to fall into that trap. She felt strengthened by her ability to resist the common pitfalls of her environment. "Just because I seen, maybe, my aunts was always getting high, didn't mean I had to get high. Just because I seen my aunt having a lot of kids and living off their mom, didn't mean I had to do it. And I wanted a better way. So everything they did, I didn't do."

While she felt her mother made mistakes that she intended not to make, she respected her ability to bounce back from hardship. But she acknowledged that there were significant differences between her mother and her grandmother's generation. Contrasting her mother's generation with her grandmothers on both sides of her family, she identified with the grandmothers for their strength of character and ambition to work. She saw these independent "go-getters" as her role models. They all worked most of their lives. She held up her mother's mom as an example. "She worked as a secretary in a hospital. She's my role model because she never took an ounce of welfare and when she passed away in 1995 she was still working. She never went back; she always went forward." She felt a special affinity with her father's mother. "She's more like me. She does independent work. She's a nanny. She chooses her jobs and she chooses her income. She just turned sixty-four."

Christina was a nontraditional student. She had to find her own path to a career and integrate personal knowledge with professional standards. She did not want to be like her parents or like the Weisses. She was determined to shape her own identity. "Well, I'm a go-getter person. If I want something, I see what I got to do and I get it done. But then I'm also a Pisces, so we kind of stray off that path sometimes. And it gets kind of confusing, but then you weigh your options and do what you got to do."

Christina's long-term goal required that she open her own shop. She reasoned that to do that she needed to be more knowledgeable about business practices so that she could set up books, monitor her expenses, and pay bills. She also wanted to become a more proficient typist and gain facility in using computers. To that end, she enrolled in a business school, did reasonably for one semester, but then dropped out. Simultaneously she explored the possibility of acquiring a loan form George Weiss to establish her own salon. She submitted a written request for a loan from George Weiss. George invited her to visit him at his New York office to discuss her business plan. George recommended that she talk with several successful African-American owners of beauty salons to get a more complete understanding of how one capitalizes a business and how to manage it successfully.

At a recent dinner with George and four additional members of the Belmont 112, the discussion turned to who felt they had used the gift to forge a better life. George reported to the Say Yes board that Christina had said to him: "I never wanted to attend college. I'm not saying you pushed me to go. But all I ever wanted to be was the most successful cosmetologist I could be."

MICHELLE

> I look at things a lot differently now. I look at things in a more realistic light now. Before I would just blow things off with "Oh well, whatever." But now . . . to some people it seems like I still have the same attitude. But to myself, now I think twice about just about everything I do.

Michelle started college a year later than most Say Yes students. Because she had been retained in tenth grade, she entered the University of Hartford in 1994. Math and English were her two favorite subjects. But sociology was difficult for her and she was puzzled by that.

> Like we have to communicate with a lot of people, not just our friends, but people we don't know. And I'm not good at that.— socializing with everybody. We had to do questionnaires. And talk to people. And it's not that I have a problem with that. But the people on campus, the way their attitudes are, I can't deal with that. I know myself. And I'm not putting myself in that position.

Outreach was difficult for her. She knew that Blacks were a small minority on campus, and interviewing a random sample of students inevitably meant talking with Whites. She was not used to that and feared the encounter. But she didn't fare much better in writing papers for sociology. She turned in a late paper and the professor announced to the class that anyone turning in a late paper that failed would not be given the opportunity to rewrite it. When her paper was returned, she saw that she had failed.

In general, her grades hovered around a 2.0 GPA, but she also failed classes. Her uneven response to her studies concerned the staff. Randall asked her how she studied for a class. Her response was a curt, "I don't." Randall persisted; not wanting her to obfuscate, he demanded an explanation.

> Usually when I sit down to study, like after class, I'll write my notes over. Or I'll go over my notes every now and then. But then when the exam comes, I'll forget it. So, if I pay close attention in class, while the teacher is giving notes or whatever, then I don't have a problem with passing my exams.

She reaffirmed her policy that she didn't need to study. "I never had to study for any of my exams before. I never studied since I'm in school, because I'm a good listener. She was capable of doing college work, but not at the degree of precision the sociology professor expected. In college math where she took pre-calculus and regular Calculus she earned letter grades of B and C respectively. Math, however, did not require her to make forays into the campus interviewing a population that she felt was hostile. College math presented difficulties for her, but it was not fraught with racial tension.

Despite her uneven achievement in college, she felt her high school curriculum had provided adequate preparation. She believed this because she felt high school had given her access to materials and an introduction to books she was currently reading in some of her college courses. If she did not understand a book in high school, she thought she had a better chance of understanding it in college, since she had read it before.

College had confirmed some of her previous beliefs, and changed others. For example, in her freshman year she considered pledging for a sorority. But the more she learned about sorority pledging she felt it would not benefit her. She developed her critique this way:

> I think pledging is a way for people to find out their identity, or have a sense of belonging. And I don't think I need to find my identity, because I know who I am and what I want to do. And I don't think I need to belong to a specific group in order to be somebody.

She was contemptuous of some of the pledging rituals that were supposed to build strength in a "sister." Her distaste for these arbitrary rituals was founded on painful home experiences. Michelle's mother had abused her physically throughout her childhood and adolescence. She asserted unequivocally about pledge hazing: "I didn't want to stand in a line for someone to beat me down telling me, 'I'm going to beat you down to make you strong' when I'm already strong."

The college experience in general had a salutary influence on how Michelle's thought processes developed. She became much more aware of the consequences of her behavior. "Like just basic everyday . . . should I cut class, and if I do, why would I cut class. What would I be missing out on? How do I handle different situations, like in my personal relationships and my professional relationships?"

In high school Michelle had little control over her anger. She was quick to solve conflicts by fighting. Slowly she became amenable to the therapy SYTE arranged for her, and she continued to seek psychological help in college. Her sense of self and development of appropriate behavior may in part be attributed to her productive use of counseling throughout her college matriculation.

From the beginning of Michelle's involvement with Say Yes, her career interest seemed focused on computers. When she entered college she listed computer science as her intended major. However, in working at the multicultural office, she gained a reputation for her empathy and willingness to help students solve their problems. Even the director of the center realized that Michelle had psychological insight and was impressed with the advice she offered regarding a problem she had with one of her own children. As the course work in computers became more theoretical, she felt disenchanted with her major. She wanted greater involvement with young people, perhaps functioning as a social worker or correctional officer. This evolution from computers to some form of social service seemed like a natural outgrowth of her upbringing.

> Because, the way I grew up. You know in my house you didn't have much, so much love. It was like, "You know what you gotta do. Do it." It wasn't no sit and ask questions. I never had any support for anything I did or didn't do. So, I would understand you know how most kids get into trouble. All my brothers got into trouble. I think I could make a difference. Or at least let them know someone cares about them.

She did not have guidance, love, or support growing up and wanted to do things differently for the next generation. She wanted to be a change agent for kids. She wanted to work with youth who came from an environment similar to hers. She felt a sense of relief that she escaped from that environment. Recalling her transition out of her neighborhood she noted, "Once I got out of that environment I thought a lot clearer." Interestingly, when the interviewer pressed her about how she would go about finding the appropriate advanced education to become a social worker, she explained that as an undergraduate she was doing an internship in a social service agency, and she expected to talk with coworkers about their preparation for a career in social work. She intended to find out ". . . what channels I needed to go through to do whatever I need to do." This statement marked development in her ability to reach out to people. Her therapy seems to have helped her to ". . . start to open up and talk to people." Michelle's attitude toward her life seems to have changed. "Life is not a matter of holding good cards but of playing a poor hand well." This quote is attributed to Robert Louis Stevenson. J. K. Felsman and G. E. Vaillant, in *The Invulnerable Child*, caution that one is not given one hand for life. Rather there are many opportunities to play the game. Initially, Michelle was fixated on the bad hand of cards she had been dealt. But increasingly through her college experience, she understood that many opportunities were open to her. She felt rejected by her family. When she wrote, they didn't write back. And if she called them, they would say they were busy. She felt hurt by their indifference. But she realized that she needed to overcome those emotions. She acknowledged, "I'm an adult now. And I don't need to worry about somebody taking care of me or worrying about me. That's my job now." Her assurance that she could manage her life came slowly. She asserted that SYTE made her into a different individual. Mentally and physically she felt like a better person. "Mentally I look at the way I used to be, and I see the way I am now. . . . I'm a young lady. And it helped me to turn myself that way. And it helped me to realize that I am intelligent. And, you know, that I can handle myself."

She worked hard to become a person who takes care of herself, even as she continued to develop a capacity to care for others. She witnessed cruelty and hatred, but knew how to protect herself against negativity and despair. Her anger, while tempered, was not lost; she found the ability to stand above the society she lives in and critique it. In the interview, she expanded her argument and introduced how class privileges certain groups because of family, wealth, or social tradition:

> Personally, I think society has a select group of people who they are satisfied with, like to run the government, who were born into wealth, wealth has been in those families since 1860 or something like that. So these people find a way to keep lower-class and middle-class people, just . . . they let you develop and go up the ladder some, but only to a specific point. It lets me know that no matter how hard I work, I will never, you know, have the prestige as most people do. I won't have the money, but I don't have the same education as the people on the higher grounds. In order to have the education as the upper class has, you have to be born into

wealth. I have two strikes against me: I'm African-American and I'm female. So, of course, I'm going to think, damn, what is my life going to be like when I graduate? Will I be able to get the job I want? And will I like the job that I get? Will I get the respect that I want from my fellow workers? That's the only thing that would bother me.

Michelle completed her bachelor's degree in December 1999. Shortly thereafter, she married and found a job as a counselor to young adults recently released from prison, advising them on how to manage their reentry into society. In addition to work, she and her husband take turns with child care for their two-year-old son. After three years of work, she and her husband saved enough money to make a down payment on a house.

Summary

Returning to the three questions posed at the beginning of the chapter, this section combines the experiences of the six students presented and reflects on their preparedness for postsecondary schooling, the development of their career goals over the course of their secondary and postsecondary schooling, and their perspectives on racism.

VIEWS ON THE EXPERIENCE OF POSTSECONDARY SCHOOLING

Five out of the six students felt that their high school experience did not prepare them for the rigors of postsecondary education. For each one who felt unprepared, the reasons were slightly different. Roger and Ebony both felt that high school should be more rigorous so that students are prepared for the demanding nature of college-level work. Ebony resented that some of her high school teachers did not hold black students to a high academic standard. She thought college professors ought to teach a course in high schools using college-level standards so that students could appreciate the differences they would face when they entered postsecondary schools.

Richard attended one of the city's most prestigious magnet high schools, Engineering and Science. He acknowledged that he received a good education for an urban school district, but he was convinced that the quality of education was superior in private schools and affluent suburban districts. He believed that his high school did not give him the edge to compete at an Ivy League university. He felt unprepared for the volume of work and the demands for high quality. In his freshman year he hardly studied. But when he understood the expectations, he studied a minimum of four hours each day.

Derrick did not complain about his high school education. His numerous absences, often due to responsibilities that he had to assume for his younger siblings, left him feeling underprepared. Derrick spent three years at Hillyard College before he could qualify for admission to Barney's School of Business and Finance. Christina constantly resisted her high school education that she thought was boring, repetitive, and unrelated to real life issues. Only Michelle, who claimed she never studied, regarded her high school education as serviceable.

Interestingly, of the entire set of students that entered a four-year college in 1993, 75 percent believed their high schools had prepared them for the challenge. But in the1996 interviews, only 50 percent of this group believed that they received the preparation needed to be successful in college. What sparked the SYTE students' complaints was that their current knowledge seemed to verify that the quality of education students from wealthy suburbs or private schools received in grade school was far superior. In other words, with exposure to students from various school districts, SYTE students were able to compare their experience and found it lacking.

CLARIFYING GOALS AND FUTURE ORIENTATION

Young adults in their early twenties experiment with different careers based on their experiences in postsecondary schools and the feedback they hear that encourages them to pursue a particular line of interest. Roger had the desire to finish college, but not the discipline. He was perpetually distracted from the narrow academic goal that required intensive study of texts and demonstrating mastery of subject matter on tests. But he also mistrusted his ability to show his professors that he could do college-level work. The first semester suggested he was capable. In subsequent semesters he continued to find ways to get in trouble even as he struggled to do class work. It took very little to rattle his sense of academic confidence and competence. When his failures compounded, he became phobic about trying to succeed in school. His objective became to remain in school, but he did not change any habits that might help him stay. By the time he had to leave school, he was the father of two children. That responsibility sobered him. He quickly mobilized his resources so that he could become a licensed cosmetologist and augmented his income by picking up additional work. His versatility made him marketable in several areas. Perhaps his greatest accomplishment was his acceptance of financial responsibility for his children and his commitment to spend time with them.

Ebony revised her thinking about career choices several times. Her interest in nursing was short-lived. She felt compelled to pursue an interest that was not hers. Subsequently, she settled on a career in communications that involved television news reporting or journalism. As she completed her associate's degree, she realized that what she really wanted to do was help people directly. Social work seemed like a natural fit. Her ambition snagged on the change in the welfare laws. The 1996 welfare regulations recognized her associate's degree as sufficient education to find a job that would provide her with an adequate income. But the salary she earned as an administrative assistant in a community organization barely paid her bills. Had she completed a bachelor's degree she might have doubled that income as a caseworker.

Christina showed great promise in becoming a well-paid cosmetologist. She was developing a professional competence that might have catapulted her into the role of trainer of hairstylists. Her dreams were stunted as she realized that health problems might curtail her ability to work in her profession. She scaled back her dreams to search for a position as a secretary, wanting a steady salary with benefits and a pension. With her grandmothers as role models, perhaps she may find work that interests and satisfies her needs for physical well-being and financial security.

Michelle seemed deeply interested in computers and saw college as a means of giving her the skills to pursue a career. However, the more technical the course work became, the less interest she took in this field. Throughout her school career, the most significant personal experience she had was through her therapy. She changed in ways that pleased her and made her more socially competent. She was praised by fellow students and professors for her psychological insight and capacity for empathy. She realized that she wanted to develop her ability to help others in need. She graduated with a bachelor's degree in communications and quickly found a job as a caseworker. In her long-range plans, she wants a master's degree in social work, specializing in counseling troubled adolescents.

Derrick hoped for a career in business and finance. He struggled with academic subjects over the five and one half years it took him to earn a bachelor's degree. After several job interviews did not land him a position, he worried about his marketability. In his fantasies, he shuttled between living the dream of emulating George Weiss' career path or following the one his father took. Eventually he found a way of shaping a career that emphasized some elements derived from both role models. He accepted a position working with his uncle selling sports memorabilia at stadiums across the country. As he built up capital, he invested in the stock market. A portion of his earnings allowed him to purchase real estate that brought him some income. The fact that George Weiss' fortune was not an inheritance, rather a result of his hard work over many years, became plausible to Derrick as he sought to build up his own resources. He is the father of one child.

When Richard entered Wharton at the University of Pennsylvania, he expected to fulfill his father's dream of becoming an accountant. By the end of his sophomore year it became obvious to him that he was not suited to pursue a career in business. Like Michelle, he, too, had a transforming experience through therapy. His work with an African-American therapist convinced him that he wanted to make his mark as a Clinical Psychologist. After successful completion of a B.A. degree in Psychology, he married and moved south. The next few years he worked as a therapist treating delinquent adolescents. He developed a critique of how depression envelops inner-city lives where poverty, unemployment offer little hope of escape. When last contacted, he was studying for the Graduate Record Exams and making applications to pursue a doctorate in Psychology.

VIEWS ON RACISM

Collectively, Say Yes students, like adolescents in general, were optimistic about their futures. As African-Americans, however, they were aware of the challenges facing them as they work to find success in and beyond postsecondary schools. The Say Yes students were not only African-Americans and thus subject to being devalued by our society and its schools, but also Blacks from Philadelphia's declining inner-city neighborhoods (Steele 1992). They knew poverty and the social context it creates. C. H. Nightingale contends that inner-city African-American children struggle with three interconnected realities: personal experiences with racism, the material abundance enjoyed by many suburban Americans in contrast to those in inner cities, and violence as an anticipated and unavoidable consequence of daily living (1993).

College offered little respite from racial indignities. Witness Michelle's experience of racism at a campus vigil honoring those that participated in the Million Man March. The women attending the vigil suffered the nasty epithets and the blatant disrespect of a white female student mooning them. Michelle withdrew from interactions with white students. She would not put herself in a position to be hurt by Whites. But Derrick, who had attended the March in Washington, D.C., could not let the incident pass. He felt the university's punishment was not appropriate. Somehow he wanted to understand the motivation behind the insulting behavior. He wanted to make rational sense out of an irrational, deliberate affront. Derrick did not assume all Whites were racist. His deep friendship with his roommate and another white student attested to the fact that he was open to relationships that were reciprocal and genuine.

Michelle distrusted "the system." In her mind the playing field was not level and did not provide equal opportunity. The "glass ceiling" prevented African-American females from rising above certain predetermined limits established by the privileged white male elite that controlled access to better positions. The elite possessed wealth that allowed them to buy superior education, making them competitive for the best positions. For her, gender, class, and racism were interrelated, overlapping concerns. Pierre Bourdieu, in describing the significant role of schooling in perpetuating the maintenance of class distinctions and the distribution of cultural capital, asserts that members of the upper classes are advantaged in their ability to extend their children's tenure in school (1977). While in school they are able to collect a greater measure of cultural capital, which eventually determines their status in society. Michelle understood intuitively how Bourdieu's theory affected her life options.

Roger kept his guard up, recognizing that racism was real and could be found in unsuspecting corners. Yet he, too, was open to friendships with Whites. To his way of thinking, friendship with Whites was synonymous with going to college. He brought white friends to his neighborhood and felt the disapproval of his old friends. His neighborhood friends felt that Roger was rejecting their lifestyle by attending college and fraternizing with Whites. His friendship with Davis cooled as Roger realized that Davis set him up to fight. While there were no overt racial slurs spoken between them, the subtext linked race to class. Roger felt used by Davis to do his dirty work, and he found the condescension unacceptable.

Neither Ebony nor Christina faced direct racist experiences at their postsecondary schools. Ebony felt keenly, nonetheless, the unfairness of needing to live the stereotypes she sensed Whites believed were true. She was willing to fight against prejudice. She asserted,

> I know that it's going to be hard for me. I'm just going to be the best I can be and show people that I'm not a statistic just because I had two children when I was young. I'm not sitting around watching Oprah, or waiting around to collect the next check. I don't want to be someone to feel sorry for. I'm trying to succeed just like anybody else, no matter what color I am.

Christina did not feel oppressed by Whites' stereotypical attitudes towards Blacks. She believed that effort and hard work brought just rewards. She was convinced that "... the opportunity is there. It's up to the individual to take hold of it." Defeating racism was not her struggle.

In contrast, Richard was very much interested in defeating racism. He resented Whites confronting his right to attend, study, and live at an elite university. A keen observer, he noticed the vast difference in expectations between people in his West Philadelphia community and the white students attending Penn. Richard was committed to helping African-Americans lift their depression and take charge of their lives. Richard believed change was possible, and he was willing to make his contribution to that effort.

Although not part of the case studies portrayed here, there were students among the Belmont group who attended Historically Black Colleges and Universities (HBCUs) and had very different experiences in college with respect to race issues. Previous research has shown that African-American students attending HBCUs are better integrated, academically and socially, compared to African-American students attending traditionally white institutions (Fries-Britt 2002). However, the experiences of those in the Belmont group who attended HBCUs revealed potential disadvantages of a predominantly African-American campus. In fact, it is not clear from my analysis that students at HBCUs had fewer obstacles, although they might have had different obstacles.

For example, Say Yes students at Virginia Union complained that gang wars initiated by New York City residents were replayed at the college; a student living on the same floor as Say Yes students was killed in a gang related fight. Two of our students left immediately after that incident, fearful for their lives. One student never adjusted to the rigors of Howard's program and flunked out. On the white campuses, while racism was clearly an issue for many of our students, some students were also relieved to find themselves in an environment so different from their neighborhoods back home.

Presumably, the HBCU environment would give African-American students a chance to focus on their studies without needing to confront the hostility of racism. For some this was certainly true. Several students attending North Carolina Central found the environment supportive and the academics challenging. Those attending Clark Atlanta had a similar experience. For others, gang issues or social opportunities proved a distraction from academic studies.

Conclusion

In concluding this chapter, I consider the following two questions that seem to capture the capacity or inability of SYTE students to use the gift: What are the key stressors that place a student at risk for completing a postsecondary education? And what factors are protective of students, making it more likely that they will finish a postsecondary education? I start with the stressors, and make a distinction between systemic inequities and personal stumbling blocks.

A critical obstacle for the SYTE students was the inadequate education they received from grades one through twelve, and especially grades one through six. The state of Tennessee under the direction of S. P. Wright, S. P. Horn and W. L. Sanders (1997) studied children from two major cities in grades two, three, four, and five over the time span from 1991 through 1995 and found that:

> . . . within grade level the single most dominant factor affecting student achievement gain is teacher effect. Groups of students with comparable ability may have vastly different academic outcomes as a result of the sequence of teachers to which they are assigned. These analyses also suggest that the teacher effects are both additive and cumulative with little evidence of compensatory effects of more

effective teachers in later grades. The residual effects of both very effective and ineffective teachers were measurable two years later, regardless of the effectiveness of teachers in later grades (1997).

While the Say Yes students certainly had some teachers who were effective, inner-city schools populated by poor minority children are likely to have concentrations of less effective teachers. Research in Philadelphia finds a system that encourages experienced and more qualified teachers to move to more advantaged schools, leaving a greater number of teachers who are new to the profession, and many who lack teaching certification, in poor schools (Neild 2003). National research confirms the concentration of unprepared teachers in poor schools; often teachers who are forced to transfer due to their poor performance are assigned to inner-city schools (Bridges 1996). Predictably, these ineffective teachers do not deliver the quality of instruction that can assist students in learning. Their ineffectiveness becomes a drag on children's ability to maintain their level of progress, let alone increase it.

In addition to the quality of teaching experienced, tracking poor students to low-level courses results in an education that does not prepare students for postsecondary coursework. In a national survey of high school students, while one in twelve white students was found to have literacy skills sufficient to learn from specialized materials, only one in one hundred African-American students had the same level of understanding (Ali 2002). The same research finds that only 23 percent of African-Americans are enrolled in college preparatory coursework, compared to 47 percent of all high school students. When SYTE students observed that students from the suburbs and private schools were better prepared to enter college than they were, they were acknowledging the failure of urban school districts to provide qualified and highly capable teachers and a challenging curriculum for those populations that for too long have been deprived.

They are also recognizing that this is an unequal society. Per pupil spending for education in Philadelphia began to decline in 1991 as a result of rising enrollments and failure to keep pace with inflation, from a high of $5,670 per pupil in 1991 to $5,009 per pupil in 1994 (*The Philadelphia Inquirer,* October 14, 1994). Large cities with high concentrations of poor minorities often do not have the tax base to provide a decent education. Beyond the city's contribution, the state abdicated its responsibility to make up the difference. It seems painfully obvious that a school district forced to operate at extreme financial disadvantage is not likely to produce high quality education. Suburban and private schools, able to collect through taxes or tuition income that consists of an additional $2,000 to $8,000 more than Philadelphia, makes hiring effective teachers a norm in those systems but impossible in inner-city school districts.

The effects of these disparities are lower rates of college attendance among poor minority youth and, for those who start college, lower rates of completion. Comparing youth by income quartiles, research from the Education Testing Service finds that 89 percent of youth from the top income quartile entered college, compared to 36 percent in the lowest income quartile (Carnevale and Desrochers 2003). When looking at completion, the data are even more grim. A low-income youth faces 7 to 1 odds that they will complete college, compared to 1.4 to 1 odds for affluent families.

Richard and Michelle were explicitly aware that poor minorities live in an unequal world. Richard noticed that expectations are different depending on the neighborhood and the wealth that does or does not exist to support its citizens. The differences are palpable and set the stage for the life one can expect. Michelle conjoined race and gender with class. Trapped by others' low expectations of her worth, she sensed a conspiracy among the wealthy to keep people like her in their place. Her concern for "respect" seemed similar to Richard's observation that the poor expect little and are not surprised when that is as much as they receive. The wealthy assume respect for their authority, their power, and their capacity to get things done. They expect to be educated and to be able to play major roles in society. In a personal letter to George Weiss, Michelle described a transformational experience that interrupted the inevitable sequence of inner-city life and allowed her to escape. The one wealthy person that she knew over several years did not disappoint her:

> If it wasn't for your generosity, I know that I would not have this chance for higher education. I probably would be just another black person who fell under the statistics of society's failures. With your help and help of the Say Yes program, I already have something that works in my behalf, and that is, I am educated. By being educated, that brings me one step closer to softening the blows of society and two steps away from stereotypes that most of us have been living up to. I know that getting a college

education doesn't automatically mean that you will become successful, but it is a start to something positive, and it can get you
a foot in the door of success.

Michelle knew that her position in life relative to George was
unequal. But she appreciated that he reached back to include her in a
world that had higher expectations of her than she knew previously.

On a more personal level, a major factor that affected students'
academic performance was their need to work. The program offered
students attending postsecondary schools a stipend and a flexible meal
plan. The stipend was adequate, but did not cover discretionary needs.
Most of these students came from working-class families. They were
used to working to earn money. But the need to work was not merely
to pay for entertainment and long distance phone bills. Students were
caught in a cycle of using credit cards as if they had the income to back
up their expenditures. For some, working overtook the primary purpose for being in college. Instead of studies being primary, in some
instances they took third or fourth place. Recall Richard's need to
work thirty hours a week to pay off large consumer debts. A heavy
workload had a negative impact on his studies as well.

Many students could retell the number of hours they should study
in comparison to the actual amount of time they did study. Roger was
eloquent in stating there could be no escape from studying. Similarly,
Derrick insisted that the middle-school youth he mentored in his college
years not get caught up in a favorite sport such as basketball. He wanted
the younger generation to take school seriously. Paradoxically, it was
only in his last year that Derrick "worked off his behind." Often he
mentioned that he was "very intelligent." That statement seemed to
cover his inability to demonstrate what he knew on tests. For Roger
and Derrick, tests were stressful. Both men had ability, but both had
major gaps in their knowledge that may be traced back to an erratic
education in grade school. These gaps were a function of irregular
attendance and lack of consistently effective teachers. While they could
verbalize for others what it would take to make up for their gaps as well
as stay on top of college demands, they were not always able to consistently invest the necessary time and effort themselves.

Moving to the second question, a key protective factor that allowed students to persist was the quality of resilience. The stressors I've
mentioned did set these students back temporarily. But they often

bounced back to continue to shape a more positive future. They were resilient in demonstrating renewed energy and commitment to find their way. Ebony fought for her education, even though the change in the welfare law put overwhelming barriers in her path; she did not want to become a "statistic." Ebony's life was hard. She worked, but hadn't figured out how to finish her degree so that she could improve her job options and salary. Richard was driven to leave a legacy. He had a sense of history and was determined to make his mark for his people as well as for his own self-interest. Derrick reevaluated his work options and realized that he would have to take responsibility for his future. He worked for his uncle, and simultaneously invested his earnings in the stock market, enabling him to purchase some real estate. He realigned his goals toward his father's lifestyle and realized that his future would not imitate George. Christina coped with her health problems and readjusted her goals for the less glamorous kind of work that would give her health benefits and a pension. Christina's identification with her productive and independent grandmothers may enable her to use these role models for inspiration and direction as she charts a different life course. Michelle worked hard to create a life different from her parents. She was reflective about her past, and proactive about her future. Roger was dismissed from college for failure to progress, but quickly recognized that as the father of two children he had adult responsibilities to pay for their upkeep and be a presence in their lives.

Difficulties adjusting to the rigors of college coursework, emotional turmoil, health problems, and family complications changed the paths of many of the students who started college with ambitious goals. In addition to the obvious benefit of a full scholarship to college, the program provided something invaluable to all the students who accepted the challenge. In their own way, each story shows a struggle to imagine different futures and the desire to make that future real. What they all got out of the program, regardless of how they used the scholarship, was an expanded sense of self, a larger appreciation of possibilities to be lived and an understanding of the education necessary to inhabit a desired future.

CHAPTER 6

Conclusion

Of the 112 sixth graders who were chosen to receive a fully paid college education and all the supports deemed necessary to achieve that goal, twenty earned bachelor's degrees. Another fourteen completed technical training and ten completed associate's degrees. While the case studies in earlier chapters reveal a complicated web of events, struggles, and distractions from the goal of getting to and finishing a program of higher education, this chapter identifies not only what made it likely for individual youth to succeed, but also what contexts facilitated their journeys. I also identify some of the structural impediments that block the way out of poverty for the vast majority of inner-city youth. In this final chapter, I explore these findings in some detail, and suggest policy implications that can be—and in some cases already have been—drawn from the experience of the Belmont 112. First, however, I turn to an analysis of the financial costs and benefits of the program.

Cost–Benefit Analysis

This study confirms what earlier studies have found: tuition guarantee programs can have a positive effect on educational attainment of inner-city youth (Schlesinger 1993, U.S. GAO 1990). These programs are also cost-effective; the investment made over a decade or more on a youth dwarfs costs to society in terms of reduced criminality and reliance on government benefits, and of increased productivity (Davis 1998). Looking just at increases in average work-life earnings, the investment in the Belmont 112 shows a healthy return.

The program spent, on average, $1,200 per student, per year, from grade seven through grade 12. Including college expenses, the program spent a total of $5 million. It should be noted here that college costs were higher than they perhaps could have been; students were given complete latitude in choosing their colleges and many chose private institutions over less expensive public universities. Despite perhaps higher than necessary costs, the program benefits far outweighed the investment. If we compare lifetime earnings of SYTE students to adults in their neighborhood based on educational attainment, we can conservatively say the Belmont group will earn an additional 11.6 million dollars over their lifetimes.

The average lifetime earnings of an African-American who did not graduate high school is $800,000 (U.S. Census Bureau 2002). This compares to a lifetime earnings of $1 million for an African-American with a high school diploma and $1.7 for an African-American completing four years of college. While these numbers are lower than the lifetime earnings of a white non-Hispanic, it is clear that regardless of race, additional education results in significant earnings differences.

Beginning at the high school graduate level, when we compare SYTE outcomes to 1990 Census data for the Belmont feeder area, we find that twenty-three additional students finished high school beyond what Census data would have predicted. The difference between not having a high school diploma and having a diploma translates into a $200,000 difference per person over a lifetime. Multiplied by twenty-three, we can say that an additional $4,600,000 of income will be earned by that group of twenty-three over their work lives.

On the other end of the education spectrum, we find that twenty SYTE students attained bachelor's degrees. Looking at Census data for the Belmont area, only 6 percent of adults had bachelor's degrees in 1990. As 6 percent of the Belmont group would have been six students attaining bachelor's degrees, we can therefore say that an additional fourteen students attained bachelor's degrees as a result of the SYTE intervention. If we conservatively assume that these fourteen would have completed some college without the SYTE intervention, the difference between "some college" and a bachelor's degree over a lifetime is $500,000. Multiplied by fourteen, an additional $7 million dollars will be earned by these fourteen in their work lives.

The more than $11 million generated by the SYTE intervention is a conservative estimate; it does not include reduced costs to government as a result of lower rates of criminality and use of public assistance. Also, I have only made estimates for the high school graduates and college graduates; an additional twenty-four students finished some college compared to Census tract data.

Defining Success

While the number of SYTE college graduates and the cost-benefit analysis might provide a sense of how much the program was able to accomplish, the case studies in earlier chapters make clear that defining success is not simple. Say Yes differs from other sponsorship programs in that it doesn't measure its success solely by the number of students it places in higher education. Rather, Say Yes measures its success individual by individual, giving each student the tools and supports necessary to become productive, self-directed, and contributing members of society. Similarly, many of the students had different ideas about success, and defined success variously depending on circumstances and context.

H. Varenne and R. McDermott (1998) highlight "the arbitrary and limiting nature of the categories 'success' and 'failure.' They are not categories that can ever capture the good sense of what children do. They directly conspire to prevent all of us from understanding the conditions within which the child's life is constructed" (p 3). While SYTE advocated for their students to reach various benchmarks of educational success, it is instructive to acknowledge Varenne and McDermott's notion of the limitation of success and failure labels. These labels tend to divert our attention from the personal experiences and the many factors of context, culture, and structure that frame student outcomes.

Explicitly, success in Say Yes was measured by several important milestones, including graduation from high school and whether a student was able to fully capitalize on the gift and obtain postsecondary certification. However, one must also consider the diverse routes of day-to-day implicit victories—moments of success and resilience that are not documented by statistics of completion.

In addition to recognizing that paths to desired goals are harder for some than for others, the very notions of success held by the SYTE students, staff, sponsors, and the media were diverse. Depending on one's frame of reference, success might be defined as being a good mother or a father, not being in jail, or simply being alive. Conversely, from a middle-class perspective, one might define anything less than a college degree as failure. Not only were these perceptions diverse, they influenced students in complicated ways. For example, Derrick states: "I'm twenty-four-years old, that's scary. I was twenty-one yesterday and thirty is not that far off. I don't want to be a failure. You know I'm very intelligent. I'm a very smart guy and I'm just scared to fail." Derrick seemed to struggle with proving to himself, the sponsors, and other observers his intention to succeed and he was frustrated with not always measuring up to his own and others' expectations. Derrick struggles as an adolescent with the upheaval of his family, the drug-dependency of his mother and the additional responsibilities of caring for younger siblings. His school performance was frequently inadequate and his attendance sporadic. He took five-and-a-half years to graduate from college and his performance was always borderline. Yet, he managed to graduate. Pushing past what would otherwise have been expected, Derrick used his broadened perception of self to mentor young black male adolescents in middle school, showing them the explicit steps needed to succeed in college and how to be educationally focused.

Marcus, on the other hand, had difficulty identifying with the notion of success the program offered. He was not successful in school; conflicting forces tore at him. In his mind, his father, in prison for murder, proved that a two-year college degree doesn't help you lead a successful life, while his mother represented a model of how to make a successful life without acquiring a high school diploma, let alone advanced degrees. He seemed to be taking his mother's path, but also realized that, in contemporary society, more education opens possibilities for better employment. Marcus expressed a dual consciousness reminiscent of that described by W. E. B. Du Bois (1903) in *The Souls of Black Folks*:

> The negro is a sort of seventh son, born with a veil and gifted with second sight in this American world—in a world which yields him no true self-consciousness, this sense of also looking at one's self through the eyes of others, of measuring one's self through the eyes of others, of measuring one's soul by the tape of a world that looks on in amused contempt and pity. (p. 8)

The social conditions that frame the lives of SYTE students are unstable yet bounded. Marcus, in particular, is keenly aware of discrepancies in the opportunities available to him. He views himself and other

SYTE students through the dual consciousness lens that Du Bois refers to. He sees himself through the eyes of the media and the outer society as he acknowledges that he is without a name; his identity has become a Say Yes composite kid (synonymous for poor, black kid). He is keenly aware that despite the opportunities and prospect of college afforded to him as well as other students in the program, they may still be destined to become negative statistics.

While the SYTE vision for the students is antithetical to the larger societal vision of a poor black student, Marcus internalizes both perceptions and feels the struggle and tension of both pressures. Marcus is aware of a dual framework in which the larger social hierarchy produces black students who become statistics, in contrast to the SYTE vision that attempts to provide supports for a counter, alternate outcome through college graduation or vocational school certification.

Richard's educational success mirrored the sponsors' higher standard of expectations, illustrated by graduation from a magnet high school and by, for the most part, above average academic performance and graduation from the University of Pennsylvania. Unlike many of his peers, this was facilitated by a number of factors: he grew up in a two-parent household, was labeled as mentally gifted, and received a strict religious upbringing. However, despite attaining a relatively higher status of education than his colleagues, Richard's path was anything but linear. His route was marked by a series of successes and setbacks as he developed his sense of self and accommodated his educational path to reflect this broadened understanding. His high school years were marked by periods of disengagement with the program and academic lows. During his college years, Richard shifted from pursuing a business degree to one in psychology, a career goal that reflected his acceptance of personal strengths and educational passions.

Richard internalized his personal notions of success, linked to fulfilling goals that were congruent with his talents and interests and translating his professional success into answering questions and presenting solutions that will help his community. Richard's larger social critique of the meaning of success sanctioned by the American white status quo found that the white establishment does not want to examine "what it would take to make most African-Americans successful. . . . I don't think they are willing to do what's necessary." Having lived in multiple worlds and having acquired a wider frame of reference, Richard perceived divergent world views:

> The biggest difference I saw was expectations, what people expect in a salary, what you expect from society, what you expect from your government. The difference was just huge. It's like one group really didn't expect, they were lucky to have a good day. And the other groups expected success in just about everything they went about.

Richard articulates an essential contribution of Say Yes to Education. The opportunity established a tension, remarked upon earlier, in which students were challenged to view the world and their potential to shape it through expanded expectations. These expectations brought many students to a place where their visions of self became a sustaining impetus in a quest for success and recognition.

When looking forward to new cohorts and new programs, a fundamental question is how success is defined and by whom. The goal of Say Yes is to build capacity within students so they can take advantage of education and thereby move out of poverty. On the other hand, decisions about how much and what kind of education ultimately must be left to the student. Is there a danger that a program like Say Yes can in effect steal a participant's identity, in an effort to replace it with one that fits the middle-class definition of success? Certainly there were those in the program who felt this was the case. In the group counseling session described in an earlier chapter, three students spoke to the pressure to "succeed," which they felt was defined by the sponsors as graduating from college. Others in the program were able to use the resources available to them to expand their worldviews, and thereby define success in a way that was different from both the program and their peers or the adults in their neighborhood. A program like Say Yes, then, must recognize the delicate balance needed between offering students the prospect of another life and imposing one's view of what that life should be.

Obstacles to College Completion

Complicating this decisionmaking process, however, was the fact that despite our best efforts, many of our students were simply not prepared for college coursework. As discussed in earlier chapters, the low state share in education spending, a state funding formula that does not equalize spending, and reliance on the local tax base has guaranteed an unequal funding system across the state, with urban and rural areas having significantly fewer resources available for education compared to suburban areas. For the Belmont 112, schools with inadequate funding were ill-prepared to address the multiple challenges youth brought to school; special education became a dumping ground for those students with learning as well as behavioral problems. Once sorted into these classrooms, special education failed many it was intended to serve. Two other obstacles that slowed or halted the progress of too many Say Yes students, the emotional strain of living in a high-poverty urban environment and the explosion in teen pregnancy in the 1980s, are also discussed in this section.

SPECIAL EDUCATION

Five of the six students profiled who did not complete high school were labeled learning disabled and placed in special education classrooms. Of the fifty-three learning disabled students in the Belmont group, only twelve (26 percent) graduated. In the comparison group, the results were four out of twenty-four (17 percent). Thirty-eight SYTE students eventually dropped out—fifteen females and twenty-three males. The majority (72 percent) was identified as learning disabled and had been placed in special education. Placement in special education classes, in the perceptions of the students and as borne out by statistics, more often than not leads to dropping out of high school. Research has found that remedial education programs actually contribute to a child's learning problems; students in remedial education often receive inferior instruction and are less likely to be academically challenged or to receive instruction in higher-order cognitive skills (Baker, Wang, and Walberg 1994, and Wang, Reynolds and Walberg 1988). This combination of poverty and a learning disability appears to place youth at greater risk of moving toward a life of antisocial behavior. As evidenced in this program and as supported by research, there exists a strong association between poverty, being learning disabled, dropping out, becoming an adjudicated delinquent and eventually being convicted as an adult felon (Fujiura & Yamaki 2000; Wolfgang et al. 1987; Kaye et al. 1996).

In five of the six case studies of the dropouts, students were involved in the drug trade. In at least four of the five cases, criminal activity led to criminal charges and in some cases incarceration. Of the thirty-nine students who did not complete high school, twenty-four

(61.5 percent) were adjudicated delinquents. Data from 2000 show that 16 percent of the original Belmont 112 were incarcerated as adults. Again, a connection can be made between involvement in the drug trade and special education status. The chapter profiling the dropouts documents efforts by program sponsors and staff to stop students from drug dealing. Students in regular education classes on the whole listened and stopped drug dealing; for those labeled as special education students, most saw no other options. Related to involvement in the drug trade, one must consider the all-encompassing effect of American consumerism on black children living in poverty; while for some the income from drug sales provided basic needs for themselves and their families, the case studies of the dropouts offer ample evidence to suggest that consumerism was a driving force for many of the youth interviewed.

Emotional Strain

The inner-city environment presents numerous obstacles to educational achievement. The multiple strains of living in a poor urban environment have been equated with the post-traumatic stress disorder experienced by a veteran of war. Random violence, financial instability, frequent relocations, and a limited support network contribute to anxiety, depression, anger, and low self-esteem (Huston 1994). In addition to psychological strain, living in a poor urban minority neighborhood also poses a physical health risk. More than gunshots or drug abuse, chronic diseases make mortality rates higher in inner cities than anywhere else (Epstein 2003) In four of the six dropout stories, there is evidence of significant emotional instability. For Cory, low self-esteem led to a suicide attempt. Anthony's defiance and difficulty communicating with his father led to him dropping out of school in the eighth grade and joining his brothers in the drug trade. Tyree was an aggressive child given to fits of rage, who ultimately committed suicide. Shamira had a history of a lack of emotional control and excessive fighting throughout her school years before eventually dropping out. In addition to the responses described above, many youth chose to bear children, perhaps in order to fill an emotional void that grew from a childhood in poverty.

Teen Pregnancy

The effect of teen pregnancy on the ability of youth to take advantage of educational opportunity cannot be ignored. The issue of teen pregnancy has now receded from the national spotlight, largely due to a decline in the teen pregnancy rate in recent years. Over the time period this book addresses, however, the teen birth rate was at its peak, and was highest in the African-American community. From 1986 to 1991, teen pregnancy nationwide rose 24 percent. In 1991 the teen birthrate was at its highest, at 114.8 births per 1,000 African-American women aged 15–19. By 2000, that rate had dropped to 77.4 births per 1,000 (Alan Guttmacher Institute 2004).

At the peak of the explosion in teen pregnancy, the phenomenon appeared to be what sociologists call "social contagion" (Crane 1991), in which there doesn't seem to be a rational explanation for what is occurring. The phenomenon continues to explode and then, inexplicably, subsides. Nationally, proponents of the 1996 welfare reform law argue that the stringent rules limiting benefits may have inhibited young women from becoming pregnant. This is, however, difficult to document. The subsiding of the phenomenon may be as irrational as the phenomenon itself.

Recognizing the potential impact of unplanned pregnancy on the educational futures of its participants, the Say Yes to Education program provided an eighteen-hour summer course to all students in the summer between seventh and eighth grade, and provided workshops throughout the high school years on relationships and human sexuality. Despite this intervention and the advantage of being part of SYTE, twenty-two of the forty-five girls in the Belmont 112 gave birth before their nineteenth birthdays. The numbers are similar for the Tell Them We Are Rising program; twenty-two of fifty-six girls had babies in their teenage years. An analysis of the Say Yes pregnancies finds that teen births in the program peaked in 1992, when the majority of the teen mothers—fifteen of the twenty-two—were seventeen or eighteen years old. In 1992, 13 percent of the Belmont females delivered their first child; 17 percent (4) delivered either a first or a second child. Nationally in 1992, the African-American teen birthrate was 111.3 per 1,000, or 11 percent (Guttmacher 2004).

Research in 1989 found that adolescent mothers experience disadvantages in educational attainment and educational well-being (Furstenburg 1989). While the same research found that these disadvantages disappear over time, the immediate effect of adolescent motherhood may have affected teen mothers' participation in the SYTE program. The chapter profiling high school graduates notes that males had significantly higher high school graduation rates than did females in the program. One explanation may be the effect on the males of intensive counseling by Randall Sims and a variety of outside mentors who were important male role models. An alternative explanation may be that because so many SYTE females had babies in their high school years, their ability to take advantage of the program was significantly affected. At the same time, the fact that the teen pregnancy among SYTE participants was consistent with TTWAR and national teen pregnancy rates complicates common assumptions about teen mothers. Despite the exhortations of R. Maynard (1997) and other economists, who point to the dramatic costs—human, financial, and social—of teen parenting, twenty-two of forty-five Say Yes girls—all of whom were exposed to hope for the future and the resources to help them achieve it—gave birth to children before their nineteenth birthdays.

One cannot assume that only those without goals or without alternatives are immersed in a culture of young parenting—the majority of Say Yes women in college were mothers. In fact, two delivered children as juniors in college. One cannot assume that access to educational resources alone will address the issue—the Say Yes students knew at the end of sixth grade that their educational futures were secure. One cannot assume that young people in the inner city share mainstream society's perception that a teenage pregnancy is a mistake. Despite the prevalent view that "when the stress of two developmental stages, adolescence and young adulthood are compressed, successful completion of both sets of tasks are compromised" (Rodriguez and Moore 1995, 687), the fact is that several of the Belmont 112 students were both successful students and responsible mothers. Several students who had children identified their new status as a mother as a critical factor in their determination to pursue higher education. Recall Ebony's sense that her children were her "most important influence." Of course, others were distracted from their education by the challenge of child rearing. However, that so many Say Yes women opted to deliver children suggests that there must be a benefit to this behavior. For young people in the inner city, a baby is a form of capital—understood, accepted, and valued. Those who influence social policy and who choose to address teen pregnancy must begin from this perspective.

Programs and institutions must reflect the needs of the students and be flexible. It is an illusion that life is rational, or a straight path for everyone. Institutions act as if development occurs by scaling levels of difficulty and complexity in sequence. The lives of the poor are out of sequence; they move in abrupt jerks rather than smooth lines. For those in the Belmont 112 who completed high school, the continuity and flexibility provided by the program in otherwise turbulent lives and the ongoing presence of supportive adult mentors were crucial factors in their success. In addition to elements of their personalities that facilitated making use of the gift, the expansion of their worldviews allowed participants to attempt to move beyond earlier conceptions of their presumed life paths. As notions of self expanded, so did a student's sense of agency to shape and influence their communities and wider world.

Sources of Success

This research finds there are three factors that can improve educational outcomes for many more youth than are succeeding in urban schools today. These factors—the presence and development of resilience; the interaction between youth and mentors; and, importantly, contexts that nurture and challenge youth to move beyond their lives in poverty—are discussed below.

RESILIENCE

A growing body of literature has emerged that considers resilience and the factors that enable individuals to achieve goals despite adversity. Resilience has been defined as "the process of, capacity for, or outcome of successful adaptation despite challenging or threatening circumstances" (Masten et al. 1990, 426). Ebony fought for her education, even though the change in the welfare law placed overwhelming barriers in her path; she did not want to become a "statistic." Christina, who developed back problems that compromised her ability to continue her work as a cosmetologist, coped with her health problems and readjusted her goals for the less glamorous kind of work that would give her health benefits and a pension. However, resilience is often not as clear as these examples suggest. A full accounting of any of the life histories of the Belmont 112 would show the unrelenting strain of living in poverty and a continuous movement forward and backward as students made their way through their adolescence. This is consistent with the current understanding of resilience, which finds that, "resilience is not a trait of an individual, though individuals manifest resilience in their behavior and patterns." (Masten and Powell 2003, 4). It is not possible for an individual to be resilient in all aspects of their lives, consistently throughout all stages of their lives. There are moments of resilience and moments of vulnerability. As M. B. Spencer finds, a limited intervention over only one period in the life of a youth who lives his or her entire life under adverse conditions is not sufficient. A key element of the SYTE program is that even when students moved backwards, when they stepped away from the program, when they became involved in drug use or criminal behavior, the program never stopped trying to support them.

In our experience with the Belmont 112 and with classes since, we have found that resilience is not a personality trait that is either present or not. We agree with recent research that finds that resilience "doesn't cause children to do well in the face of adversity. Rather, resilience reflects the developmental process by which children acquire the ability to use both internal and external resources to achieve positive adaptation despite prior or concomitant adversity." (Yates et. al. 2003, 250). The SYTE program, by intervening in school systems on student's behalf; by providing tutoring, mentoring, counseling, exposure to alternative career paths; and even by providing a safe and quiet place to work, allowed students to be resilient.

The sources of success among SYTE students are varied and complex, and a dynamic process of personal development accompanied gains and widened perceptions of self. As discussed in the high school graduates chapter, navigating the status passage toward higher education requires resilience. Richard stripped his environment of all distractions and willed himself to study and achieve. Students like Ebony, Roger, and Derrick complained about the pressure, but often found ways to use the program to help them move forward; others like Christina and Marcus found the pressures to live in the new status passage too foreign and discomfiting. For them, their comfort zones hewed to the lives they had always known.

TRUSTING RELATIONSHIPS AND CONTINUITY OF CARING

A key quality of people who exhibit resilient behavior is that they learn to appreciate the value of people who can help them develop productive goals and effective behaviors in the pursuit of their goals. Numerous studies on tuition guarantee programs point out the turbulence in the lives of inner-city youth and the persistence required of program staff in keeping students connected to the program. Research conducted by the U.S. Department of Education recognizes the important role of mentors and suggests that mentoring can have a significant impact on a youth (Nunez and Cuccaro-Alamin 1998). A U.S. GAO report on tuition guarantee programs found that half of operating programs cited strong mentor and staff relationships as a key factor in the success of the program (1990). At one time early in the life of the SYTE program fifty mentors were actively participating with at least one student. Over a period of years, as is typical in a mentoring program, this number dropped to twenty-five. The mentors who remained were those who could relate to the students and invest the time and energy to provide real support.

Sometimes more powerful than the formal mentor pairings are the relationships that develop with project coordinators, teachers, a therapist, or even a parent. These were also mentors, without the official title. SYTE sponsors and staff made a long-term commitment: Randall Sims was with the program for fourteen years; George Weiss and I for over eighteen years. The continuity of caring had an invaluable effect on the development of the SYTE students.

Research on tuition guarantee programs acknowledges the central importance of the project coordinator (PC). He or she is the person students bond with. The PC, like a parent, makes a full time commitment to help students sustain their interest in the long climb toward high school graduation and then matriculation in some form of postsecondary education. Many of the students felt particularly close to Randall. Several students thought of him as their father. Three quarters of the Belmont 112 did not live with their father or didn't know him. An abiding male presence was hard to find in many of these families. The Say Yes students felt that Randall would always respond to their needs. As Michelle recalled, "Sims follows up on how we're doing in education and work. But he goes beyond that, he gets into personal business. Sims, you know, just making sure everything's cool." Several students noted that Randall was "cool," someone they could relate to much like a parent or older brother. It was Randall's unfailing persistence that sent a message to the Say Yes students that he would not give up on them. Martin, whose father was not to be found and whose mother abandoned him in early childhood was graphic in describing the level of Randall's commitment: "He made sure I came down to

SAT tutoring, made sure I got out of bed, made sure that if he asked me to go on a trip that I went even though I didn't want to get out of my bed and go. He's just cool and I consider him somewhat like a father, you know, a person I can look up to."

The degree to which staff and sponsors became a strong presence in the lives of these children cannot be overstated. Ebony connected to the Weisses and responded to their difficulties as though they were her own parents. More commonly, many of the students developed strong relationships with one or more of the staff or sponsors, and came to rely on them for emotional support.

These relationships also enabled the expansion of the student's worldviews, an essential component in envisioning their futures. In Roger's case, for example, the University of Pennsylvania scientist, Aunt Nicole, Mike Christiani, and Ms. Vaddy mobilized to help him visualize a life different from his mother's. For Michelle, the people who expanded her understanding of a better future for herself included her therapist, Mr. Muller, her English teacher, and Randall Sims. Ms. Little and Diane mentored and supported Ebony so that she could move forward after her mother's death. And George and the Human Services staff helped Derrick survive his stressful and debilitating home life. In addition, SYTE staff was available to coach, cajole and support students who showed signs of receptivity to accepting their help.

This receptivity does not always come naturally or easily. I saw repeatedly how students resist accepting help with academic, social, or personal problems. They have internalized a macho/cool attitude that makes help seeking a sign of weakness (Nelson-LeGall & Jones 1991). Students are afraid they will suffer derision by their peers if they are seen to accept help. But some of the reluctance to ask for help goes beyond peer culture, growing from a definition of school as hostile, intrusive, and unreliable, especially for low-income students who experience frequent failure. An attitude of "hypermasculinity" some youth adopt may be a coping response to a society that does not respect young African-American males; this reactive behavior may be more effective in generating respect by peers when respect is not forthcoming in schools or larger society. By contrast, Michelle, Roger, Derrick, Richard, Christina, and Ebony learned to use help in varying degrees because the context in which they received it was perceived to be caring and trustworthy.

In accepting help, they learned to value their abilities to learn and succeed academically, and developed an appreciation for interdependence—not independence (without others) or dependence (on others). The pressure of higher expectations was motivating. They began to appreciate the value of standards and the connection between knowledge and their capacity to improve their life's circumstances. In the past, "possible selves" for Roger and Michelle were mostly negative. Now they could expand their self-concept to include selves they would very much like to become (Markus and Nurius 1986). I am not suggesting that their lives were problem free. They were not. George's public criticism of Derrick, Roger's baseball bat incident, Richard's financial difficulties—these stumbles could set them back, sometimes dramatically. They walked an emotional tightrope between their negative reactions to stress and adversity and the more positive response of resilience (Rutter 1987; Newberg and Sims 1996).

Michelle, Derrick, Ebony, Christina, Richard, and Roger's stories are about individual resiliency. They did bounce back, and for them as individuals, that is important. But their stories may be more generalizable, because they are about the contexts that create and sustain resiliency. Human Services and the Motivation Program are the kinds of school environments that grow resilient students by building trusting relationships (Noddings 1992). These organizations avoid the traditional stance of a school organized to make success a scarce commodity. Instead, they present contexts that instill and engage commitment and challenge students as well as teachers and administrators. The partnerships that emerged from Say Yes's engagement in the public schools that were serving the Belmont group had an effect that extended beyond helping its participants. In Philadelphia, Say Yes has been able to promote restructuring at the elementary and high school levels in several schools that resulted in closer monitoring of student progress and advocating for greater responsiveness to all children's academic and social needs, including specialized learning problems. The resulting continuity of caring provided a sense of stability in the lives of students whose lives outside of school were often chaotic.

Considerable recent research has shown higher reading, math, and science scores in K–8 schools compared to middle schools (Pardini 2002). It has been posited that part of the reason for the superior performance of students in K–8 schools is the continuity of experience in the K–8 models (Colardarci and Hancock 2002). Fewer transitions into new and different environments and smaller schools offers the advantage of being known by teachers over the course of multiple years and provides a continuity of caring that we have seen is so essential to inner-city youth. Beyond the school itself, by working with higher education institutions, Say Yes has helped integrate social services, educational programs, medical and mental health services that promote a caring environment in schools.

Beyond the Belmont 112: Impact of the Program

The Belmont 112 were active participants in reshaping their futures; they also guided the program staff and sponsors through development of the program, illuminating the strengths and weaknesses of the original vision for SYTE, which evolved in two major ways—to start earlier and include the whole family.

STARTING EARLIER

As SYTE started new chapters, each of these reflected course corrections learned from older SYTE programs. The original program (Belmont) started with entering seventh grade students. Experience as well as educational research urged us to start earlier. Previous research has shown that it is possible to identify potential dropouts very early in their educational careers (Meyer et al. 1991). Others have shown that early school achievement is a strong predictor of high school completion (Stroup and Robins 1972). We were also interested in reaching students before the "fourth grade slump," the sudden drop-off between third and fourth grade in the reading scores of low-income students (Chall et. al. 1990). Recognizing the need to intervene earlier in the lives of the children chosen to participate in the SYTE program, subsequent classes of SYTE have been identified as early as kindergarten. The new model recognizes that establishing a connection with children early allows the program the best opportunity to capitalize on their strengths and requires less remediation of neglected problems (Bogaines 1993). In 1990 the Hartford chapter was launched with seventy-six students in fifth grade; in 1991, the Jane and Robert Toll chapter began in Philadelphia with fifty-eight third graders and Cambridge, MA with sixty-nine children in third grade. With the Bryant chapter in Philadelphia, the program began with fifty kindergartners and their families (2000). Starting at kindergarten offered opportunities to capitalize on preferred practices that should produce students who feel more confident and competent as learners. Educational research asserts that children must be competent readers by the end of third grade if they are to succeed in the mastery of academic subjects in fourth grade where reading for information takes precedence over the mechanics of reading. To meet that need, Say Yes added a reading teacher to its staff that works with Say Yes children from kindergarten through the end of fourth grade (Thomas-Reynolds 2005). Parents were pleased that their children received help in reading, but they informed staff that their children also needed additional instruction in math. To that end, we invited a math education professor from Penn's Graduate School of Education and one of her doctoral students to work with students and parents to improve math skills. Preliminary data suggests that SYTE children at Bryant were improving their math and language arts skills at a higher rate than an in-school comparison group (Gold and Hartman 2004). While these data are promising, they represent only one year, 2003–04. We will be able to make stronger statements about results in two or three years. We can tentatively say that the added support in reading and math appear to be making a positive difference in student outcomes.

INCLUDING THE FAMILY

It was never the intention of the program to become a surrogate family for the participants. Research on resilience in children, however, confirms that "adaptive distancing" enables resilient children to move away from disordered families and access other adults and resources that are more beneficial to their growth (Chess 1989). Given the difficulty several families had in caring for their children it was inevitable that SYTE would pick up the slack. Rather than accepting that resilient children will move away from less positive family connections and connect to a program sponsor, staff or mentor, the retooled model targets the whole family for intervention, offering parents and siblings scholarships for education. This move is also supported by research that shows the importance of good parent/child relationships in the development of resilient children (Rutter 1990). Fostering family involvement in schools has been shown to have multiple positive affects, both for the youth and for the parents. Parents who participate in family involvement programs were found to feel better about themselves and were more likely to enroll in courses that advanced their own educations (Flaxman & Inger, 1991). The changes implemented in the Bryant chapter were more inclusive of the entire family in significant ways. Both parents may receive support in completing a GED and tuition to a community college or vocational training program. And siblings receive partial support toward tuition at a four-year college.

Of course, not all families have the capacity to accept the challenge. There may be families that are too stressed and resource poor to be able to help their children. In these instances the child is at great risk and even extraordinary intervention may not be enough to make a positive difference. Shantih, a mother who asked authorities to label her child as incorrigible is one example; also Kenny's mother, who fought violently with him, forcing him to live in one home after another. Say Yes is a powerful intervention, but it cannot address some of the deepest kind of familial dysfunction and criminal behavior.

Each Say Yes chapter shared the same common overarching goal for Say Yes in improving the educational outcomes for poor minority children. But each chapter had autonomy in how they would pursue their objectives based on the staff and the talents they brought to the work. The Hartford Chapter began in October 1990, when seventy-six fifth-grade students from the Annie Fisher Elementary School visited the University of Hartford and received the same promise of assistance that the Belmont students had received just three years earlier in Philadelphia. Hartford recruited high school faculty and staff to mentor the Say Yes students. The chapter was linked to the University of Hartford's Scholars Program, which contributes half of tuition expenses at the University of Hartford for public school graduates. In addition, Hartford staff and local sponsors Morton and Irma Handel organized weekend retreats with students that focused on human sexuality, respect, and responsibility in relationships, and conflict resolution within school and the workplace.

The Jane and Robert Toll chapter began in October 1990 with fifty-eight third grade students from a West Philadelphia elementary school. The Tolls built relationships with their students and their families by advocating for their academic and social needs. They were especially interested in encouraging students to read for pleasure and to improve writing skills. Students in the Toll program, like the Belmont students who preceded them, benefited from links to the University of Pennsylvania.

In June 1991, the fourth chapter of SYTE was established in Cambridge, MA, when Lesley University entered into a partnership with the SYTE Foundation and the Cambridge public school district.

Sixty-nine entering third graders at the Harrington Elementary School comprised the new Say Yes group. The collaboration with Lesley University has provided the Cambridge Chapter with access to varied human and institutional resources available through the University's many programs. One of the unique features of the Cambridge Chapter is the ethnic background of its student population. Most of the students are either immigrants or first generation Americans, representing many cultures and ethnic origins including African-American, Caribbean Black, Portuguese, Haitian, Asian, Hispanic, and Caucasian. The Cambridge Chapter has played a key role in restructuring efforts at the Harrington School, the elementary school most SYTE students attended. SYTE staff worked closely with the Harrington administration and faculty to develop strategies for team teaching and grade level cluster development, interdisciplinary and thematic teaching, portfolio assessment and before-and-after school programs (Hurd et. al. 1999).

The Bryant chapter in Philadelphia was launched in the fall of 2000 with fifty kindergartners and their families. At the opening event George Weiss offered the following challenge to the expectant parents: "If you pledge to do your share, I promise to educate you and your entire family." In addition to intensive instruction in language arts and math, the Bryant chapter emphasizes a rich Afrocentric curriculum each summer through a six-week Freedom School program. Students study academic skills in the morning and the afternoons are devoted to arts, crafts, history, and values derived from various African cultures. The summer program involves siblings and parents as members of the school community.

Say Yes intends to expand nationally. New York will be the first city to have five chapters operating simultaneously. Those chapters opened in the fall of 2004 and use the total family model of intervention that is in operation at the Bryant school. Each New York chapter will consist of seventy-five families with a total of 400 families participating. Once these chapters are in operation, Say Yes will expand to an additional ten cities. SYTE also served as a model for national legislation, the GEAR-UP program.

GEAR-UP

In 1998, Congressman Chaka Fattah (D–PA) scored a legislative victory when his first major education initiative, GEAR-UP (Gaining Early Awareness and Readiness for Undergraduate Programs), was passed.

Modeled after Say Yes to Education and Tell Them We Are Rising, GEAR-UP partners students from low-income schools with colleges and universities to significantly increase the number of low-income students who are prepared to enter and succeed in postsecondary education. Similar to SYTE, and unique among federal early intervention programs, GEAR-UP focuses efforts on cohorts of low-income students rather than on individuals. This unified focus compels school systems and postsecondary institutions to focus on systemic change that will have lasting effects for the cohort and beyond. As of FY 2002, 251 university partnerships and 28 state programs were serving nearly 1.3 million students. It is currently the federal government's only whole school 7–16 reform model. An early evaluation of the GEAR-UP program finds that the projects offer tutoring, college planning activities, summer programs, and professional development (U.S. Department of Education 2003). Data on high school and college outcomes will not be available for several years.

Giving Back

In addition to helping this group of students through their education so that they could improve their own lot, the program hoped to provide them with the tools so that they could make their own contribution to their community. As described in chapter one, M. Mauss' notion of giving engenders indebtedness. The paradox in the case of the gift given by SYTE is that a high quality education is not something someone should have to ask for. In our society, the wealth of one's parents should not determine the degree of access one has to quality education. In a reconsideration of Mauss' important work on gift-giving, A. D. Schrift finds that the gift "must also be unnecessary to the receiver; it must be excessive, for if it is needed, it loses its status as gift" (1997). Certainly the larger community (through the media) perceived the offer made by the Weisses as a very generous gift. In my view, quite possibly shared by some of the now older and wiser Belmont 112, an empowering education, once it is experienced, does not feel like a gift as much as it does a necessary part of one's growth and development. While this may be a sentiment felt by some of the SYTE students, it is also true that many voice that sense of indebtedness and a desire to share their gift with others who face the same obstacles they did. Recall Richard's commitment to a Belmont graduating class that he would raise funds to contribute to their college educations. Others made career decisions reflecting their desire to help their community. Ebony explains her career choice this way:

> That's why I'm going into the field that I'm going into. Somebody has to care about these children, these low-income families. Somebody has to give back because everybody's just taking and leaving and that just leaves everybody out here to fend on their own. And some people need the help. . . . So I mean, I do feel it's my duty, not even as a Say Yes, but as a human being to help other people.

Like Richard, Christina intends to establish a scholarship fund. Hers would be available to females who graduate high school and wish to become cosmetologists. But her interest in giving back was not limited to helping the next generation progress. She felt that SYTE students had an obligation to rescue those SYTE students who had dropped out and were struggling. She mentioned her idea to Randall Sims who agreed to organize a few SYTE students into an outreach committee. "We need to talk with them and see what's wrong." Articulating a plan for helping the dropouts, she questioned:

> Where did we lose them at? We need to try to help them get back on track. Instead of people belittling them and putting them down, try to bring them back to reality. Because times are about to get real hard and they need that kind of support. And if they know we care and that somebody does care, then maybe they'll straighten out and become better people. So, for example, I know that Rolland is getting ready to come out of jail. So the outreach committee was thinking about having people that have been in jail like Malik who has been in jail and is now out and doing good, talk to Rolland. Maybe he won't fall back in the same trap again. Maybe he'll take up a trade and become something.

Illustrating her point, she described her interactions with a SYTE student who was a chronic user and seller of drugs:

> Whenever I see him standing on that island in the middle of the street, I give him a hug. He can look the worst I ever seen anybody look, I give a hug and I give him a couple of dollars, even though I'm quite sure I know what he'll do with the money. Or sometimes, I'll take him and feed him. Recently I heard he was

doing all right and I want to make sure he keep doing all right. I want him to get some kind of education so he can get a job. If he sees his peers care, that will make a difference.

In sharing their worlds, George Weiss and the Belmont students are inspired by the same motive: to make a difference in the lives of others. Walter Annenberg illustrated this very point when he showed his disapproval for George's admiring applause in acknowledgement of his major gift to Penn. When Annenberg heard the applause, he returned to the podium to make sure all understood his motivation in giving the gift when he said: "It's simply a matter of good citizenship." At this moment George understood the difference between giving charity or alms and doing the right thing to make a difference. These distinctions are nicely drawn by Mauss when he explained the evolution of the meaning of the Hebrew word *Zedaqa* and the Arabic *Sadaqa*. Originally, as stated in the Bible and the Koran, those words meant "justice." Only later as Christianity and Islam spread did it mean "alms" (Mauss 1954, 17). "Generosity," according to Paul Dresch, "is doing right action" (Dresch 1998, 117) or, as Annenberg said, a matter of good citizenship. Good citizenship is about doing the right thing, the just thing. George extends these concepts by defining justice to mean making a difference in the others' lives by providing what should rightly be his or hers. It is right for philanthropists to make this world a better place, especially for children. And it is just for a society to provide for its youth so that no child is left to the serendipity of the gift.

George Weiss, in assessing the value of the program, felt he received more than he gave. In public speeches he often said that the program made him a better person, more compassionate, more in touch with his feelings. Kenny's death at age fifteen was devastating to him. He appreciated his quick mind and his brave spirit in confronting adversity. George cried at Kenny's funeral. He had not cried since he was a child. Kenny made him feel the terrible loss, the pain of a life barely lived. The Belmont 112 were his kids. "I'm interested in what happened to them. When we first started Say Yes, I thought we would succeed with every kid. I expected As and Bs on their report cards. I was a tad naïve. But I firmly believe we were successful and that five million dollars I spent was money well spent." George pauses for a moment and then rejoins, "How do you place a price tag on this kind of work? You put forth your best effort into saving each child so that they have a good future." As if to illustrate his point he told me this story. "Michelle came to visit me. Her baby was asleep in her stroller. She told me about her life since she finished the University of Hartford. She found a job counseling troubled youth. She was married to an ex-marine who also attained a bachelor's degree. 'We both work,' she said, 'so that we can save up enough money to buy a house.'" George leaned back in his chair and reflected, "She's doing just fine. I'm proud of her."

Throughout my professional career, I have searched for more effective ways to educate poor minorities so that they were not always playing a losing game of catch-up. In Say Yes, I came closest to realizing that goal. Say Yes became a learning community in which change and experimentation were possible and desirable. Living with an extended family like Say Yes expanded my understanding of how children learn across the span of childhood, adolescence, and young adulthood. Poverty limits opportunity. Most apparent was how few resources were available for helping children with learning disabilities. But it was not just the availability of resources, it was how inflexible the bureaucracy was in servicing the needs of these children. I saw our students thrive under the instruction of capable, dedicated teachers. But I also saw our students wither under teachers who were inadequately trained. It is painfully obvious that inner-city children will not bridge the achievement gap without highly qualified teachers working with them every school year. Earlier in the book, I mentioned the important research in Tennessee which showed that the difference in achievement between students who attended classes taught by high-quality versus those taught by low-quality teachers for three consecutive years is sizeable: approximately 50 percentile points on standardized tests (Sanders & Rivers 1996). In Texas, economists have found that while schools are seen to have powerful effects on achievement differences, these effects appear to derive most importantly from variations in teacher quality. (Hanushek, Kain & Rivkin 1998). Children at risk should not be subjected to teachers who were insufficiently trained to teach them.

This book is a way to pay back for the gift the students gave to the Weisses, to me, and to others involved in the program. What was this gift? The students were generous in sharing their lives candidly and often with deep trust that we would respect their ambitions and challenges. They held their lives up to public scrutiny. They broadened our appreciation for how they helped each other survive. They allowed us to share in their joy and their sorrow. The students' gift mirrors the asymmetry that was caused by the original act of offering the program and the scholarship to the students. We, too, became indebted, and to some degree equality was established between the professionals, the sponsors, and the students.

Conclusion

The varied experiences of participants illustrate the complexities of the lives of poor urban youth, the obstacles they encounter, and the factors that allow them to succeed. The Belmont 112 provide us with several important lessons. First, as others have shown, resilience, defined by the ability to pursue one's goals despite considerable obstacles, is essential to the academic success of inner-city youth (Spencer, Swanson and Cunningham 1991). More importantly, this research finds that resilience can be fostered. A network of individuals and institutions that care about a child's well-being can enable resilience in most situations. It must also be said that resilience is not a lifelong inoculation; a few stable family years, a short-lived connection with a mentor, an after-school program in middle school cannot ward off the inevitable stumbles on the long road out of intergenerational poverty. The SYTE study confirms that it is not possible to swiftly and neatly improve educational performance among inner-city youth. Poverty is just as intractable as it seems, and a long-term commitment is required to even the odds. The program for the Belmont 112 began in seventh grade and extended through college; currently SYTE devotes up to seventeen years to youth, starting the program in kindergarten. This brings us to our final point; the SYTE experience makes glaringly apparent the inadequacy of the government's role in making urban communities viable. The voluntary philanthropy of George and Diane Weiss certainly improved the life chances of a few hundred poor children; more generally, the SYTE program demonstrates how in-depth, sustained intervention with at-risk students does make a positive difference. It also reveals the inadequacy of governmental efforts to make inner-cities places where youth can thrive.

America has been callous to the plight of the poor. We continue to believe that individual effort alone will lift someone out of poverty, while not acknowledging the insidious effects of structural inequalities. Consider the case of Richard, the student most likely to succeed among the Belmont 112. Despite being part of a two-parent family with strong religious beliefs and having above average intelligence, there were clearly moments in his life where he very nearly took the wrong path. Richard was fortunate to have several protective factors in his life in addition to SYTE that facilitated his progress. But risk factors such as inadequate schooling, high rates of crime and drug use were constant pressures in his neighborhood that inhibited resilience. Richard also had to reconcile his desire to succeed academically with his peers, among whom high academic achievement was not the norm. Even for Richard, the pressure of living in a high poverty inner-city neighborhood almost derailed his ultimately successful academic career. It was in large part because SYTE was a strong presence for many years that Richard was able to succeed.

A clear lesson we can learn from SYTE is that programs operating in the inner city should have the long-term in mind. A recent study of community-based organizations finds that "These CBOs provide community sanctuaries and supports that enable youth to imagine positive paths and embark upon them" (McLaughlin 2004, 7). These sanctuaries are caring communities, where trusting relationships can be fostered and self-esteem can grow. Milbrey McLaughlin also makes an important connection between youth development and community development. Youth are a vital part of community, and organizations serving youth can be a driving force in revitalizing a community. The SYTE experience makes clear that local, city, state, and federal resources should be targeted to youth programs that encourage youth to give back to their communities and involve adults in the community in making positive change. McLaughlin makes a powerful point in confirming that cultivating youth is community development.

The SYTE program is significant and important and as such it deserves replication; GEAR-UP is a promising intervention in the lives of inner-city youth. However, neither SYTE programs nor GEAR-UP can substitute for equal government spending in inner-city communities on quality education, improved housing and generating a viable legitimate economy. Schools as presently organized provide a set of sluice gates that allow only so many through and offer insufficient supports for those left behind. Ultimately, SYTE intervened in dysfunctional schools and often in impoverished homes, and made a long-term, individualized commitment that enabled individual resiliency to develop and promoted the creation of contexts in which resilience is supported. SYTE provides a proxy for middle-class support, allowing many more to be successful and showing what is possible.

The greatest weakness of the program is its limited capacity to serve the many youth trapped in unsupportive urban schools. The Belmont 112 were but a fraction of the youth who graduated middle school in 1989, destined for underfunded, overcrowded high schools where tracking, referral to special education, and dropping out were all more likely than high school graduation. The philanthropists who support programs like Say Yes are pathfinders, forcing us to reconsider who can learn and what it would take, especially in minority communities, to give every child the same opportunity. While the reader can see the value of the generous philanthropy of the sponsors of Say Yes, it is the government's responsibility to provide an adequate education for every child in this country, regardless of race, class, or geography. Early in the book I quote the Say Yes mother who thanked the Weisses for giving them the "privilege to dream." Her assumption suggests that for those living in poverty, dreaming is a luxury they cannot afford. Programs like Say Yes demonstrate how adequate funding and long-term commitment to inner-city youth pays off. The payback becomes possible when minds are enabled to dream of a better future and, through education, gain the capacity to take steps towards realization of those dreams.

Appendix A

Say Yes To Education
(August, 1993)

Comparison and SYTE Students Six Years after Leaving Elementary School

Group	Graduates N	%	Dropouts N	%	Still Enrolled N	%	Total2 N	%
All Students★								
Comparison	22	28%	43	54%	15	19%	80	100%
SYTE	44	44%	36	36%	20	20%	100	100%
Regular Education Students★★								
Comparison	18	32%	28	50%	10	18%	56	100%
SYTE	32	60%	11	21%	10	19%	53	100%
Special Education Students★★★								
Comparison	4	17%	15	63%	5	21%	24	100%
SYTE	12	26%	25	53%	10	21%	47	100%

Reasons for being classified as a "dropout" include being a non-attender, i.e., a student over the compulsory age of 17 who has been absent (unexcused) for 30 consecutive days, being committed to a correctional institution, and joining the Job Corps before graduation. Most of the students who dropped out were classified as "non-attenders."

Twelve SYTE students and five comparison group students were excluded from this analysis. Students were excluded because they moved from Philadelphia, transferred to a parochial or private school, had incomplete records, or were deceased.

★ (X2 = 6.53, df = 2, p < .05)
★★ (X2 = 11.25, df = 2, p < .01)
★★★ (X2 = .80, df = 2, Not significant)

Source: A Study of a Tuition Guarantee Program by Michael Schlessinger, 1993.

References

Ainsworth-Darnell, J. W., and D. B. Downey. 1998. Assessing the oppositional culture explanation for racial and ethnic differences in school performance. *American Sociological Review* 63 (August): 536–544.

Alan Guttmacher Institute. 2004. U.S. teenage pregnancy statistics: Overall trends, trends by race and ethnicity and state-by-state information. New York: Author.

Alexander, K. L., D. R. Entwisle, and C. S. Horsey. 1997. From first grade forward: Early foundations of high school dropout. *Sociology of Education* 70 (2): 87–107.

Ali, R. 2002. The high school diploma: Making it more than an empty promise. Washington, DC: The Education Trust.

Anderson, Elijah. 1990. *Streetwise.* Chicago: University of Chicago Press.

Anderson, E. 1999. *Code of the street.* New York: W. W. Norton & Co.

Baker, E. T., M. C. Wang, and H. J. Walberg. 1994. The effects of inclusion on learning. *Educational Leadership* 52 (4): 33–35.

Berrueta-Clement, J. L., L. J. Schweinhart, W. S. Barnett, A. S. Epstein, and D. P. Weikart. 1984. Changed lives: The effects of the Perry Preschool Program on youths through age 19. *Monographs of the High/Scope Educational Research Foundation 8.* Ypsilanti, MI: The High Scope Press.

Bingaman, J. 1988. Better Off Under Reagan? Mostly, No. *New York Times*, January 30.

Block, J. 1971. *Lives through time.* Berkeley: Bancroft Books.

Bogaines, B. 1993. "Radio Times." Interview with Norman A. Newberg and Harold Shields. Philadelphia: WHYY, July 27.

Bourdieu, P. 1977. *Reproduction in education, society, and culture.* Beverly Hills, CA: Sage Publications.

Bracey, G. W. 2002. Summer loss: The phenomenon no one wants to deal with. *Phi Delta Kappan* 84 (1): 12–14.

Brennan, J. 2002. *The funding gap.* Washington: The Education Trust, Inc.

Bridges, E. M. 1996. Evaluation for tenure and dismissal. In *The New Handbook of Teacher Evaluation*. Eds. J. Millman and L. Darling-Hammond. Newbury Park, CA: Sage Publications.

Brim, O. G., Jr., and J. Kagan, eds. 1980. *Constancy and change in human development*. Cambridge, MA: Harvard University Press.

Brofenbrenner, U. 1979. *The ecology of human development: Experiments by nature and design*. Cambridge, MA: Harvard University Press.

Bronfenbrenner, U. 1993. The ecology of cognitive development: Research models and fugitive findings. In *Development in context: Acting and thinking in specific environments*. Eds. R. H. Wozniak and K. Fischer. Hillsdale: Erlbaum.

Brooks-Gunn, J., and G. Guo. 1993. Who drops out of and who continues beyond high school? A twenty year follow-up of black urban youth. *Journal of Research on Adolescence* 3 (3): 271–294.

Bureau of Justice Assistance. 2000. A second look at alleviating jail crowding: A systems perspective. Washington, DC.

Cairns, R. B. 1994. *Lifelines and risks: Pathways of youth in our time*. New York: Cambridge University Press.

Cambell, R. T. 1982. Status attainment research: End of the beginning or beginning of the end. *Sociology of Education* 56 (1): 47–62.

Canale, J., and L. Dunlap. 1987. Factors influencing career aspirations of primary and secondary grade students. Paper presented at the annual meeting of the Eastern Psychological Association, Arlington, VA.

Carnevale, A., and D. M. Desrochers. 2003. Standards for what? The economic roots of K–16 reform. Princeton, NJ: Educational Testing Service.

Centers for Disease Control. 2002. Teenage births in the United States: State trends, 1991–2000, an update. NVSR 50 (9): (PHS) 2002–1120.

Chall, J. S., V. A. Jacobs, and L. E. Baldwin. 1990. *The Reading Crisis: Why poor children fall behind*. Cambridge, MA: Harvard University Press.

Chess, S. 1989. Defying the voice of doom. In *The child in our times*. Eds. T. Dugan and R. Coles, 179–199. New York: Brunner/Mazel.

Cichetti, D. 1993. Child abuse, child development, and social policy. In *Advances in Applied Developmental Psychology*. Ed. S. L. Toth. Vol. 8. Norwood, NJ: Ablex Publishing Corporation.

Coladarci, T., and J. Hancock. 2002. Grade-span configuration. *Journal of Research in Rural Education* 17 (3): 189–92.

Coleman, J. S., E. Q. Campbell, C. J. Hobson, J. McPartland, A. M. Mood, F. D. Weinfeld, and R. L. York. 1966. *Equality of educational opportunity*. Washington, DC: U.S. Government Printing Office.

Coleman, J. S. 1988. Social capital in the creation of human capital. *American Journal of Sociology* 94, supplement: S95–S120.

———. 1990. *Foundations of social theory*. Cambridge, MA: Harvard University Press.

The College Board. 2002. Annual survey of colleges and trends in student aid. New York.

Crane, J. 1991. The epidemic theory of ghettos and neighborhood effects on dropping out and teenage childbearing. *American Journal of Sociology* 96 (5): 126–129.

Davis, A. E. 1998. "I Have a Dream" program—class one evaluation report. Portland, Oregon: Northwest Regional Educational Laboratory.

De Lone, Richard H. 1979. *Small futures: children, inequality, and the limits of liberal reform.* New York: Harcourt Brace Jovanovich.

Devine, Joel A., and J. D. Wright. 1993. *The greatest of evils: Urban poverty and the American underclass.* New York: Aldine de Gruyter.

Donley, E., and J. von Seideneck. 2003. We could learn something from Kentucky. *The Philadelphia Inquirer*, March 18. 1998.

Dresch, Paul. 1998. Mutual deception: totality, exchange, and Islam in the Middle East. In *Marcel Mauss: A centenary tribute.* Eds. Wendy James and N. J. Allen. New York: Berghahn Books.

Du Bois, W. E. B. 1903. *The souls of black folk: Essays and sketches.* 2nd ed. Chicago: A. C. McClurg & Co.

Eccles, J. S., and C. Midgley. 1989. Stage-environment fit: Developmentally appropriate classrooms for young adolescents. In *Research on motivation in education.* Eds. C. Ames and R. Ames, 139–186. 3rd ed. San Diego: Academic Press.

Eccles, J. S., C. Midgley, A. Wigfield, C. M. Buchanan, D. Reuman, C. Flanagan, and D. MacIver. 1993. Development during adolescence: The impact of stage-environment fit on adolescents' experiences in schools and families. *American Psychologist* 48: 90–101.

Elder, G. H., Jr. 1998. The life course and human development. In *Handbook of child psychology: Theoretical models of human development.* Ed. W. Damon. Vol. 1. New York: Wiley.

Elliot, D. S., D. Huizinga, and S. Menard. 1989. *Multiple problem youth: Delinquency, substance use, and mental health problems.* New York: Springer-Veriag.

Emerson, Ralph Waldo. 1909. Essays and English traits. New York: P. F. Collier.

Ensminger, M.E., and A. Slusarcick. 1989. Paths to high school graduation or dropout: Family and individual characteristics. Paper presented at the annual meeting of the American Educational Research Association.

Epstein, H. 2003. Enough to make you sick? *The New York Times Magazine,* October 12.

Erickson, F. 1987. Transformation and school success: The politics and culture of educational achievement. *Anthropology and Education Quarterly* 18: 335–57.

Erikson, E. H. 1950. *Childhood and society.* New York: W. W. Norton.

Farkas, G. 1996. *Human capital or cultural capital? Ethnicity and poverty groups in an urban school district.* New York: Walter de Gruyter.

Farrington, D. P. 1986. Stepping stone to adult criminal careers. In *Development of antisocial and prosocial behavior: Research, theories and issues*. Eds. D. Olweus, J. Block, and M. Radke-Yarrow, 359–384. New York: Academic.

Felsman, J. K., and G. E. Vaillant. 1987. Resilient children as adults: A 40-year study. In *The invulnerable child*. Eds. E. J. Anthony and B. J. Cohler. New York: The Guilford Press.

Fine, M., ed. 1994. *Chartering urban school reform*. New York: Teachers College Press.

Fine, M., and A. Burns. Forthcoming. Class notes: Toward a critical psychology of class and schooling. *Journal of Social Sciences*.

Fishkin, J. 1983. *Justice, equal opportunity and the family*. New Haven, CT: Yale University Press.

Flaxman, E., and M. Inger. 1991. Parents and schooling in the 1990s. *ERIC Review*, 1 (3): 2–6.

Fordham, S. 1993. "Those loud black girls": (Black) women, silence, and gender "passing" in the academy. *Anthropology & Education Quarterly* 24 (1): 3–32.

Freedman, J. 1993. *From cradle to grave*. New York: Macmillan Publishing Company.

Freedman, M. 1993. *The kindness of strangers: Adult mentors, urban youth, and the new voluntarism*. San Franciso: Jossey-Bass Publishers.

Fries-Britt, S. L., and B. Turner. 2002. Uneven stories: Successful black collegians at a black and a white campus. *Review of Higher Education* 25 (3): 315–30.

Fujiura, G. T., and K. Yamaki. 2000. Trends in demography of childhood poverty and disability. *Exceptional Children* 66: 187–199.

Furstenberg, F. Jr. 1989. Teenaged pregnancy and childbearing. American Psychologist (February): 313–320.

Gewertz, C. 2001. Forces target Pennsylvania school aid changes. *Education Week*, November 28.

Gilligan, C. 1982. *In a different voice*. Cambridge, MA: Harvard University Press.

Glasser, B. G., and A. L. Strauss. 1989. *Status passage*. Chicago: Aldine Atherton.

Gold, E., and T. Hartman. 2004. "SYTE Outcome Study," (unpublished preliminary report). Philadelphia: Research for Action

Griffin, L. J., and K. L. Alexander. 1978. Schooling and socioeconomic attainments: High school and college influences. *American Journal of Sociology* 84: 319–47.

Hanushek, E. A., J. F. Kain, and S. G. Rivkin. 1998. "Teachers, Schools, and Academic Achievement." National Bureau of Economic Research.

Hayre, R. W., and A. Moore. 1997. *Tell them they are rising*. New York: John Wiley & Sons, Inc.

Hechinger, F. M. 1992. *Fateful choices: Healthy youth for the 21ˢᵗ century*. New York: Carnegie Council on Adolescent Development, Carnegie Corporation of New York.

Howard, M. P., and R. J. Anderson. 1978. Early identification of potential school dropouts: A literature Review. *Child Welfare* 57 (4): 221–31.

Hrabowski, F. A., K. I. Maton, and G. L. Greif. 1998. *Beating the odds: Raising academically successful males.* New York: Oxford University Press.

Hubbard, L. 1999. College aspirations among low-income African American high school students: Gendered strategies for success. *Anthropology & Education Quarterly:* 363–83.

Hugh, M. 1992. Understanding inequality in schools: The contribution of interpretive studies. *Sociology of Education* 65 (1): 1–20

Hugh, M., A. J. Hertweck, and J. L. Meihls. 1985. *Handicapping the handicapped: Decision making in students' careers.* Stanford, CA: Stanford University Press.

Hurd, T. L., A. Larkin, and J. Ribeiro. 1999. The benefits of a philanthropic-university-school community partnership: the Cambridge "Say Yes to Education" story. In *Serving children and families through community-university partnerships: Success stories.* Eds. T. R. Chibucos and R. M Lerner. Boston: Klewer Academic Publishers.

Huston, A. C. 1994. *Children in poverty.* New York: Cambridge University Press.

Jimerson, S. R., G. E. Anderson, and A. Whipple. 2002. Winning the battle and losing the war: Examining the relation between grade retention and dropping out of high school. *Psychology in the Schools* 39 (4): 441–458.

The Justice Policy Institute. 2002. *Cellblocks or classrooms? The funding of higher education and corrections and its impact on African American men.* Washington DC: Author.

Kahne, Joseph, and Kim Bailey. 1999. The role of social capital in youth development: The case of 'I Have a Dream' programs. *Educational Evaluation and Policy Analysis* 21 (3): 321–343.

Kaye, H. S., La-Plante, Carlson and Wenger. 1996. Trends in disability rates in the United States, 1970–1994. *Disability Statistics Abstract*, Number 17. Washington, DC: National Institute on Disability and Rehabilitation Research.

Kellam, S. G., C. H. Brown, B. R. Rubin, and M. E. Ensminger. 1983. Paths leading to teenage psychiatric symptoms and substance use: Developmental epidemiological studies in Woodlawn. In *Childhood psychopathology and development.* Eds. S. B. Gunn, F. J. Earls, and J. E. Barrett, 17–51. New York: Raven Press.

Kellam, S. G., L. Werthamer-Larsson, L. J. Dolan, C. H. Brown, L. S. Mayer, G. W. Rebok, J. C. Anthony, J. Laudolff, G. Edelsohn, and L. Wheeler. 1991. Developmental epidemiologically-based preventive trials: Baseline modeling of early target behaviors and depressive symptoms. *American Journal of Community Psychology* 19: 563–584.

Kellum, S. G., and R. C. Hunter. 1990. Prevention begins in first grade. *Principal* 70 (2): 17–19.

Kobasa, S. C. 1979. Stressful life events, personality, and health: An inquiry into hardiness. *Journal of Personality and Social Psychology* 37 (1): 1–11.

Kotlowitz, A. 1991. *There are no children here: The story of two boys growing up in the other America.* New York: Doubleday.

Kozol, Jonathan. 1991. *Savage inequalities.* New York: Harper Perennial.

Labaree, D. 1997. *How to succeed in school without really learning: The credentials race in American education.* New Haven, CT: Yale University Press.

Lamont, M., and A. Lareau. 1988. Cultural capital: allusions, gaps and glissandos in recent theoretical developments. *Sociological Theory* 6: 153–68.

Lanasa, P., and J. H. Potter. 1984. Building a bridge to span the minority-majority achievement gap. Paper presented at the National Conference on Desegregation in Post Secondary Education, Durham, NC.

Levine, A., and J. Nidiffer. 1996. *Beating the odds: How the poor get to college.* San Francisco, CA: Jossey-Bass, Inc.

Lipsky, D. K, and A. Gartner. 1989. *Beyond separate education: Quality education for all.* Baltimore, MD: Paul H. Brookes Publishing Co.

MacLeod, J. 1987. *Ain't no makin' it: Leveled aspirations in a low-income neighborhood.* Boulder, CO: Westview Press.

Markus, H., and P. Nurius. 1986. Possible selves. *American Psychologist* 41 (9): 954–969.

Massey, D. S., and N. A. Denton. 1993. *American apartheid: Segregation and the making of the underclass.* Cambridge, MA: Harvard University Press.

Masten, A. S., K. M. Best, and N. Garmezy. 1990. Resilience and development: Contributions from the study of children who overcome adversity. *Development and Psychopathology* 2: 425–444.

Masten, A.S., and J. L. Powell. 2003. A resilience framework for research, policy, and practice. In *Resilience and vulnerability: Adaptation in the context of childhood adversities.* Ed. S. S. Luthar. Cambridge: Cambridge University Press.

Mauss, M. 1954. *The Gift: Forms and functions of exchange in archaic societies.* Trans. I. Cunnison. Glencoe, IL: Free Press.

Maynard, R., ed. 1997. *Kids having kids: The costs and social consequences of teenage childbearing.* Washington, DC: Urban Institute Press.

McCord, J. 1986. Instigation and insulation: How families affect antisocial aggression. In *Development of antisocial and prosocial behavior: Research, theories and issues.* Eds. D. Olweus, J. Block, and M. Radke-Yarrow, 343–358. New York: Academic.

McLaughlin, M.W. 2004. Community counts: How youth organizations matter for youth development. Washington, DC: Public Education Network.

McMullan, B., C. Snipe, and W. Wolfe. 1994. *Charters and student achievement: Early evidence from school restructuring in Philadelphia.* Bala Cynwyd, PA: Center for Assessement and Policy Development.

Meyer, L. H., and D. R. Williams. 1991. Inclusive middle schooling practices: Shifting from deficit to support models. Paper presented at the Annual Meeting of the American Educational Research Association, Chicago.

Mezzacappa, D. 1987a. Sixth grade class is offered a gift of college tuition. *The Philadelphia Inquirer*, June 20, pp. 1A, 6A.

———. 1987b. Gift of schooling may be hard to accept. *The Philadelphia Inquirer*, November 1, pp. 1, 1B.

———. 1988a. A struggle of dream and reality. *The Philadelphia Inquirer*, June 26.

———. 1988b. Clayton targets North Philadelphia for school improvements. *The Philadelphia Inquirer*, July 31.

———. 1992. Urban obstacles make diplomas precious at Kensington High: Their pomp defies the circumstances. *The Philadelphia Inquirer*, June 18, pp. B1, B4.

———. 1993. A gift changed his life's path. *The Philadelphia Inquirer*, January 17.

———. 1999a. Dreams deferred. *The Philadelphia Inquirer Magazine*, April 25.

———. 1999b. The $5 million lesson: Connecticut philanthropist George Weiss's twelve-year odyssey. *Philanthropy*, July/August.

———. 1999c. Offered a college dorm, he sits in a prison cell. *The Philadelphia Inquirer*, November 26.

Myers, D., and A. Schirm. 1999. The impacts of Upward Bound: Final report. Washington, DC: U.S. Department of Education.

Neild, R. C., E. Useem, E. F. Travers, and J. Lesnick. 2003. *Once and for all: placing a highly qualified teacher in every Philadelphia classroom*. Philadelphia: Research for Action.

Nelson-LeGall, S., and E. Jones. 1991. Classroom help-seeking behavior of African-American children. *Education and Urban Society* 24: 27–40.

Newberg, N. A. 1991. Bridging the gap: An organizational inquiry in an urban school system. In *The reflective turn: Case studies in and on practice*. Ed. D. Schon, pp. 65–83. New York: Teachers College Press.

Newberg, N. A., and R. B. Sims. 1996. Contexts that promote success for inner-city students. *Urban Education* 31 (2): 149–76. Reprinted by Permission of Corwin Press, Inc., 1996.

New York Times. When a college scholarship buys a car. November 4, 2002, Editorial Desk.

Nightingale, Carl Husemoller. 1993. *On the edge: A history of black children and their American dreams*. New York: Basic Books.

Noddings, N. 1992. *The challenge to care*. New York: Teachers College Press.

Nunez, A. M., and S. Cuccaro-Alamin. 1998. *First generation students: Undergraduates whose parents never enrolled in postsecondary education* (NCES

98-082). U.S. Department of Education, National Center for Education Statistics. Washington, DC: U.S. Government Printing Office.

Oakes, J. 1985. *Keeping track.* New Haven, CT: Yale University Press.

Ogbu, J. 1991. Minority responses and school experiences. *Journal of Psychohistory* 18.

Ogbu, J., and S. Fordham. 1986. Black students' school success: Coping with the burden of "acting white." *Urban Review* 18 (3): 176–206.

Olson, L. 2003. Quality counts 2003: "If I can't learn from you" *Education Week,* January 7.

Orlofsky, G. F. 2002. The funding gap: Low-income and minority students receive fewer dollars. Washington, DC: The Education Trust.

Oxley, D. 1994. Organizing schools into smaller units: Alternatives to homogeneous groupings. *Phi Delta Kappan* (March): 521–526.

Pardini, P. 2002. Revival of the K–8 school. *School Administrator* 59, No. 3 (March): 6–12.

Patterson, G. R., and T. J. Dishion. 1985. Contributions of families and peers to delinquency. *Criminology* 23: 637–639.

Peterson's Guides. 1995. Peterson's Guide to Four Year Colleges, 1996. Princeton, NJ: Peterson's Guides.

Pittman, K. J. 1996. Preventing problems or promoting development: Competing priorities or inseparable goals? International Youth Foundation. http://www.iyfnet.org.

Rauch, J. 1989. Kids as capital. *Atlantic Monthly,* (August): 56–61.

Robins, L. N., and R. Price. 1991. Adult disorders predicted by childhood conduct problems: Results from the NIMH Epidemiological Catchment Area Project. *Psychiatry* 54 (2): 116–132.

Rodriguez, Cleo, Jr., and Nelwyn B. Moore. 1995. Perceptions of pregnant/parenting teens: Reframing issues for an integrated approach to pregnancy problems. *Adolescence* 30(119): 685–705.

Rose, M. 1990. *Lives on the boundary.* New York: Penguin Books.

Ross, M. 1989. Relation of implicit theories to the construction of personal histories. *Psychological Review* 96 (2): 341–357.

Rutter, Michael. 1990. Commentary: Some focus and process considerations regarding effects of parental depression on children. *Developmental Psychology* 26 (1): 60–67.

Rutter, M. 1987. Psychosocial resilience and protective mechanisms. *American Journal of Orthopsychiatry* 37: 317–331.

Ruvolo, A. P., and H. R. Markus. 1992. Possible selves and performance: The power of self relevant imagery. *Social Cognition* 20 (1): 95–124.

Sampson, R. J., and J. H. Laub. 1993. *Crime in the making: Pathways and turning points through life.* Cambridge, MA: Harvard University Press.

Sanders, W. L., and J. C. Rivers. 1996. "Cumulative and Residual Effects of Teachers on Future Student Academic Achievement." Knoxville: University of Tennessee Value-Added Research and Assessment Center.

Schlesinger, M. 1993. *A study of a tuition guarantee program*. Ph.D. doctoral diss. Philadelphia, PA: Temple University.

Schlossman, S., and S. Wallach. 1978. The crime of precocious sexuality: Female juvenile delinquency in the progressive era. *Harvard Educational Review* 48: 65–94.

School District of Philadelphia, Office of Accountability and Assessment (1990a). A study of the ninth-grade class of 1984–85 (No. 9024, pp. 1–2). Philadelphia, PA.

School District of Philadelphia, Office of Accountability and Assessment (1990b). Superintendent's Management Information Center, 1989–1990. (No. 9021, pp. 98, 158). Philadelphia, PA.

Schrift, A. D., ed. 1997. *The logic of the gift: toward an ethic of generosity*. New York: Routledge and Kegan Paul.

Schweinhart, L., H. Barnes, and D. Weikart. 1993. Significant benefits: The high/scope Perry Preschool study through age 27. In *Monographs of the High/Scope Press 10*. Ypsilanti, MI: The High Scope Press.

Schweinhart, L., and D. Weikart. 1980. Young children grow up: The effects of the Perry Preschool Program on youths through age 15. In *Monographs of the High/Scope Educational Research Foundation 7*. Ypsilanti, MI: The High Scope Press.

Serbin, L. A., P. L. Peters, V. J. McAffer, and A. E. Schwartzman. 1991. Childhood aggression and withdrawal as predictors of adolescent pregnancy, early parenthood, and environmental risk for the next generation. *Canadian Journal of Behavioural Science* 23: 318–331.

Shapiro, J. P., Sewell, T. E., and J. P. DuCette. 1995. Reframing diversity in education. Lancaster: Technomic Publishing Company.

Sowell, T. 1981. *Markets and minorities*. New York: Basic Books.

Spencer, M. B., and J. Youngblood, II. 2002. Integrating normative identity processes and academic support requirements for special needs adolescents: The application of an identity-focused cultural ecological (ICE) perspective. *Applied Developmental Science* 6 (2): 95–108.

Spencer, M. B. 1997. A phenomenological variant of ecological systems theory (PVEST): A self-organization perspective in context. *Development and Psycholpathology* 9: 817–833.

———. 1995. Old issues and new theorizing about African-American youth: A phenomenological variant of ecological systems theory. In *Black youth: Perspectives on their status in the United States*. Ed. R. L. Taylor, 37–70. Westport, CT: Praeger.

Spencer, M. B., D. P Swanson, and M. Cunningham. 1991. Ethnicity, identity and competence formation: Adolescent transition and identity transformation. *Journal of Negro Education* 60 (3): 366–387.

Spencer, M. B. 2001. Resilience and fragility factors associated with the contextual experiences of low resource African American male youth and families. In *Does it take a village? Community effects on children, adolescents, and families.* Eds. A. Booth and A. C. Crouter. Mahweh: Lawrence Erlbaum Associates.

Sroufe, L. A., and E. Waters. 1977. Attachment as an organizational construct. *Child Development* 48: 1184–1199.

Stack, C. 1974. *All our kin: Strategies for survival in a Black community.* New York: Harper & Row.

Stanton-Salazar, R. D. 1997. A social capital framework for understanding the socialization of racial minority children and youths. *Harvard Educational Review* 67 (1): 1–40.

Statistical Abstract of the United States. 1997. *Labor force employment participation by sex, race and age.* U.S. Department of Commerce, Bureau of the Census and Bureau of Labor Statistics: Washington, DC: Government Printing Office.

Steele, C. M. 1992. Race and the schooling of black Americans. *Atlantic Monthly* (April): 74–75.

Steele, Shelby. 1990. *The content of our character: a new vision of race in America.* New York: St. Martin Press.

Stevenson, Howard C. 1998. Raising safe villages: Cultural-ecological factors that influence the emotional adjustment of adolescents. *Journal of Black Psychology* 24 (1): 44–59.

Stroup, A. L., and L. N. Robins. 1972. Elementary school predictors of high school dropout among black males. *Sociology of Education* 45 (2): 212–222.

Swanson, D. P., and M. B. Spencer. 1991. Youth policy, poverty, and African American youths' identity and competency. *Education and Urban Society* 24 (l): 148–161.

Thomas-Reynolds, A. M. 2005. Knowledge, practice and inquiry: Influencing teacher learning to build collaborative partnerships in schools. Ed. diss. Philadelphia: University of Pennsylvania,

Tierney, J. P., J. B Grossman, and N. L. Resch. 1995. *Making a difference: An impact study of Big Brothers/Big Sisters.* Philadelphia: Private/Public Ventures.

Traub, J. 2000. What no school can do. *The New York Times,* January 16.

Tuskegee Syphilis Study Legacy Committee. 1996. Final Report. http://hsc.virginia.edu/hs-library/historical/apology/report.html.

U.S. Census Bureau 2002. *The big payoff: Educational attainment and synthetic estimates of work-life earnings (P23-210).* Washington, DC.

U.S. Department of Education. 2000. *Twenty-second annual report to Congress on the implementation of the Individuals with Disabilities Education Act.* Washington, DC.

U.S. Department of Education. 2003. National evaluation of GEAR-UP: A summary of the first two years (2003–13). Washington, DC.

U.S. Department of Health and Human Services. 1993. *Creating a 21st century Head Start: Final report of the advisory committee on Head Start quality and expansion.* Washington, DC DHHS.

U.S. General Accounting Office. 1990. *Promising practice: Private programs guaranteeing student aid for higher education* (GAO/PEMD-90-16). Washington, DC.

Varenne, H., and R. McDermott with S. Goldman, M. Naddeo, and R. Rizzo-Tolk. 1998. *Successful school failure: The school America builds.* Boulder, CO: Westview Press.

Wang, M. C., M. C. Reynolds, and H. J. Walberg. 1988. Integrating the children of the second system. *Phi Delta Kappan* 70 (3): 248–251.

Warburton, E. C., R. Bugarin, and A Nuñez. 2001. *Bridging the gap: Academic preparation and postsecondary success of first-generation students.* U.S. Department of Education, National Center for Education Statistics. Washington, DC: U.S. Government Printing Office.

Werner, E. E., and R. S. Smith. 1992. *Overcoming the odds: High risk children from birth to adulthood.* Ithaca: Cornell University Press.

Willis, P. 1976. *Learning to labor.* Lexington MA: D.C. Heath.

Wilson, W. J. 1987. *The truly disadvantaged: The inner city, the underclass and public policy.* Chicago, IL: University of Chicago Press.

Wilson, W. J. 1997. *When work disappears: The world of the new urban poor.* New York: Vintage Books.

Winfield, L. F. 1991. Resilience, schooling, and development in African-American youth. *Education and Urban Society* 24: 5–14.

Wolfgang M., T. Thornberry, and R. Figilo 1987. *From boy to man, from delinquency to crime.* Chicago, IL: University of Chicago Press.

Wright, S. P., S. P. Horn, and W. L. Sanders. 1997. Teacher and classroom contexts effects on student achievement: Implications for teacher evaluation. *Journal of Personnel Evaluation in Education* 11: 57–67.

Yates, T. M., B. Egeland, and A. Sroufe. 2003. Rethinking resilience: A developmental process perspective. In *Resilience and vulnerability: Adaptation in the context of childhood adversities.* Ed. S. S. Luthar. Cambridge: Cambridge University Press.

Zweigenhaft, R. L., and G. W. Domhoff. 1991. *Blacks in the white establishment? A study of race and class in America.* London: Yale University Press.

Index

217